Must I Grow Up!!!

a fraction of the life of Freddie Giles ~ so far

by

Freddie Giles

Compiled and Edited with Jan Giles

Published by
Farmer Giles Publishing

Farmer Giles Publishing
The Courtyard
Meadows Works, Court Street
Trowbridge, Wilts BA14 8BR

Published by Farmer Giles Publishing 2008

ISBN: 978-0-9558289-0-4 (HBK)
ISBN: 978-0-9558289-1-1 (PBK)

Typeset by Farmer Giles Publishing in Times New Roman

Printed and bound by
Cpod, Trowbridge, Wiltshire

Winner of the Seaman Trophy Race Oulton Park 1976
Photo courtesy of Cheshire Life

The author, Freddie Giles, is a well known figure in National and International competitive motor sport and equally renowned for his exploits in his home county of rural Wiltshire.

He's a 10/10th man whether racing, wild days with the Art College crowd, his expulsion from Round Table, sailing in tall ships or indulging his attraction for women.

Born in the 'workhouse' of a busy dairy, taken out of grammar school on his 15th birthday, sent by the army to Belsen and kicked out of home by his father, he emerged at twenty as a natural entrepreneur to start his first business as chimney sweep and window cleaner. Since then he's worked hard and played hard, both with considerable success.

Rallying and Racing have taken him all over the world in British vintage and classic cars and on the way he has won over 200 trophies including an outright win of the prestigious Around the World Rally in 2000.

His story epitomises 'the naughty boy' nascent in all men.

Read and enjoy.

JMG

CONTENTS

Mending a Frazer Nash bevel box in the French Alps 1973.

*When Motor Sport Magazine 'inadvertently' referred to Freddie as
'Frillie Giles' some kind soul lent him her knickers so that he could
live up to his reputation.*

Acknowledgements

The rage these days is to do your family tree in the hope of having descended from an illustrious family but as a chap said to me on a little beach in Spain. "I've looked at my family tree back to the 1600s and do you know, we were peasants then and we're still peasants today" The two of us were sitting around a fire eating fresh caught sardines with our teeth and our hands – we are all still peasants at heart.

Nowadays we are better off peasants but rather than a table of births and deaths I felt that our family should know where part of their good fortune comes from and what life was like not that long ago. Materially, as Harold Macmillan once said we've never had it so good but sometimes the present worries me with its violence, its Big Brother surveillance but I won't jump onto my soap box. 'Twas ever thus. I would instead like to thank those who have allowed me and helped me achieve so much.

My father first – did he act in anger or in calculation? I hope the latter. Thanks to the various skilled tradesmen who have allowed a small boy and grown man to watch and ask questions of their skills enabling me to become a Jack of All Trades and Master of None. A bricklayer in particular who let me borrow a shovel for a moment with the adage "Yes boy, you can, but remember it ain't got legs" – I still use it when I lend out my own tools. Arthur Poulsom for his invaluable business advice when I was starting out. The many staff – mostly women – who have worked with me over the years and without whom I couldn't have succeeded in business. Tony Coles, a good friend, who has worked with me for almost 40 years and without whom I wouldn't have succeeded in business or my motor sport activities. John Ford for the last thirty years and his many and varied building skills . He has the ability to make so much from a simple workshop and a basic sketch and to find the solution to countless problems in our shops and commercial premises. All of the women in my office who have looked after me so fantastically including Lesley who continues to do so. John Naish – "Big John" who has always been on hand to get me out of trouble, to repair anything and to give me in his very quiet way his huge and never faltering friendship.

Thanks to Alan Wilkinson for starting me off writing my story, Geoffrey Rogerson, Michael Scott and Suzanne Smith for reading early and revised drafts and offering constructive suggestions, to the Wiltshire Gazette for early photographs and press cuttings and to the photographers who haven't been credited because I don't know who they are. Special thanks to my wife Jan for the many hours of work on the book - and for everything else.

I wish now that I had listened more to older people; knew more about their lives and the way they lived. Every generation thinks that they have invented the wheel and they certainly think they've 'had the best'. They haven't. Everyone's life is different but it's up to all of us to get the best out of it.

For my grandchildren with love

Moon Leith	*13th April 1987*
Mishka Leith	*20th February 1989*
Amy Giles	*8th July 1994*
Fletcher Giles	*6th December 1994*
Edward Frederick Giles	*28th April 1997*
Alice Davis	*16th June 1997*
Harrison Giles	*22nd August 1998*
Sarah Davis	*25th May 2000*
Alexander Giles	*4th April 2001*

Happy New Year

```
To : Mr.F.GILES           From E.F.GILES
     HAWKSTREET DAIRY           HAWKSTREET DAIRY
     BROMHAM                    BROMHAM
                           1st Jan. 57
```

Sir,

In reply to your letter of the 30th Jan.
stating you wish to terminate your employ
on Jan. 13th 57, this I accept, and in return
you can pack all your personal belongings
and leave on or before that date.

Yours faithfully,

E. F. Giles

I read father's letter again. The miserable bugger I thought. How could he kick me out of home? I loved working with the family and my letter to him had only meant to suggest what I thought were improvements to the business. My mistake had been to threaten to leave if he couldn't agree to some of my ideas for change. Perhaps I was getting too big for my boots and he knew it even though I didn't then. I left the army on the 3rd August. Home by 2.30. In the dairy by 3.30. Since then I hadn't missed a day's work; seven days a week and not a single day off; the army paid me £14 per week and father paid me £4; and now I was to be homeless!

As these things turn out it was the best thing he ever did for me and January 13th was to recur repeatedly as a significant date in my life.

But before then I still had two weeks notice to work out in the dairy.

Home in the Dairy

The dairy was our life and my earliest memories were of working there. Milk; churns; bottles; work. Always work; seven days a week for everyone in the family; ours was a family firm and we were all part of it. I made my own first contribution whilst I was still in nappies – or, in this instance, not in nappies as the photograph which was intended to demonstrate the healthy properties of our un-pasteurised milk shows a bonny baby wearing nothing but a rug.

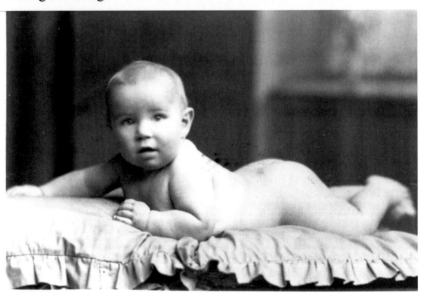

"You can whip our cream but you can't beat our milk" was the substance of the flyer which father circulated around the local villages and I was the illustration. The business was my father's and his word was law. On 13 January 1923 he'd bought a pony and trap, a churn and a bucket, for £40 from John Trueman of Durlett just a mile from the present dairy. Next morning he set out on his rounds, delivering about eight gallons of milk.

It was hardly an empire, but he soon had it expanding. That first month he took £28, and by the autumn he was doing sufficiently well to be able to marry his childhood sweetheart. Neither of them was afraid of hard work. Alice Elizabeth Philips had been born out of wedlock in 1902, and in those days of course there was a terrible degree of shame attached to any illegitimate child. However, she was lucky enough to be taken in by an aunt, her mother's married sister Nan Bolland, and that was an end to the matter.

Ted – Edgar Frank Giles - came from a proper family, a big family of ten children. In 1899 he was, quite literally, born in a field – appropriately enough, since his parents were peasant farmers, making a living out of a few cows and a vegetable small-holding. Nothing extraordinary about that either: that's how a lot of people got by in those days.

There was a little story we were told about Granny Giles who had a pony and trap and used to go into Devizes once or twice a week. There was a market there Thursdays and Saturdays, and she'd go selling whatever they were harvesting at the time: peas or broad beans, new potatoes or celery. Now to get from Bromham to Devizes you have to climb Dunkirk Hill, which is quite steep and long and sometimes the pony would be reluctant. One day Granny Giles was stuck at the bottom of the hill with all her produce and a new pony when along came a roadman. He would naturally carry his lunch with him: a bottle of cold tea, a chunk of bread, a lump of cheese and a raw onion. "Roadman, roadman" called Granny "canst 'elp I? Thik pony wunt go up thee ill" "Oh ar missus" said the roadman spotting the situation, "that be easy" and with that took out of his knapsack his pocket-knife and his raw onion. He cut the onion in half, lifted up the pony's tail and rammed it up his a***. The pony took off like a rocket, right to the top of the hill. Granny was amazed. "Thas wonderful roadman" she said "but there's just one problem. The pony 'n cart be up thee 'ill an I be down yer still at the bottom". "Dussnt worry missus" he replied "I thought about that an so I cut thik onion in 'alf!" At least that's what they told me as a small boy!

One of Granny's regular calls together with Ted was at the Bolland household, where the girl who would grow up to be my mother was being raised by her auntie. And that's how my father came to meet her. The Bollands were doing quite well for themselves, running their own bicycle shop in town, so you might say that business was in my blood one way or another.

Father was conscripted into the Navy in 1917, signing up for five years and finding himself involved in the Russian Revolution. Well, not exactly, but his ship did serve the White Russian cause, helping a pair of fugitive Tsarist princesses escape by way of the Black Sea. His travels enabled him to really see the world and I wouldn't have been surprised to discover that he was a true sailor with a girl in every port. He confessed to me in his dotage that he had always wanted to make love to a black girl. When he discovered that we had a lovely buxom coloured girl working for us his eyes lit up. "Well boy" he said "you go and do her and come back and tell me what it's like!" Next time I was in Yeovil I mentioned this jokingly to Dawn. "That's all right Mr Giles" she replied "I could do that and spit you out for breakfast". I never mentioned the subject again!

Work was almost impossible to find in rural Wiltshire in 1922 when Ted came out of the Navy and two of his brothers had already departed for Canada. Going into business seemed as good a plan as any – even if it did take a sizeable chunk of the money he'd saved out of his pay as an ordinary seaman. As well as the money, he'd gained another benefit from his Navy years: iron self-discipline.

When Ted and Alice got married they rented an old timbered farmhouse dating from the sixteenth century and built by an arrow-smith. If you go over to Hill Farm, Seend today you'll see a highly desirable property with well tended gardens, burglar alarms, and expensive cars parked on the drive. The arrow motif indicating the original owner's profession is carved in the timbers of the gable.

Back in the 1920s, however, it was pretty run down. The paint was peeling, the roof was leaking, and it was overrun with rats. Ted and Alice tolerated them for a while but the day they found one in the baby's cot they decided it was time to get out. The baby, born in 1924, was my sister Betty. Ted used the rest of his savings to build a house in Hawk Street, Bromham, not the customary two-up two-down cottage but an imposing double-fronted house with three bedrooms. Perhaps he overstretched himself as mother remembered him being forced to hide under the stairs when the bank manager came knocking at the door.

Although he had added a smartly sign-written Model T Ford van to the pony and trap, he was still serving his customers from a bucket. From the churns he carried on the van he'd fill a two-gallon milk pail with a lid; he carried this from door to door; and then he'd use a pint or half-pint dipper to dispense milk into the jugs which the lady of the house would leave on the doorstep – twice a day in many cases at the posher houses. In the summer milk didn't keep. Bottles were introduced soon after the family moved to Bromham, because that's when the tin shed which would become the dairy was put up, 50 yards from the house. They'd without doubt expanded into butter, because at certain times of year – in spring, mostly – there was an excess of milk from the herds, and, in order to keep the relationship with the dairy farmer going, dairymen like my father had no option but to buy every gallon the herd produced, and find a use for it – that was the contract. The Milk Marketing Board came into being in the '30s and was the saving grace of the whole dairy industry. The farmer was guaranteed a price for his milk. The summer surplus milk went directly to a wholesale dairy and vice versa in winter, the dairyman could buy as much as he needed from the wholesale dairy. The MMB undertook the advertising for the whole of the industry and increased the sale of milk all over the country. It certainly enabled my father's business to take off. Sadly with the demise of the MMB farmers are left to negotiate their own contracts and the small dairy farmers are going out of business at an alarming rate.

Mother admits I was the result of a challenge. They already had my brothers Frank, born in August 1927 and John in January 1931. In those days Dad would often walk down to The Bell for a couple of pints and a warm summer evening in 1935 was no exception. They were only in their mid-thirties and a balmy night is a balmy night in any year. "Go on with you" said mother when he came home later that evening "you're not the man you used to be. I don't think you've got it in you anymore." Off came his shirt – for then the same shirt was worn night and day for a week – he'd show her! And nine months later on 20th March 1936 young Freddie Giles made his first appearance.

By January '37 Nan Bolland, who was by then living with us, had died and mother had added a shop to the side of the house with the money Nan left her. She soon needed help. Phyllis Clarke, then a teenager, may have arrived as a hired help but she would soon become a member of the family, the sister that Betty always hoped for. I think I was about ten before I realised she wasn't actually my sister. She'd just left school and had been looking for a job where she could `live in` to ease the pressure at home, where there were nine other children. Not that our place was all that spacious. I distinctly remember as a small boy sleeping between Phyllis and Betty, but that may have been when the war was on. When dad was out on fire service I would creep in with mum and listen to the planes going over; enemy aircraft returning from Bath or Bristol, looking for somewhere to dump their bombs on the way back home to Germany.

When I was born my sister Betty would have nothing to do with me for three weeks. I was meant to be a girl; she certainly didn't want another horrible brother. Of course she relented and I know she loved me because she spoiled me and still does. I was born lucky because I came into the world with a caul over my face – rather like the stuff they wrap faggots in –and this was supposed to be a sign of great good fortune – according to the neighbour cum midwife who helped with mum's labour. It may be an old wives' tale but I've had a lot of luck in my life.

Frank, Father, Betty, Mum and John and in the middle a grumpy Fred with a Giles pout on – because I had to wear boots for the photograph!

I've got a feeling I was a bit of a handful as a child – always up to mischief whenever I could. I left home for the first time in 1940 on Christmas Day when I was not yet five. Father Christmas had left me a little tricycle, the first wheeled vehicle I'd ever owned and naturally I couldn't wait to try it out. Being Christmas morning there was no-one around to keep an eye on me; the whole house was at work delivering milk or preparing for the Boxing Day deliveries. I was off; ploughing through a layer of freshly fallen snow and pedalling furiously across the tracks which criss-crossed the small-holdings so particular to the neighbourhood. I was going to the pub, the Bell, and I'd almost achieved the few hundred yards and the main road before they caught up with me. Not too difficult to follow a single set of wheel ruts through the virgin snow. But the practice was useful. It wouldn't be so very long before I was out on a bike and at work. By the time I was eight or nine I was a vital part of father's operation every day; pedalling along the muddy tracks to outlying cottages in Cling Hill Woods with six or seven bottles of milk hanging in bags from my handlebars.

Later on, in my early teens, Raleigh Bicycles brought out a brand new sports model. It was only the late forties and we had been at war until 1945. It's difficult to imagine now how poor the country was and how low were our expectations. Nevertheless several lads in Scouts had a new Raleigh and I pushed mum into buying me one. We went to Devizes to buy this bike and I cycled home so proudly. What I didn't know was that mum had never said anything to dad about it . He hit the roof. "We can't afford it". "But lots of boys in the village have them" I pleaded. They were going off Sundays for anything up to 80/90 miles in the day. But no, "he's working weekends and there's no money for this bike. Take it back; I won't have hire purchase. We will not borrow money!" It went back, how mum got on about the HP I don't know but that was that until father said he'd spend a bit of money on a bike John had discarded. A bike which Frank had second hand from Dick Breach. John had then taken it over and now it was my turn. In the village, Den Hard's father, besides being the village postman, was also the bike repair man with a little shed up his garden. He was very kind to me and I spent many hours with him trying to make a silk purse from a sow's ear. I stripped and painted; renewed all the ball bearings even though I couldn't renew the ball casings themselves. I was pleased with it and though never allowed to go off with the other lads I had a very presentable bike and finally left home on it.

It's funny really but I love old machinery, equipment and cars especially and I've still never had a new bike. My present bike is a 1920s ladies model, very tall with a basket on the front and a single gear, a string guard to stop skirts billowing into the back wheel and a chain guard to keep oil at bay. It's called Rusty and I love it although it did get me into trouble a few years back.

Collecting bean sticks for the vegetable garden with Rusty and Kate in '92

Jan and I had a monumental row culminating in me leaving her to find her own way home from Cadwell Park Race Circuit in Lincolnshire. I had been competing for a top trophy in the VSCC[1], an aggregate points trophy which involved competing in every discipline of motor sport throughout a year, and I was doing well. I was working hard and at the same time preparing my own cars with Tony Coles and this was the last circuit event of the season. Another young friend was trying for the same trophy but with the benefit of several borrowed motor cars. He is a good driver but at this meeting he won a handicap race by a mile. His patron was well up in the club and Jan, who can be over-competitive on occasions, hinted that the patron had influenced the handicap committee and the race had been rigged. I was furious with her and told her that if she wouldn't take that back I would go home without her. I drove

---

[1] The Vintage Sports Car Club

home alone; 230 miles non-stop and still furious.   She finally arrived in the small hours of a Monday Bank Holiday having taken the train – first class as she pointed out to me! – and thrown pebbles at the bedroom window until I opened the door. But we still weren't speaking and the following morning I took off on Rusty in a foul temper.

My first pint was in Devizes at coffee time – and that's where I acquired my Bart Simpson helium balloon for the back of my bike. By tea time I seemed to have drunk myself sober and was thinking that the whole argument was rather silly and it was about time we made up. I phoned home and Jan agreed to meet me at a local pub but we hadn't been there five minutes before the argument was raging once more. Off I went on Rusty to drown my sorrows yet again. All I can remember is cycling home at midnight with no lights on my bike and chattering away to myself when the next moment I am flying through the air thinking you've bloody well done it now Giles, this is serious. An off-duty police officer – female – had hit me with her mini. Police and ambulance arrived on the scene and were very perturbed to be told that I'd lost Bart. "Hell" said the copper, "there's two of them. One must be in the ditch." They searched the ditch and finally came back to ask me what Bart looked like and how old he was. When they found he was a day old and yellow they were less than amused and I was carted off to hospital. Jan was phoned – "this is Melksham police and we have your husband." You can bloody well keep him was her reply until she realised I was a hospital case and had to relent. They tried to prosecute me for being drunk in charge of a bicycle but an out of town solicitor called their bluff and they finally backed off with a £25 fine for having no rear light. There was no motor so no breathalyser and Rusty was soon restored to its former glory.

Before I got into bikes and helping out on the milk-rounds though, my early days revolved around the kitchen and the shop. Mother of course was always there. She had the shop to look after from 6.30 in the morning, although that was right next door.   There were

10

actually several other shops in the village at that time, including a butcher, three grocers and two bakers, but she sold most of the things the villagers needed from day to day: butter, cheese, milk of course, tea, coffee, loose biscuits from those big square tins, tobacco and cigarettes. These included some evil black Turkish things that were sold loose – and naturally found their way into grubby little boys' hands to be smoked up in Cling Hill Woods on a summer's evening. When Ted found out he decided to teach me a lesson. He smoked a pipe which he filled with "Black Beauty Shag", a totally politically incorrect label in today's climate with a drawing of a smiling, headscarfed Negro girl as its trade mark and made in the tobacco factory in Devizes' Snuff Street in the '40s and '50s. As I wanted to smoke he had no objection and filled his pipe for me. Of course I had just one puff and it was disgusting so I handed it straight back to him. "Oh no boy" said father, "you wanted to smoke and you'll smoke all of it". I was so violently ill that I have never touched tobacco in any form since.

When our eldest boy, Rob, was in the same position we thought we would try the same trick. Jan was then smoking Benson and Hedges and we offered him a cigarette which he smoked with no problem. Another? Yes please until he had almost smoked the whole packet and insisted he was both enjoying it and feeling fine. We were panic stricken. What had we done? Somewhere about number eighteen he slowly changed from pink to green and like me he became a non-smoker from that moment on.

I think my mother was the stronger of the two. Ted's nickname was 'scrabbler'. During and immediately after the war the whole family was scrabbling with him to make a living and there was no time to plan any strategy. Not that they would have been able to implement many of their ideas. Milk was on ration and there could be no increase in sales. They couldn't keep pigs as there were no permits for pig-meal. Dad had seen sailors drowned in WW1 and would have absolutely nothing to do with the black market or with anybody who did. They had tried all sorts of ways to keep going, even serving pots of tea on the front lawn, and Ted was at his wits end. Mum was the one who encouraged and refused to give in. Whereas dad's family had lived hand to mouth, mum had been brought up in a successful business, living above the bike shop where Fred Bolland repaired and sold the best makes. He'd taught her at a young age that "a nimble nine-pence is better than a slow shilling", meaning that it's better to make a lot of sales at a small profit than a few sales with a larger return. It's something I've remembered all my life.

All of us children were steeped in bloody work. From the youngest age I remember the shop takings were counted out on the kitchen table. The milk money was sorted in the front room every day. We were all expected to contribute to the running of the dairy, the rounds and the household in whatever way we could. Sometimes, however, our efforts weren't appreciated as much as we hoped.

It was a cool spring afternoon, a Sunday. Sunday was the only afternoon off in the week. We did the milk rounds that day at a run so that we could get home for Sunday lunch and have a few hours respite. The only thing left to do then was to collect the afternoon milk from the farm and rather than bottle it we would all get up extra early on Monday morning. I had on my best Sunday suit, my only suit in fact. Tweed jacket and short trousers: chafed your thighs in winter and stifled you in summer. I'd gone out for a walk with Scamp, our little Jack Russell. It was a good walk, across the fields and up onto Roundway Hills. I was getting tired and had started on my way home when I heard the gun go off. Ahead of me the long stems of last year's grass rustled and twitched as some creature or other made a run for cover. Scamp gave chase of course, and the next thing I saw he'd put up a hare, and chased it out into the open. Normally he wouldn't have got near it, although he'd always try, but it had obviously been hit, and Scamp soon closed in on it. After he'd put it out of its misery he stood over the corpse grinning at me, proud as punch – but not half as proud as I was when I carried the trophy home. It was too heavy to carry it in my arms, and I didn't want to drag it through the dirt, so I did the sensible thing and slung it across my shoulders, never giving a thought about who'd tried to shoot it. I couldn't wait to get home. They'd be so pleased with me. This was war-time after all, and meat was on a tight ration – all except offal, pig's heads, ox-tails and the like, all available cheaply from Harris's pig factory in Calne, but that became monotonous week after week. I marched jauntily into the kitchen. "Look what I've got," I said, beaming from ear to ear. I was a provider, a man of the world, a hunter returning from the chase.

Mother looked up and I think she was about to break into a smile – until I slung my catch onto the table, and turned round to close the back door.

"Look at you!" I knew I was in trouble, but couldn't for the life of me think why. "Just look at the state of that suit." She grabbed me, whipped the jacket off and turned me around all in one movement, then pushed it up to my face. It was warm, sticky and it stank to high heaven. It was smothered in blood, with a few tufts of hair and a smear of purple gut for good measure. For an awful moment I thought I was in for a hiding and looked over at the hazel switch she kept by the side of the fire. "Well, I suppose you were only trying to help." She was really very pleased and by the time we tucked into the hare my little escapade had become a laughing matter.

Bromham was full of 'Holdings', the two-acre plots where generations of local families made a living growing produce on some of the richest land in the county. We had our own holding, part of which was taken up with the house and dairy but out the back was a large vegetable garden. The garden produced almost everything we ate, hardly anything was bought, and although us boys had to do the digging, father's pride and joy were his runner beans, for which he prepared a fresh patch of ground every year. The secret was in a big old bucket that lived in the outside privy next to the back door and was emptied into a trench once a week or so. It was our toilet. And it wasn't to change until mains drainage and water came in quite a few years later, in the 1950s. Father wouldn't hear of a chemical loo which a few people had – he wasn't wasting good material – and us boys didn't use it just to pass water, there were several places outside where that happened. Throughout my childhood the toilet seat was the wooden lid of a box, more like a small cabinet. A neat circular hole on the top, and a hinged door on the front. We had proper toilet paper, pretty posh really - although like everyone else we reverted to newspaper in the war. Father used to empty the bucket as and when it needed it. He would tip the contents into his bean trench and bury it with a few spadefuls of soil, digging on his trench by a couple of spits for the next contribution. He must have hated this job because he would never empty it until it was as full as possible and then it was very difficult to carry without spilling – ugh! If we had to get up in the night we used pots under the beds to be emptied by our cleaning lady, Gladys.

It can't have been much fun cleaning up after a family of seven with no indoor plumbing. Water came from a well between the house and the dairy. Some neighbours used a rope and bucket but we had a hand-pump in the house and the dairy had an electric pump! The electric pump meant we could even have a bath - albeit not in the house. For that we had to go to a tin shed built by father on the side of the dairy and where he had installed a fixed enamel bath, a very large water tank and a wash basin. There was no insulation and the single skin walls and roof dripped condensation. The tank was heated by the steam boiler in the dairy so there was gallons of hot water. The only trouble was it cooled off pretty rapidly, especially in winter. You'd be lying there luxuriating in the warm water, knowing that eventually you'd have to step out onto the concrete floor and do your best to get dry before you froze to death, although usually someone was banging on the door before you got to that stage. In the end it was a matter of gritting your teeth, jumping out and grabbing the towel.

Keeping warm and keeping the family fed took a great deal more time than it does today and you only realise how great is the difference during a prolonged power cut or a long lasting snow which closes the roads. Before the war dad kept pigs, most country folk did. You bought in a weaner and fattened him up. As well as meal we would supplement the pig's diet with whatever we could get hold of - like left-over parsnips off the Holdings, anything that wasn't up to market standard – and we'd stick them in an old milk churn, run a steam line from the dairy into it and cook them up. When the pig was nicely fattened we got the butcher round to deal with it. Killing the pig was quite an occasion, as far as we were concerned. The pig might have thought differently of course. The last pig we killed I must have been about five or six.

The pig wasn't one of those little plump pink things you see nowadays. It wasn't what you'd call cuddly. In was a black and white saddle-back. A big hairy brute. Had it been a boar you wouldn't have got in the sty with it. We were always hearing stories about people who'd been crushed or even killed by angry boars. Later on, when we lived at Frome and Jan was teaching our eldest daughter Jill to drive, the two of them came quite close to making pigs angry. From the narrow lane we had quite a tight entrance into our drive around the end of some old cow sheds and on the opposite side of the drive was a dry stone wall. Jill had very little experience and when she was told to slow down and change gear ready to turn into the drive she hit the accelerator pedal instead of the brake and careered into the stone wall at full chat.

Fortunately the wall collapsed – as did a large part of the yellow Marina she was driving – but less fortunately next door's pigs escaped through the gap and began rampaging along the lane. I came home from work and found my drive blocked by a crumpled car and a wife and daughter haplessly trying to round up a herd of pigs. Luckily we had another entrance and I must admit I left them to it. "You got yourselves into it girls; you get yourselves out of it!" Perhaps that was a bit mean and had I known that one of the pigs was indeed a bad tempered boar I might possibly have given them a hand. Luckily Alan, our next door neighbour and owner of the pigs, came to their rescue, telling them how his boar could get extremely cross if he wasn't handled with care!

Mother was injured by a boar helping father when he was breeding pigs pre-war but on the other hand all fattened pigs, although huge, were quite gentle as they would have been castrated early on. Old Mr Amor "bit off" bits to castrate pigs. I'm sure that's not right but that's what us boys were told and we were never allowed to see what was happening although we knew what he did. Killing a full-grown pig needed a couple of grown men just to turn it over so that it could be scraped clean of its hair, and tin baths were borrowed to collect all the parts as it was disembowelled and dismembered. It was a mucky old job. The fatty intestines would have to be very well cleaned of the stomach waste before being boiled to make chitterlings. They would then be served cold with mustard, vinegar, pickled onions and plain bread – delicious. The head had the jowls removed. These became Bath chaps and the head would be made into brawn – sheep heads also made a delicious brawn. Then the fat boiled up to make lard, the hams salted and the bacon cured; mother was kept busy for days making faggots and sausages while we children, in traditional fashion, blew up the bladder, tied it off and played football with it. Not real football of course – real football was played with an old leather ball, wet and heavy, the laces hard enough to open up your forehead if you caught it wrong with a header.

At Christmas we'd kill a goose. That provided us with a splendid dinner plus lots and lots of goose-grease to put into jars - a precious commodity. You could waterproof your boots with it – we all wore boots, day in and day out – and you'd waterproof yourself too, having it rubbed it into your chest and back to keep out the winter damp. The only heat source in the entire house was the kitchen range, which explains why we never ventured far from that room in the winter, once the day's work was done. In the bedrooms we regularly had to scrape the ice off the windows. But then so did everyone. We just learned to sleep with our clothes under the pillow so that they were nice and warm when we got dressed in the morning.

Like most families we knew, we supplemented our diet with rabbits. There was never any shortage of them, and as a young lad it was a bit of a game to go out shooting. I don't remember ever being taught how to use a gun; I must have learned by watching the others. There was always a single-barrelled .410 shotgun by the back door. You just picked it up, grabbed a few cartridges out of the drawer, and set off. It was nothing extraordinary. By the time I was twelve or thirteen I'd often pop out on an evening, shoot a few rabbits, paunch and skin them, then sell them for half a crown apiece on the milk round.

There were airguns about the houses too, and these were more or less toys. My older brother and Geoff Weston got me to hold a penny between my thumb and forefinger once. Geoff hit it but Frank missed the penny but didn't miss my hand, and it bloody well hurt. Another time, at the Westons, Chink Weston was at the bench in the garden shed and I found an air rifle behind the door. With no thought I levelled it at his back and pulled the trigger. Bloody hell did he yell! I wasn't punished but the person who left it loaded should have been. Chink wasn't seriously hurt but by then I should have known better than to point a gun at anyone. Brother Frank had a double barrelled 12 bore shot gun. He was a very good shot and used it for all sorts of rough shooting for the pot and he seriously upset a few foxes too. We didn't play games with that.

What we did play was soldiers. We knew all about Cowboys and Indians but instead of putting on feathers and war-paint we'd dig slit-trenches out the back and throw clods of earth at each other. War had broken out when I wasn't yet four, and the influx of soldiers after they built the Army camp made a huge impression on us all – it was less than half a mile from home in the grounds of a country house on St Edith's Marsh. With British or Canadian troops we never attempted to go near it but when the Yanks arrived in `43, and word got round about how well provided for they were, the older boys were over there as often as they could and I tagged along with them. Sometimes the GIs would get us involved in a game of baseball. If it was cold we'd go into their huts and sit on their beds or gather round the big pot-bellied stoves, listening fascinated to their drawling voices, and being given gum or sweets. They were always ready for a laugh and they were a generous lot. One day they gave a couple of us boys a rare treat, two balloons each. We'd never seen a balloon before so we were thrilled beyond words. We set off home proudly trailing them behind us on strings, and breezed into the kitchen just as father came in. He nearly exploded – and, looking back, I can see why. In those days there were certain things you just didn't bring out in public. Among them were inflated condoms. How were we to know?

The yanks wanted to know if we had older sisters and I did, so it was no surprise when Phyllis started dating a Yank. Later she would marry him, leaving the church in her white wedding dress seated on a tank. This was just before D-Day. There was little money around and precious few luxuries but the Americans came to the rescue with tins of peaches, meat and frankfurters for their reception at the local pub. Not long after her husband had been shipped off to the continent Phyllis found she was pregnant. When news came that he was wounded, but safe, it was soon followed by an announcement that he had been repatriated to the U.S. For some reason Phyllis never followed him out there. She had the baby, naming him Alan Le Roy after her absent husband. It would be many, many years later – 2004 in fact - that Alan would trace him. Sadly before he could make the trip across the Atlantic he received news that his father had been involved in a car accident and killed.

My sister Betty was married three weeks after Phyllis – her wedding had been in the planning a long time but Phyllis pipped her to the post. She married a lovely local man, John Wheeler, and they bought a corner shop in Swindon, coming to Bromham twice a week to collect vegetables from her father-in-law's Holding so that it would be fresh to sell the following day. My sister really did spoil me. In the spring when primroses were in abundance I, as a 9 or 10 year old, would pick bunches for her to sell in her shop. I never found out if she sold them all but she always paid me for them. I still pick a bunch every year to put on my mum's grave on her birthday March 28th. I've always done this since I was a child and although I'm breaking the law now I'm sure she appreciates the gesture. Betty and John also invited me to Swindon for holidays. It was very exciting to be in a big town and to have two of John's cousins to play with. Both were girls, one a couple of years older than me and her sister Diana, my age, who became a fairly serious girlfriend in our mid teens. I still have very fond memories of her.

Dad brought the milk in from the farm twice a day in heavy ten gallon churns; early morning and late afternoon. Three of us would unload and bottle the milk ready for the next day's deliveries. An hour and a half mornings before school or after tea. I wasn't involved in the dairy work until I was maybe eleven or twelve, but earlier still had my round to do on the bike before setting off for school. At the heart of the dairy was the boiler, maintained at forty pounds of steam pressure. It provided hot water for the bottle-washing plant, and power to turn the individual brushes which scoured out the insides of the bottles before they went into steam chests. We loaded the bottles into crates upside down, and when they were sterilised we hauled them out, scalding hot, and put them ready for filling. The chests were just about big enough to walk into – especially if you were a young lad; so it always fell to one of our weekend or Saturday lads from the local schools, and later on to me, to be sent in loading and get locked in by one of the older chaps. Very funny if you were on the outside; not exactly a laugh a minute if it was you in there in the pitch black listening to the pipes cracking and hoping to God your fellow workers didn't decide to turn on the steam. You could hear them opening a tap to frighten hell out of you and it did. A great joke. They played the same trick of course with the walk-in cold room. Once the door was slammed behind you there was no way of getting back out. Once sterilised, the bottles could be filled with milk. Each bottle was put by hand under a teat on a revolving table where the machine pushed the bottle upwards, releasing a measured amount; pints, half-pints, thirds for the schools, as well as one-and-a-half and two-pint bottles. To finish the job a cardboard cap was put in place by machine. Again by hand we loaded them into their respective crates.

Milk wasn't all we sold on the rounds; we packaged cream and could deliver goods from the shop too. One of Frank's schemes when he came back from his National Service in '47 was to try and increase ice cream sales. While he was away father had hired Rosemary, a smashing looking girl from the village to work a milk round. I was her Saturday boy and I'd already decided that she would be good for Frank and that I'd better mind her for him until he came home from the Navy. There were a couple of chaps on Rosemary's round who also had their eye on her, Charlie Harraway and Ron Ferris and they both had big motor bikes. Being offered a ride on a big bike was bound to impress her and that worried me for Frank's sake, especially when she took up their offer one Saturday and left me to mind the van. Little sneak that I was, I went straight to father and told on her! By God did she have a telling off but it worked and she didn't go near them again – at least not when I was looking! Rosemary and Frank used to go round the villages on summer evenings selling. Usually it was a Friday or a Saturday when the men had been paid and the children had their pocket money to spend. They had a hand-bell and I can hear Frank shouting "ICEY! ICEY!" now. Good practice because later Frank became unofficial town crier in Devizes with his bell and still now if you are quiet you can hear his laughter from the Market Place to the Brittox. Frank had no difficulty in agreeing that Rosemary was a lovely girl and three years later they were married.

I'd started school in Bromham, a simple country school still with a dirt playground. All country schools had allotments and little or no playground equipment. I was very slow to pick up reading and writing and by the time I was seven father was obviously worried about this. Mr Rolfe who looked after the firm's books, such as they were in those days, was also the headmaster of the school in Rowde, the next village. Rowde took pupils from 5 to 15 – if you didn't pass the 11+ you simply stayed on there so Mr Rolfe was used to both younger and older boys and had a reputation as a bit of a disciplinarian. He'd soon sort me out, he told father.

And he did. Despite his reputation he was a very fair and decent head who believed in the punishment fitting the boy. I loved cricket. Playground cricket. One day as I was idly throwing a ball against the school wall I noticed a swallows' nest under the eaves and thought it might be 'fun' or 'good practice' – perhaps I just didn't think anything – if I could knock it down. Of course I could and Rolfe saw me do it. For a whole term I was made to stand in the playground every playtime and watch the other boys playing cricket. That hurt as much as the caning he would occasionally hand out. One morning, Brian Bull and I were playing up our young teacher more so than usual and she had enough of us. Rolfe was taking a class of older boys and she sent us in there. There was a silence as all heads turned to look at us and an expectant "Well?" from Rolfe himself. "Please Sir, Miss Springbett says will you cane us". He made us stand for a moment while he gave his class some work to do and then slowly walked over to his tall cupboard – where the cane was kept. "Follow me" he ordered, leading us back into our own classroom. There we stood in front of all our classmates, our hands held out as the cane swished up and down on them, desperately trying not to blub. We didn't go there again –

any of us. But the head's discipline wasn't the real reason my school work improved. That was down to Miss Springbett – a young teacher straight out of college – who made us want to learn for her sake rather than our own. I thought she was beautiful and she filled me with such enthusiasm that I never looked back.

If there was discipline at school there was plenty at home. Ours was a small village where everyone knew each other and everyone was 'a potential customer'. That included a friend of father's, Mr Schofield. He worked for a big building firm in Devizes who'd landed a contract for supplying the wooden huts that accommodated the soldiers at the Army camps. I often met him as he came out of his gate to cycle to Devizes when I was cycling to school. He and I would cycle and chat together and I got to know him quite well. Father always called him by his first name and so I did the same – until Mr Schofield casually mentioned to dad one night that young Fred called him Jock as well. Not only was I a cheeky little beggar but I deserved a sound thrashing – and I got one.

We were taught to speak civilly to everybody and even now neither Frank nor I can stop ourselves calling people 'Sir' or 'Madam' when we don't know their name. Or couldn't pronounce their names, like the German and Italian prisoners of war who came into the shop for their tobacco. Initially they were controlled by armed guards but they were only country people themselves and had no desire to escape. They worked the land or in the huge complex of glasshouses growing tomatoes and cucumbers. My mum was fond of them and bought the little items they made during their evenings in the camp; slippers with rope soles and woven rag uppers; little wooden boats; toys. Reminders of the real war, however, were never far away. The red glow on the horizon as Bath was blitzed. The crackly radio in the kitchen which demanded our silence for the latest news. British and American troops arriving and departing in ever increasing numbers, erecting huge fences protected by barbed wire. We knew something big was going on – the preparation for D-Day – we just didn't know when.

Father was too old to be called up but he wasn't quite 'Dad's Army' material. His involvement in the war effort consisted of setting up the village's Auxiliary Fire Service, towing the fire pump behind a milk van with ladders on the top. He was the officer in charge of a team of half a dozen men and girls (including Betty, Phyllis and Frank) who took turns to spend the night in a shed in the village and be ready for call out.

You never knew with father. He could be a very kind and thoughtful man, but he could fly into a temper at a moment's provocation. Other times he'd withdraw into himself for seemingly no particular reason and refuse to talk to any of us. When that happened, woe betides anyone else who broke the heavy silence – especially at the meal-table. I can see him now, slurping his tea as noisily as he could and glowering at us over his cup, daring us to utter so much as one syllable. If ever you met his gaze when he was in that sort of mood you made darned sure you looked away quickly. Otherwise he might just throw a plate at you. His most spectacular withdrawal came when I was still quite young. For seventeen consecutive days not a single word passed his lips. Two and a half weeks of absolute silence as far as his family were concerned. It was as if he'd been struck dumb. In the midst of one of these spells a customer might come knocking at the door and we'd hear him being his usual polite and friendly self. How are you? How's the wife? No, it isn't as warm as it ought to be this time of year. They loved him. He was such a charming man, so kind-hearted. Then he'd shut the door, come back inside, set his jaw and clam up again - until suddenly one morning he'd come downstairs and start to talk perfectly normally, as if nothing had ever happened.

The silences weren't so bad, really. He had other ways of letting out his temper and these were much more frightening. Around the time Frank came home from his service in the Navy there was an almighty row. He must have fallen out with mother over something or other and was having a go at her one night. We boys were in bed next door, and through the wall could all hear him, screaming at

23

her, calling her a bastard – not a nice thing, since he knew full well that she was born out of wedlock and had carried that stigma through her life. Frank decided enough was enough. He got up from his bed, barged into the next room, and pushed the old man onto the bed. "You lay a hand on my mother one more time and I'll sort you out." He was more than capable. In the Navy he had become a boxing champion. Father never abused mother again like that.

Less threatening than his occasional outburst against mother was his violence against inanimate objects. It was the winter of 1947, bitterly cold, with the snow piled up along the roadsides for weeks on end, and a critical shortage of every kind of fuel – coal, electricity and petrol. One morning we went out to start the vans which were only garaged under tarpaulin. We had no anti-freeze so they were drained every night and we then had no hot water so they were difficult to start. The last one just wouldn't have it although we pushed it up and down the yard. Ted and Frank wound it on the starting handle but it was still no go. Ted finally lost his temper and the last I saw of him before I went off to school he was beating the bonnet furiously with the starting handle and turning the air blue.

Frank didn't inherit father's temper and was slow to rouse – John did, with a cruel and nasty streak, and I inherited the tantrums and temper born of frustration, the inability to suffer fools gladly. But Frank shocked me the first time I heard him use the f-word in anger – when he was chopping gnarled and knotty wood with only a slow progress. He was my hero and in those days heroes didn't use bad language! Nobody used bad language.

All this time I was still doing my early-morning round, but at this stage it wasn't interfering with my education. We never had homework when I was at Rowde, and we never did any extra preparation for the eleven-plus exam which was looming. The rounds-man would often get back and tell us he'd run out of milk before the last two or three houses. As 'the boy on the bike' I'd have to pedal a couple of miles each way to deliver it – it made me cross that the rounds always finished at the furthest point from the dairy when with a bit of thought they could have been organised the other way round. Every Saturday and Sunday I'd go out with Rosemary on a round in the van –on a Saturday there was the money to collect and extra pints to deliver, and other bits and pieces. But of course I was still a lad, and always likely to get distracted – like the morning she delivered to a house where she had to walk a hundred yards up a path to the front door and I had to wait with the van. There was a big pond near the gate and this particular morning it was frozen over. Naturally, I had to try it out, inching my way out on the slippery surface until I became aware of this horrible creaking noise and – splash! – I was in it up to my waist. Rosemary just sent me home where I cleaned myself up, changed into some dry clothes, and ran back to pick up the round where I'd left off. You couldn't let a little escapade like that interfere with getting that morning pint on the doorstep.

The dairy was quite a modern affair by the time I was working in there full time.. Quite often it was me who had to fire up the coke-fired boiler mid morning and get the steam power going for all of the cleaning. If I let it almost go out then I was in trouble. As a rule it ticked over nicely, but now and then it would be a bit reluctant because I hadn't got the clinker out of the bottom. I remember one time when I was under pressure, so I threw half a bean tin of petrol on it. "That'll get the bugger going," I thought, and it did – except that it took half the hair on my head, my eyebrows and all down my right arm as the flames whooshed out from the open fire-door. I didn't get shouted at, I had the fire going so what did it matter. I forgot that, twenty years later, and really dealt severely with my two boys who I found firing oil cans at the gas fire in the workshop. The flames came back up the oil like a flame thrower and was obviously great fun. They hadn't thought about father's toys – the Bentley and the Frazer Nash sitting around them.

It's strange really how small fires seem to have cropped up in my life but perhaps the fact that Mum would have a fire in the garden as often as possible and burn virtually anything that she deemed superfluous no matter who owned it has something to do with it; I was lucky to save my school report book still in its original envelope. Although father was the war-time fire officer for the village, one of the fires that his vintage fire pump didn't put out was our street's VE Day bonfire. The weather was so terrible that the bonfire had been postponed to the following night. Everyone was celebrating and a group of chaps who had drunk a pint or two thought differently about waiting and set the bonfire alight as they left the pub. Father saw the glow as he came home from the same pub and immediately set about the culprits, smashing the ringleader's glasses with his wild assault. Ted and another friend thought they had finally brought them to order when they made a grab for their bikes to run away. John Sims had had the foresight to take out their tyre valves and they were well and truly caught! Their punishment was to build another bonfire for the following night which they duly did. Thereafter the ringleader was known to us all as "Bonfire Billy".

Our children have had their moments with fires too. Rachel kept her pony in a field about a quarter of a mile from our house at Clink. 'Robbie' wasn't in the field so she thought she would burn off the dry grass under the hedges by simply putting a match to it. Very quickly the grass, the hedge bordering the road and the main line railway embankment were all ablaze. Panic. Tears. The fire brigade and an understanding police force brought the episode to a close but a few months later a very local farmer had his hay barn go up in flames during the day time. It could have been natural internal combustion but our two boys were blamed because of the Rachel episode.

But the funniest and not quite the most serious fire was years later, an evening Jan and I came home quite late. The kitchen light was on but the room was full of smoke and son Jon was slumped over the kitchen table. For reasons which became obvious much later, the back door was locked. I had to smash the window to get in and haul Jon outside before I went back to deal with the fire. The cooker was in flames. He had obviously come home boozed and decided to cook a bacon sandwich – only he'd fallen asleep instead. Was I angry! Daft bugger! He was OK and I went to bed not best pleased. Half an hour later and Jan still hadn't come to bed so I stormed back down to the kitchen in the noddy. What the bloody hell was going on now? Jan was talking, not to Jon who had been put to bed in the recovery position, but to Robert, our eldest son, – and a lovely girl. They had been at the far end of our long narrow Somerset farmhouse taking advantage of the shag rug in the lounge and were blissfully unaware of any commotion. No longer. The sight of a naked flaming Fred jumping up and down in full flow must have frightened the young lady away because she never went out with Rob again! Drink and Cooking together was henceforth banned.

School, Scouts and Starter Sex

The dairy rounds were so much a part of daily life, the pattern so ingrained, that fifty years on I can still recite my customers from the early days: and not just their address, but what their daily order was. I have to say I wasn't always as good at reciting my school lessons. Nevertheless, while I was at Rowde I wasn't doing badly, and when the eleven-plus finally came around I was one of five in my year who passed it. Again, I have to thank Miss Springbett. Previous to her arrival I don't think many pupils from Rowde School had got through, but she inspired something in us – perhaps just a desire to do well for her. I can't thank her enough. Sadly some years later she was knocked off her moped on Caen Hill and never recovered.

Frank had passed his eleven-plus several years earlier, but he never went to the Grammar School. By the time he was fourteen he was at work. I don't think it ever entered anybody's head that he would do otherwise. In any case, that was before the 1944 Education Act when you still had to pay fees to go on to the Grammar. Plus the fact that as the oldest son he was lined up to take over the business one day. He was ear-marked as father's right-hand man. It was in the natural order of things, so I shouldn't think he ever questioned it. On the other hand, John and Betty had both gone on to Cannings College, a fee-paying school over in Chippenham. They cycled there every day, seven miles each way. Nothing was ever said at home about my passing the exam –no praise, no congratulations. But then we weren't that sort of family. You were expected to do your best, and then come home and carry out your duties. Work came first, second and third on the agenda. Nevertheless, I was pretty pleased with myself at being kitted out with a brand new school uniform and walking down Hawk Street at eight o'clock my first morning for the bus into Devizes. Unlike my schoolmates, however, I'd been up since six, done my chores in the dairy, collected my milk, done my round, dashed back for breakfast, then got changed and run for the bus – still in my short trousers and boots.

My first thought when I arrived at Grammar School was that I'd never seen anything like it. I don't think I knew enough at that age even to have imagined such a place. Rowde had been three rooms, three teachers and ninety children. Here there were over 300 of us, with a different teacher for each subject. As well as the individual classrooms, there was an art room, a woodwork shop, a metalwork shop, domestic science kitchens for the girls. There was also a library, and there were playing fields. Beyond the fields, still inside the grounds, were the woods. It all seemed so huge, and the first day seemed so long, what with finding my way from classroom to classroom, meeting the new teachers, making friends, and then when it was all over riding home on the bus at twenty past four. Time to get changed, grab a slice of cake and a cup of tea before the van came into the yard with the evening's milk, whereupon it'd be all hands on deck in the dairy for bottling, followed by high tea and bed. We worked hard and we slept soundly. And to be fair, I was paid for my efforts. At fourteen I was paid four shillings a week, but I saved most of that in a little tin money-box we got from Lloyds Bank.

With all the work to be done we didn't have much time for amusement. The highlight of the day might be listening to *Dick Barton* on the radio, or weekly Wilfred Pickles in *Have A Go*. We occasionally went to the pictures. Like every other child of my generation I was taken to see *Bambi*. Unlike most other children of my generation I was so frightened by the film that I hid under my seat and refused to come out. It was the scene where the forest caught fire that terrified me. Brother John amused himself on Sunday afternoons with his money box. He would take all his savings – the £1 and 10/- notes that is – screw them into tiny balls and throw them around the bedroom. Then he would collect them all up, straighten them out and count them. A strange chap.

I did get a holiday. That was at the invitation of our neighbours across the road, Mr and Mrs Paget. They used to rent a caravan down at the seaside and spend a week there with their son Ryal, who was a good friend of mine, probably my best mate as I was growing up. Most of the coast at that time, in the aftermath of the war, was a no-go area, much of it mined and just about all of it littered with barbed wire and concrete bunkers against the German invasion that we'd fully expected in 1940 and '41. But by the mid to late 1940s the beaches were being cleared, and Bowleaze Cove, just to the east of Weymouth, was declared accessible. There was no running water in the caravan, and no electricity. At night we read by the light of oil lamps, and Mrs Paget cooked over a paraffin stove.

Ryal and I always swam before breakfast and we learned for the first time about limpets on the rocks. We could knock them off with a stone, cut them out and tie them to a string which we would then dangle in rock pools. Sitting on the rocks we pulled in small crabs by the bucketful. They hadn't been disturbed for years because of the war and they certainly weren't edible but we didn't need complicated gear to catch them. We learned to catch hold of them across the shell so that they couldn't nip us!

Poor Ryal came to a tragic end. He loved to play football, but one day he suffered a nasty injury when he was kicked by an opponent, quite accidentally. Something went badly wrong with his leg and a cancer took over which rapidly spread through his body and killed him. He was sixteen.

After Ryal died, I became best friends with Bernard Smart. Bernard had been born on the same day as myself and was a good looking boy; later he never had any problem attracting the girls. I called on his mother on the milk rounds and I would sometimes ring up for her from the box in the village to the bookmakers to put on a bet. "This is for Snowdrop" I would say before relaying the message. Bernard and I went on his new Douglas motorbike to the Grand Prix at Silverstone and watched Fangio racing, an early inspiration for when I later raced myself, and we both learned to dance in what was to become Devizes' first coffee-bar.

A huge part of my enjoyment came from Scouts which I joined when I was ten – there were no cubs in those days. Our leader was the Rev. St.John Battersby "BATT" to us all. He was the vicar of Chittoe and Spye Park, all part of the parish of Bromham and he was extremely charismatic. He got about on a tin leg and wore thick lenses in his glasses as a result of the 1st World War.

Both of my brothers had been in Scouts before me, FWANKIE and GILER and then me NIMROD, so named because I was a bit handy with a bow and arrow. I had a longbow which I later passed on to Frank's two boys and then a year or so ago when he moved house he found it again and gave it back to me. Now our grandchildren use it for target practice. I remember shooting a rabbit and cooking it over an open fire on a spit. We all had nicknames. Scouts had been re-formed by BATT after the war in

1947 and we would meet at the vicarage and use the grounds for woodcraft, camping or cooking activities in the summer or go to Spye Park for wide games and swimming in the lake. In the winter we met in the disused village school room.

I was very keen and loved scouts. I got lots of badges – pioneer, woodcraft, cooking, nature, swimming, sport. We were very smart, about 15 of us and I went on my first away camp – the Wiltshire Scout Jamboree in 1948 – at Corsham Court, home of Lord Methuen who was with Baden Powell in South Africa. It was an experience, the London Olympics were taking place at the same time and we would listen to it on the radio – no TV of course. We were very short of food and Batt went out to a hotel each night to eat. We were not very happy about that and so we raided the stores tent! A year later nine of us camped at Bridport. One of the parents took us down in his open top 30 cwt lorry with our gear and we sat on the top. No thought of safety! But great fun, cooking on open fires and walking each day to the sea at West Bay about 2 miles away. The next year it was Beaulieu in the New Forest. Memories of clubbing rabbits as they ran out from the machines cutting the corn. They couldn't run over the stubble and it was easy to catch them there were so many. We had rabbit every day, stewed, roasted, it was very good especially as meat was on ration. At times you could hear the rabbits screaming in fear as they were being stalked by a stoat. The ponies and donkeys in the forest were neglected during and after the war. They were all crippled as their hooves hadn't been trimmed and were turned up in a dreadful manner.

By this stage I was a very keen Scout and aiming towards my 1st Class Scout badge, no-one in the troop had it. I had passed all of the test except the solo overnight hike and so one Sunday in the Easter holidays just after my 14th birthday I walked up to the telephone box at the Pound in Bromham at 2pm. My instructions, a sealed envelope and an OS map 1" to 1 mile, were handed to me by Eric, BATT's assistant, who then left me. My companion was Prince, a beautiful black Labrador belonging to brother Frank. In my unframed rucksack I carried an ex US Army open fronted bivouac, a wash bag, my mess tin and a small pot plus food for 24 hours, an ex-Army water bottle, my sheath knife, a blanket, cycling cape and 6' of rope. Naturally I wore a full uniform including a scarf, a woggle I had made from the spine bone of a sheep skeleton found in Spye Park, lanyard and whistle, flat rimmed hat as per the Canadian Mounties, shorts, long socks and my work boots.

I first had to pick up an old coaching road, a rutted farm track over Roundway Hills, and find a milestone on Beacon Hill recording the miles to London and Bath. Next to the monument and White Horse at Cherhill to find the date it was erected and from there to Calstone to find and ask permission for a place to camp. I stayed at a farm close to the church where I was given water. I'd covered approximately 10 miles and by the time I had heated a tin of stew and bread for my supper, written up my log book and washed I was ready for bed.

Next morning I was woken abruptly by Prince. At the front of my tent and peering in on me was an unshaven man with a strange foreign accent. He began quizzing me in guttural broken English. What was I doing and why? I was very frightened and began to wonder what I could do. As it happened there was no problem. He was a German prisoner of war going milking! By the time I had cooked my breakfast of beans, bacon and bread, the weather had turned to drizzle and as I broke camp this became heavy rain. I was heading for home, about seven miles on country roads. By Hedington I was soaked to the skin and was more than grateful for the group of electricity board workmen who had their brazier going. They dried me out a bit and gave me hot sweet tea before sending me on my way. Over the tracks after Turnpike Farm and I was back at the telephone box and only a mile from home. We'd done it!

My log was written up; I had to record the birds I'd seen, and in fact that Sunday was the 14th April and I had seen the first swallows; together with the weather conditions, wet; and the heights I had reached, 725' at Cherhill. With this I had passed my First Class Scout Badge which put me in the running to be chosen as one of 24 Scouts from Wiltshire to represent our County at the World Jamboree in Austria in 1951.

I was getting on all right at the Grammar school too although I was the only kid to show up in boots – every day for the first two or three years and the last to go into long trousers at 14. It seemed normal enough to me: we all wore boots in the village, and I don't believe I possessed a pair of what you'd call shoes, unless it was my Sunday best. Whatever I had were probably re-studded several times over on the heavy cobbler's last that father kept in the kitchen. We had to make do and mend because of clothes rationing after the war.

My first reports were encouraging and I was beginning to do well at Geography and Science in particular. In English I had "a tendency to dissolve into helpless laughter at the feeblest joke" and an ability to "get into mischief if he has an idle moment". But the fact is that I wasn't destined to achieve academic success. I was destined for business, and, to tell the truth, when father remarked a couple of weeks before my fifteenth birthday that I wouldn't be going back to school after the Easter holidays I was delighted. "Great," I thought, "I can start work." I was also relieved. I'd got behind with my homework. I rarely had time to think about it as I juggled the school day with my morning and evening chores – not to mention scouting, which was becoming quite a hobby. It even got to the stage where I would deliberately leave my exercise books on the school bus and tell the teacher I'd done my homework but lost it. On another occasion I bullied – yes, bullied – another boy into doing my Latin exercises for me. He was in the year above me and he certainly got his own back. The following lesson our Latin teacher, Mr Howell, congratulated me on a very good piece of work which I had handed in. However he wanted to know how I was clever enough to cope with the grammatical problems that he didn't anticipate teaching us until the following year! Found out and in trouble again!

I loved games, we had a double period one afternoon per week but we had to walk nearly ¾ mile to the football or cricket pitches and back to catch the bus home. No showers just a changing shed. Summer term gave us one lesson of swimming each week. The pool opened mid-April, in the open air and with no heating, and no matter what the temperature you swam. We loved it, it had a springboard and a three height diving stage. The Superintendent, Sid Dowse was the life saver, the cleaner, the money taker and in fact the only person employed by the Town to look after the pool. He sold 1d Oxo cubes in boiling water for 3d and by golly you needed it some days.

I rarely got into real trouble, but I was once singled out for the Headmaster's disapproval. It all came about after the school had been having sex education lessons. Revolutionary stuff and we loved it. Now, we were adolescent boys; and we lived in the country. We knew about the birds and the bees. But our knowledge was pretty rudimentary. Here was a teacher going through the whole business scientifically, with diagrams of boys' parts and girls' parts, and everything described and explained to us. It worked us up into a kind of sexual fervour. All we could think of was getting to grips with the girls and investigating further. The poor girls, I have to admit, came in for some rough treatment. Most resisted, but some succumbed. What I didn't know at the time was that we boys weren't the only ones touching them up, pestering them to let us have a look at what they'd got and so on. One or two teachers were guilty of the same thing. But that didn't come out until a few years later.

The whole sex craze came to a head one day when the Headmaster called a special assembly and lectured the school on morals. The school, he told us, was like a bridge, and we the pupils were like the water flowing under it. My mates and I nudged each other and started to smirk. What was he on about? Most of that water, he continued, was pure and sparkling, but some of it was... dirty. By this time we were nudging each other and sniggering, and of course once that started we couldn't control it – nor the explosion of anger that it provoked. "Yes," the headmaster's voice rang out. "At the back there." Everyone turned to look. "Giles, Dowse and Neate. We all know that you're some of that dirty water, don't we?"

We felt pretty small, and it did calm it down. Later when I was Den Hard's boy on the milk round, he was a bit of a ladies man, he gave me lessons in love, teaching me the rules of engagement. Every time I took a girl out he wanted a full match report with edited highlights. Aha, so I'd got me hand on her breast, had I? Good lad. Well, next time you need to try this… and so he coached me every inch of the way. Now that's what I call sex education. Den's philosophy was that a girl will always forgive you for being too fast but never for being too slow.

These days, I suppose, the school would have tried to get my parents in for a talk; but back then that's not how it worked. As far as I recall neither my mother nor my father ever set foot on the school grounds. It didn't mean that they didn't care; just that they never thought it was any concern of theirs. Education was what the teachers were paid for, and presumably the teachers knew best. Besides, I wasn't doing badly; I was always in the `A` stream but work at home was the real reason I wasn't doing as well as I could.

However, when the school got to hear that I wasn't coming back they certainly expressed their concern. In my final report the Headmaster wrote, "From Fred's point of view I am sure his leaving school at fifteen is a mistake." My form teacher added a more personal note: "He has added quite a lot to the pleasure of those around him, for he has shown that it is possible to be a boisterous boy and, at the same time, courteous and pleasant. He will be missed, particularly on dull days!" He even took the trouble to have a chat with me. He was surprised I was leaving and wondered whether it was because my parents felt I wasn't doing very well. He told me he'd never had any concerns about my ability to progress. "We expect you to be a bit of a nuisance in Year 4, but we know you'll settle down. Boys always do."

I left school the day after my fifteenth birthday, elated and relieved. I was going to leave all my troubles behind: Latin verbs, mathematical formulae, overdue homework, deadlines. It was such a weight off my shoulders. On the Friday lunchtime of my final day a few of us sloped off to the woods beyond the playing-fields and lit a little fire. Then I made a pile of all my books, peeled off my cap, my tie, tore the badge off my blazer, and burned the lot. It seems now like a gross act of vandalism, the sort of thing a really disaffected youth might do after a miserable career at a rotten school. It wasn't any of that. I didn't hate anyone. I was just glad school was over. Burning my things was, like so much else in my young life, a bit of a laugh. Years later Taffy Watkins, our P.E. teacher, told me he'd seen what took place. Why didn't he apprehend us? He realised there was no point – and I know he realised too that we meant no real harm. Work at home meant I just hadn't been able to keep up.

My brothers thought I had been expelled and couldn't understand how I was allowed to go to the World Scout Jamboree in Austria that same year in June. Only in the last year or so has Frank learned the truth.

Of course at fifteen I wasn't ready to take over my own milk round – I didn't have a driving licence for a start although I'd learned how to drive the vans years before with Den Hard. I had also learned a bit about basic mechanics. We had to. The vans we used were old Austin 10s, petrol-engined, 1936 models. They didn't have the sides out, like a conventional milk-float, so you still had to lean in through the rear doors and pull the full crates towards you. Later, when Pat Garrett set up his workshop in the village he re-sprayed and modified them for us, which made things a lot easier. Those old vans frequently ran rough, so you needed to be able to whip the plugs out and clean them, top up the battery, that sort of low-level maintenance. And of course you had to be able to get them going with the old starting-handle. Nobody taught you these basic every day skills; you just picked them up by observing and then having a go.

I helped out on all the rounds in turn, Frank, Rosemary, John, Den and one day when I was out on the rounds helping Doreen Shell, a pretty girl but married by then, we stopped to watch a steeple-jack scaling Bromham church steeple. It was being overhauled, and they'd rigged up a lattice-work of scaffolding and ladders right to the very top. They'd removed the cockerel for re-gilding, and we could see one of the steeple-jacks way up the top, clinging to the steeply angled sides as he checked over the lightning conductor.

"You wouldn't catch me going up there," Doreen said. "I can't imagine how they do it."
"Why not? I could do it. Be easy"
It was true: I liked heights. I was always climbing trees. Never felt the tiniest bit scared.
She looked up at the steeple-jack again, and shuddered. "I bet you wouldn't dare go up there, though."
"How much?"
"Ooh, got to be worth half a crown."
"Make it five shillings."
"Right you are then. Five shillings – but you got to prove you was up there, mind."
"Oh, I'll prove it alright."

I don't know where I got the idea for the welly from. But there were always plenty of old worn out wellies in the dairy, so late that night as I sneaked out I grabbed a size ten, tied it round my middle with a bit of string, and set off towards the church on my bike. I have to admit it wasn't quite as easy as I thought – not least because the steeple-jacks had removed the bottom ladders as they did every night. This meant shinning up posts and cross members and diagonals until I got to the ladders which had been left. Although these were completely straight up I found it easy and I was soon looking down on the white plumes of smoke that curled around the sleeping village from damped-down fires. The hardest part was untying the welly from around my midriff, but I soon got it loose and wedged it firmly over the blunt tip of the spire.

Next morning on the early round Doreen gave me my five bob. She was impressed, thought it was a great joke and gave me a big smile. Mother wasn't so struck. I knew I should have kept my mouth shut, but that's never been my strong point and when I got home for lunch I found everyone in the village had been talking about the sight that greeted them as they went to work. I had to tell her. I just couldn't contain myself. The upshot was mother made me hand over the five shillings to the vicar when I went, tail between my legs, to apologise. By the time the escapade was written up in the paper – with my name right there in cold print – we all treated it as a bit of a joke, which is what it was supposed to be.

I could have done with that money too for I was saving hard to raise the £25 I needed to take part in the World Scout Jamboree. We'd already been on a couple of weekend camps to sort ourselves into patrols and get to know each other but now came the problem of affording the trip. The only way I could do this was by earning it but the rounds men were only paid £5 a week and as a mere boy of 15 I was worth only ten shillings (50p). Batt, my scout master, gave me a log-sawing job paying me by the hour and I picked strawberries on the Holdings. Mother found a bit too from the till but luckily I had been in the habit of saving since my original money-box and so somehow it was all found. A Wiltshire White Horse badge together with the Union Flag was stitched onto my uniform and after being inspected by the Mayor of Swindon we were marched to the station for the London train. Seeing the Skylon, part of the Great Exhibition of 1951, impressed us before we even left the train but the overnight stay in London really added to our excitement. We were billeted in an underground railway station, narrow metal stairways going forever down and down until finally we were in a very deep shelter with metal bunks three high.

A relic of the war of course but now containing the whole of the British Scout contingent with their sandwiches and cocoa and non-existent washing facilities. The next morning we had the climb to do in reverse with all our gear but nothing was going to daunt us now we were on our way. We were to see sights and enjoy experiences which we had never dreamt of. After a calm channel crossing the foreign trains were waiting for us and we were crammed eight to a compartment into their dirty smelly carriages. Thirty six hours of sleeping two in the luggage racks, two on the floor and four on the seats until we reached the American Zone of occupied Austria, Bad Ischgl near Salzburg. More sardines as we changed into a narrow gauge train that would take us into the mountains. We were seriously overloaded and the train set out with much spinning of its wheels until they finally bit the track. Some three or four miles before our campsite we got slower and slower until finally the wheels spun to a stop. At last a relief engine appeared and tired and weary we were unceremoniously pushed into the camp.

The rain poured down as it can do only in the mountains and wet through and exhausted we were more than relieved to find that earlier arrivals had pitched our tents for us; we could scrape a hollow in the ground where our hip would be and climb gratefully into our sleeping bags. The days of mattress and air bed camping had not yet arrived! The next morning we rose early to build our 'Gateway', poles and ropes shaped into standing stones and lintels to represent Stonehenge; all over this huge camp of twenty odd thousand scouts from all corners of the world, magnificent Gateways were being erected. We had a lot of free time to meet and talk with those from other countries; to understand and see and talk of our differences but with Scouting as the aim over all of us. The American contingent came off best; we were all being helped by the US Army but they had lounges with armchairs and settees, coca cola machines, hot dog stands in marquees. Good for them but we were a bit jealous.

A Jews Harp, a small instrument held in the mouth and played by twanging a metal strip, effective in the right hands or perhaps that should read teeth, was given to everyone of us as a symbol of music and peace. I had the symbol branded onto the leather of my sheath knife which I wore everywhere. Here were twenty thousand teenage boys with virtually all of them wearing open bladed knives, my own knife blade is 5"(125cm) long, using them, cleaning their razor sharp edges, and all with no violence – but that was fifty years ago. Have we progressed?

This was my first taste of foreign travel and I loved it. Wonderful camp fires with national costumes and dancing, ice-cold lakes, mountains to climb, friendships to make and something I shall always remember. Very early one morning , because our tent was next to the boundary fence, I was woken by a steady and regular SWISH, SWISH, SWISH. I looked out to find an old Austrian in

full national costume, whiskers and all, cutting grass with a scythe. It was beautiful. But all too soon it was the closing camp fire, the singing, the farewells, and back to reality. It had been wonderful and I had been very lucky.

I'm proud of Scouting; I was able to continue while I was in the Army and to see my two sons in both Cubs and Scouts. Now Jonathan is a Leader and nearly sixty years later I am able to give something back as Executive Chairman of Corsham Sea Scouts, a very thriving group. I'm also pleased that I can still get into my original uniform.

Once I was home, life now settled into a bit of a routine. Work, work and more work, seven days a week. The idea of taking on extra help so that we could get a day off was never an issue as far as father was concerned. He'd worked all his life, so why shouldn't we? I don't believe he and mother ever had a holiday until after he had a heart attack at the age of 61 and had to ease up. After that they occasionally went away with me or Frank, but never on their own.

As to wanting time off, and any feeling that we were hard done by, we only had to look around us at our neighbours. Most of them were still travelling to Melksham or Calne or Chippenham to put in long hours at the various factories, the rest were on the land, cycling in with their tools lashed to their cross-bars and putting in endless hours of ploughing and planting and hoeing and harvesting out on the Holdings in all weather, spurling the pig-muck with their forks or burning last season's weeds. They weren't suburban gardeners, tilling the soil for a bit of relaxation: they got a living from that fertile, light land but by golly they worked for it. When the beans were ready for market, or the new potatoes, or the sprouts they had to be picked there and then, no matter whether it was blowing a gale or the rain lashing down. No, we were doing all right with our rounds, our dairy work and the daily banter with our customers. We could have been a lot worse off, and I think we realised it.

At fifteen and sixteen, I wasn't actually that bothered about time off anyway. I was keen as mustard about the business. I suppose, being the youngest boy, I always wanted to prove I was as good a man as Frank, John and Den, and so I would charge into things without a care for my own safety. It was partly their fault in a way, because they were always winding me up about being a boy doing a man's job. When I saw Frank lift five crates full of empty milk bottles out of the van and into the dairy, I naturally couldn't rest until I'd matched him. So I had a go. I felt something give, but I had no idea what I'd done for several days until I felt the same pain

43

again. What I'd got was a hernia – and a two-week stay in Devizes Hospital. It was a life of Riley in there. Just plenty of rest and three square meals a day not to mention surrounded by pretty nurses.

Once I'd had my seventeenth birthday I was ready – itching – to take the next big step: pass my driving test and take over my own round. The driving test was going to be a piece of cake. I'd been driving off-road for four or five years now. What did I need to know? There were no lessons in those days: you taught yourself, more or less.. All it meant was a trip to Bath and a date with the examiner.

I failed – miserably. It was one thing lurching around the villages and up farm tracks in a milk van but driving in traffic in a city centre - and an unfamiliar one at that for I'd never driven there at all – was a different matter. I forget what the bloke failed me for, but it took a hell of a time for him to go through the entire list as I shrank lower and lower in my seat. I seem to remember the words "due care and attention" cropping up once or twice. I was not looking forward to going home and telling Ted that I still couldn't drive a milk van on my own.

Back home I swore a bit, then got a copy of the Highway Code. I'd gen up on that and have another go. This time I knew I'd pass. No problem at all. And to celebrate I'd ask Mary Hobbs out on a date. She was a farmer's daughter and she was gorgeous. We'd go to the pictures in father's car. She'd like that.

Imagine my shame when I had to ring her and tell her I'd failed - again. I had to meet her on the bus! Anyway, I may have been a failure as regards the driving test, but I'd still had my date with Mary: Charlie Chaplin in *Limelight*. You never forget these things. When we moved to Seend in '88 I realised that Mary's parents still lived in the same house, Melksham Park Farm, and they were now our nearest neighbours. Mary and her husband visited regularly and not only did we become good friends but I was able to see that Mary was still gorgeous and I still fancied her like mad! Jan teased me a little as I drooled over both the old and the new 'Mary from the Dairy'.

Not only was I smarting from the ignominy of failing my test again, but I'd had a right ear-bashing from the old man. So long as I was unable to go out on my own he had to pay another man's wages, and outside help cost more than we did. To make things worse, John got on to me. He and I were always chafing at each other. He could be a really nice chap when he wanted to, taking me on a trip now and then – to London to the Motor Show on one occasion – but he took after father in his moods, and when he was in one of those you did well to stay away from him. At the best of times he was a hard task-master. One bitter winter's day when I was about to go out on the rounds with Den, he spotted me wearing gloves. What was the matter with me, he wanted to know? Getting soft already? Not up to the job, maybe? Carrying those freezing bottles from door to door would toughen me up, he said, make a man of me. And just to make sure he snatched the gloves away from me. Den said nothing, but after a while on the round he peeled off his own and passed them to me. "I'll make do with these," he said under his breath, slipping on a pair of old mittens.

Not only could John be mean, he could be dangerous. It wasn't so long before this that he'd lost his rag with me and thrown an empty milk crate – metal, not plastic – right into my face. Frank laid him out and re-arranged his features for him. Of course, keeping away from John when he was in a mood was easier said than done: we worked side by side in the dairy most days. Anyway, he couldn't resist having a dig at me over the driving test and this time I completely lost control. I grabbed the nearest thing handy, which happened to be the ice-pick, and went for him. In my rage I fully intended to kill him; no doubt about that. So you could say that Den Hard, coming up behind me and wrapping his strong arms around me, saved my brother's life – not to mention my future. But the strange part of all this was that – just as with father – John's customers thought the world of him.

Third time lucky, I went to Swindon rather than Bath and passed my test with no problem.

Now I was ready to assume my inheritance, as it were. After ten years of scuttling up the lanes on foot or on my bike, of riding shotgun for the others, I would have my own vehicle, my own round, and my own list of clients – or customers, as we called them in those less sophisticated days.

But first a word of warning from my father.

"You'll get offers" he told me. "And you take 'em my boy, take 'em all. BUT,"….

There was a pause in which I considered with anticipation the certain women along the rounds.

And then father continued

"…..BUT. YOU FINISH YOUR BLOODY MILK ROUND FIRST!"

It's one thing to sit here today and write this, saying I loved the work and was having a grand old time of it, but I'm overlooking the fact that at times I was unhappy enough – maybe angry enough – to run away from home. Maybe it was John winding me up – which he delighted in doing. Maybe it was a feeling of being trapped. I don't know, but when I was around that age, fifteen or sixteen, I twice got on my bike and set off for Southampton, fully intending to join the merchant Navy. Both times I got no more than fifteen or twenty miles before I ran out of steam, my anger dissipated, and I turned around. My family never said a word. They never even reacted when I managed to run away and stay out overnight. I packed a few things, got on the bike, and hid out in Spye Park. Lit a fire, slept in an old hunting lodge and cursed everybody roundly, then went home again. Nobody had come looking for me, and nobody said a word when I came back. So long as I got on with work, so long as the business wasn't disrupted, that was okay.

I wasn't the only one to run away, as it happened. John was clearly unhappy when he ran away to Salisbury to join the Guards. He hadn't passed his medical for the services on the grounds that his hearing wasn't up to scratch and certainly couldn't withstand the battering his ears would get from gun-fire,. The Guards were known to take anyone who would join up voluntarily – as opposed to the conscripts they were getting who wanted nothing more than to see out their eighteen months and get back to civilian life. That particular adventure lasted twelve weeks – until they too discovered John's weak hearing wouldn't tolerate the noise of rifle fire, so he was soon back home once more. But in that short time the Guards had made him mad, totally indoctrinated him. He marched everywhere, even to the outside toilet, where he would stamp his feet to attention, raise his right hand and hammer three times on the door before stepping smartly back and opening the door. Everything was spit and polished and each night our trousers, for I was included in this campaign, would be wet down the creases and placed under the mattress between sheets of newspaper to be pressed for the next day. His desire to get away was unabated, however, and would culminate later in his emigrating to Canada.

It was a fine evening in late spring, and my cousin Richard was at the dairy door in a bit of a state. He was about Frank's age and lived maybe half a mile away on the other side of Cock Road where his father farmed. Adjacent to their fields was a stretch of Rowde Common where gypsies used to camp two or three times a year. We were all a bit wary of them, but by and large they caused us no real bother and they generally moved on after a week or two. The problem arose, as it had in the past, when they let their horses stray onto private grazing. It was always a case of "some-one must have left the gate open": very hard to prove one way or the other, and always a cause of friction. This time they'd let them get into Richard's fields once more just when the hay crop was ripe for cutting. They'd made a right mess of it and Richard's dad had had enough. Would we come and help sort the buggers out?

We needed no encouragement. At the end of work we three brothers fired out of the dairy and set off towards Richard's farm. By the time we arrived there were about eight to ten of us. We found eight caravans parked on the common. In the near-dark we could see the gypsies cooking over their open fires, their faces illuminated by yellow and red flames as they stirred the contents of black iron pots. The men were making clothes pegs, holding the little work tops between their knees and shaping them with a round mallet rather like a stone mason's made from a single piece of wood 5/6" diameter. As they spotted us they got to their feet and an argument started but it wasn't going to resolve anything so we charged. Wow. Could those men throw their mallets; we were repulsed with some nasty hurts.

We were having second thoughts until old Bill Sheppard, a farm labourer well into his fifties, decided to lead a second charge, and we were with him. This time the gypsy men all ran and to our amazement it was the women who stood their ground with one old lady wielding a bill hook – a short handled wood chopper – and Bill dealt with her with his stick across her arm. Blood was spilt, and one of the gypsies went for the Seend police force – a solitary copper who lived in a cottage on the edge of the village. The women were strong and tough as old boots but they took shelter behind the vans and a stand off formed. It was nasty, and it could have got a lot nastier had the village bobby not arrived and called us to order. It was then a classic case of old-fashioned community law enforcement. He told us to stop being naughty boys and go home, which we did. What he said to the gypsies we never found out, but by next morning they were gone, and never returned.

It all seems a bit vicious looking back, but from our point of view an injustice had been done, a good crop of hay spoiled, and so we took the law into our own hands. I should add that none of us lads were strangers to fighting. Punch-ups outside dances were a fairly regular occurrence; but unlike today they were pretty fair fights. You didn't get gangs attacking an individual; you didn't get people using weapons; and you certainly never saw a man kicked when he was down. Years later when we lived in Frome and I had lost a little Jack Russell I went along to Gypsy Lane to see if they had him. After all that time the women recognised me and although it was water under the bridge by then and they weren't at all aggressive or threatening I thought it politic not to overstay my welcome!

By the time I'd turned sixteen I was starting to go out with John and his mates on a Friday or Saturday night. I had a nice suit, a pair of decent shoes, a keen eye for the girls, and I'd tag along with them for a couple of pints in the local and a night's dancing wherever there was a band playing.

There was no live entertainment in the village, so wherever we went - Bath, Devizes, Melksham - involved transport. Neither of my brothers could afford a car so as often as not John would hire one from the village taxi firm, Nelson King. If we squashed six or eight of us in it worked out quite cheap. Later on father was happy for us to borrow his car – although he must have known he was running a risk. In 1953, when I'd just passed my test, he splashed out on his first ever new vehicle, and a thing of wonder it was: a black Morris Oxford, like the ones the police had. If you've ever watched old films like *The Lavender Hill Mob* you'll know what it looked like. It had a touch of class about it, even if it was built like a tank.

When we went out in those days, of course, we did what I'd call proper dancing. And the music was always `live`. At Bath Pavilion we might have Ted Heath or Johnny Dankworth, swinging modern big bands. In Melksham Assembly Rooms we'd have a twelve or sixteen-piece band, playing everything from Strauss waltzes to swing to Frank Sinatra songs. Sometimes it'd be foxtrots, sometimes old-fashioned numbers like the military two-step. Or it could be a snowball, where one couple took to the floor

A nice suit, a pair of decent shoes and a keen eye for the girls
Brother John and I off to a dance

and every time the music stopped both the man and his girl took a new partner until everybody in the place was out there having a good time. One of the joys of it all was that you could go for a night out on your own, knowing that if you spotted a pretty girl you were perfectly entitled to ask her to dance with you. It might go no further than that, but at least you could enjoy her company for a few minutes. If she was with a partner already, then you could "excuse me". It was good old-fashioned fun – even though there was never any alcohol on sale. Of course, we liked to have a beer or two but we did that before the dance started, slipping out again

50

in the interval; but you had to hurry back in before they locked the doors on you at ten o'clock. The dances would go on till about midnight, and if one of us got lucky with a girl and the others were ready for home, well, they'd give you half an hour – and if you weren't back by then the lucky lad would be left to hitch-hike, or walk.

One night we were all off to the Policemen's Ball at the Pump Room in Bath, a pretty swanky black tie do. Could we borrow father's car? Yes, help yourself. Just bring her back in one piece and pay me for the petrol. It was still only a few weeks old and had hardly been run in. There were five us in the car that night, with John driving. We had a great time at the ball but it was about three in the morning as we made our way home. It was a wild old night as we headed back to Bromham, blowing a gale and the rain lashing down. Just the sort of night when you don't want your windscreen wipers packing up on you. John was driving and finding it harder and harder to see where the hell he was going. In the end he lost his rag and pulled up in Atworth, about six or seven miles from home. He got out and opened the back door.

"Come on, you drive. Time you pulled your weight."

I'd been asleep and before that I'd been drinking – fairly heavily as we all had before the breathalyser, but I climbed into the driver's seat and set off, nice and slowly.

"Get a bloody move on, will you; we've got to be up in three hours." I did my best, but all I could see through the rain cascading down the windscreen was about ten yards of scrubby hedge illuminated by our dim yellow lights. I don't think we'd gone a mile when we rounded a bend and met an Austin Seven coming straight towards us with just his sidelights on. I said the Morris Oxford was a built like a tank, and we now had every reason to be glad it was. We rammed the little Austin side on, shoving it into the ditch and pushing in the driver's side door.

The driver suffered a broken arm, the police arrived after we'd roused someone in a nearby house, and only after they'd interviewed us in the car and got all our details down did they tell us to "bugger off home" and leave the car where it was. With no wipers it wasn't fit to drive, they told us. We staggered in an hour and a half later after a five-mile hike in the rain. I was already in tears. I didn't think the accident had been my fault but I still felt responsible. As soon as father saw us coming in the back door, soaked through, we knew what to expect. He listened to our explanation in silence. "Right, now get your bloody evening suits off and get to work," he said. "It's six o'clock." We were just in time to load up the vans and do the rounds.

I ended up getting a summons out of that, for driving without due care and attention. The fine was seventeen pounds and ten shillings, or four and a half weeks' wages. Good job I'd developed an early habit of saving a bit every week. Father washed his hands of the whole affair. We'd got into trouble; we could sort it out – the repairs, the fine, the solicitor's fee, the lot. Thank goodness he'd got fully comprehensive insurance. From that point on, though, he would only insure me to drive the milk vans.

All the time this was going on I was well aware that the clock was ticking. At eighteen, like every other able-bodied man of my age, I would be liable to the `call-up`. National Service. Two years rather than eighteen months in Her Majesty's Armed Forces thanks to the added demands of the Korean War.

End of Innocence

I have to admit I was looking forward to going into the Army. Maybe it was hearing Frank talk about his experiences in the Navy. He had been stationed for some time in Ceylon – now Sri Lanka – and loved the place and the people. He told me stories of being locked up there in Trincomalee for trading navy petrol with the natives, incarcerated in a cell next to a man who was waiting to be hanged. I had to visit The Gut in Malta where his ship had docked and where father had been 25 years previously when he was in the Navy. I did go tho' it took me fifty years to get there but by then I found all the trade gone! Naval ships may still call into the port but the ladies of the night no longer grace the steep steps under the arches by the docks! The main advice I got from father as I awaited my call-up papers was the complete opposite of what many an old soldier will tell you. "Always volunteer for everything."

I turned eighteen on 20 March 1954 and it wasn't more than a few days before the Army called me in for my medical. I passed, but only Grade 3. The problem? Not flat feet, not bad hearing, not eyesight, but a much more mundane affliction suffered by many a teenager. Acne. At that time Britain maintained quite a large force in the Far East and other tropical areas where numerous contagious diseases were rife. Acne, with its broken skin, laid a man open to all sorts of infection – and as they pointed out to me, one sick man deprived a fighting unit not only of his strength but also of whoever had to look after him. Even getting sunburn out there, and thereby disabling yourself, was a chargeable offence.

A few months after the medical I got my orders and a travel warrant. I was drafted into the Royal Artillery and was to report to Oswestry camp on the fifth day of August. On the slow train up the Welsh borders into Shropshire there were hordes of other fresh-faced eighteen-year-olds, all of us wondering what we were in for. At Oswestry station we found a convoy of trucks waiting for us. There were no seats. What did we expect? We were "in the Army now". We piled in, grabbed hold of the metal stanchions that supported the taut canvas sides and top, and tried not to lean against each other too closely as we lurched off down the road.

We spilled out from the back of the trucks and were immediately surrounded by snapping terrier-like Bombardiers in shiny boots armed with swagger sticks shouting at us. "Right you lot. Face the front and get yourself into three lines." We shuffled and shambled and eventually found ourselves in three ragged lines. "Right you lot. We're going to make you into bloody soldiers." We were well and truly in the Army now, and this is the way it was going to be until they licked us into shape. After a lot more shouted insults they got us divided up into squads of 28 men. .

"Right, you 'orrible lot. Some of you lucky sods will have been in the Army cadets. Am I right?"
"Yes."
"Yes what?"
"Yes sir."
"No, not 'yes sir'; 'YES SIR!!!'"
"YES! SIR!"

"Better. Right, those of you who have been in the Army Cadets step forward in your best soldierly fashion. *On* the command… MOVE*!*"

Several of them stepped forward. Old hands showing up the rural greenhorns. They stood smartly to attention, trying not to smirk.

"Right, you will forget every thing you ever learned in the Cadets. The Cadets is for boys. This is the Army, where we make men of you. You know nothing about soldiering. We know everything. IS THAT UNDERSTOOD? "
"YES! SIR!"

Everything in the camp, our home for the next twelve weeks, seemed to be built of timber or tin. The barracks were called 'spiders' because they were in a sort of H formation, with the cross-member being the ablutions and the four legs being four separate huts, each one housing a squad. Our beds were iron-framed and our blankets itchy. Into the barber and out with a short-back-and-sides. Into the stores and out with our uniform, leaving our civvies behind, even our underwear. The unfit were weeded out with PE tests. How do you fold everything army style? How do you polish the brass parts of your uniform? Blanco your webbing? Polish your boots, then take a spoon, heat it over a candle and iron out all the little pimples on the toe-cap and heels until it is as smooth as glass, and then polish again to use it as a shaving-mirror? We were given a number; one that you would never forget as long as you live, and then took turns with the assorted metal stamps to impress that number on every piece of kit that would take it: our boot-brushes, our boots - underneath the arch - even the little button stick that we slid under our buttons to make sure that we didn't get Brasso all over the cloth. My spit and polish training imposed by brother John came in very useful.

Everything we did and everywhere we went it was at the double, generally while being shouted at and called all the f---ing idiots under the sun. Basically, they broke us in. We were to show no initiative, but to obey orders quickly and efficiently. In spare moments we polished our aluminium mess-tins till they shone like mirrors, and if, upon inspection, our beloved Bombardier (equivalent in rank to a Corporal) decided they weren't shiny enough he'd scratch them with a fork and leave us with hours of hard graft and elbow-grease until they were one hundred per cent perfect again.

Our beds, our kit, and the entire hut was inspected every morning - and believe me, they looked everywhere for faults. They'd poke at your blankets with their swagger sticks to see if the corners were nice and tight and if they weren't – crash! – over went your bed, scattering your kit all over the floor and leaving you to start again.

Most of the lads coped with it; some hated it; some really struggled, and had to do things over and over again until you were sure they'd break. As for me, I loved it. I enjoyed the discipline, and revelled in the challenge. Whatever they wanted me to do I was determined to be the best at it. There were quite a few public schoolboys at this early stage – before they got siphoned off for officer training – and some of these were a bit lacking in practical skills. As I watched them struggle with taking their belts to pieces and doing all the Blanco and polishing before re-assembling them, I thought of what father always said: "Better a shovelful of common sense than a barrow load of brains."

After we'd ridden this tidal wave of activity there came the aptitude tests. Here my good subjects at school – maths, geography and so on – came to the fore. They soon had me down as a trainee Technical Assistant. My job was to learn all the technical aspects of giving the gunners the information for setting their guns: reading maps, plotting co-ordinates of the gun's position and the target, then working out the range and the required angle of elevation. Here I finally found a use for all the logarithmic and trigonometric exercises I'd done at school; I took to it like a duck to water. Although I was then put forward to see if I was officer material, I wasn't. I suspect now that my broad Wiltshire accent weighed heavily against me.

But now I was a trained soldier and off home for two weeks' embarkation leave - and a fortnight's work in the dairy - before my orders came in the post. I opened the envelope and wondered; where on earth was Luneberg Heath?

How the men who were transported to Hong Kong, which took six weeks, survived I shall never understand. We spent only one night in bunks on a troop-ship, stacked three high down in the bowels of the craft, awaking next morning as the ship entered Holland at the Hook. From there the train took us across the flat Dutch landscape into Northern Germany, to Celle where we were greeted by a familiar sight: a convoy of three-tonners ready to take us to the barracks at Hohne, home of the Fourth Royal Horse Artillery, out on the blasted heath between Hamburg and Hanover. It was here that Montgomery received the surrender from the Germans at the end of WW2 and it was a perfect place for gunnery ranges.

Built by the Germans in the 1930s for their own tank and artillery crews, these barracks were a far cry from the draughty wooden huts we'd had at Oswestry. They were two-storey stone blocks, divided into individual rooms rather than dormitories. Some had three beds, just like the room I'd shared with my brothers but some had 8 beds and held a complete gun crew. Down the corridor were toilets and hot showers. No outside toilet? This was better than home! In all, six regiments were housed here, a total of 4,000 men.

I had only been in my new quarters for two to three weeks when I found myself in trouble and not of my own making. We had a Brigadier's inspection coming up. Everything had to be spick and span. But that was no problem to us lads in our room. We were all good soldiers. We applied the usual copious amounts of Brasso, Blanco and Bullshit, made sure everything was neatly stowed or folded, dressed in our very best uniforms, looked proudly around and went off for breakfast.

"Left - right - left – right! About TURN"

The strident voice of the Sergeant Major rang in my ears. I was in the guard room and I was on a charge. So were my room-mates.

The sight of the smoke billowing from our window was etched on my mind. It had only been half an hour since we left it pristine and suddenly the beds, the mirrors; my carefully folded blankets were splattered with the contents of the fire extinguisher we had used on the waste-bin. What bloody idiot had thrown his cigarette end in it?
"Well Giles. What do you have to say for yourself?"
The Battery Commander looked up from his papers. I was close to tears and feeling suddenly a long way from home. My throat

constricted. Was I going to be able to say anything at all. I had tried so hard to get things right and now I was totally shattered.
"I don't even smoke, Sir" was all I could manage.

I was dismissed without punishment. Fortunately there was no real damage to either the room or to my ongoing army career. Soon after this episode it was December and Christmas was on top of us. So many chaps had leave and I was so dreadfully homesick. Not sure now that I liked this army life. That first Christmas I went to an army hotel in a small town in the Harz Mountains. The only thing I really recall was being in uniform, a very new soldier, drinking too much beer and then a hazy recollection of being picked up by the red caps – the military police – and thrown into the back of a jeep, not noticing the bruising where I hit the rifle and tool racks until the following morning. When I woke, still fully dressed, boots and all, my army pay-book – the army passport – was open on the locker besides me. God, not another charge! I needn't have worried. Even the MPs recognised a homesick young soldier and were merely teaching me a lesson.

Life on the Heath soon settled down into an apparently endless series of exercises. I was a TARA – a Technical Assistant Royal Artillery – and it was our job to make sure that the guns ended up firing at the correct targets. The fact is that as a Gunner you could very rarely see what you were aiming at. It was all worked out on paper by us from information supplied by an OP – observation post. My job was to take note of the grid references for our position and the target handed to me by the radio operator, then plot both on a map. After that I would take a sheet of scaled grid paper and, with the aid of a ruler on a swinging arm, measure the angle and distance between the target and the gun. We'd also have to take into account other factors such as the wind speed and direction, and even the wear of the barrel calculated by the number of times that gun had been fired. Then we would calculate how many degrees left or right to swing the gun and the elevation to raise or lower in degrees and minutes. The 25lb guns were mounted on Sherman tank chassis and unlike the ordinary artillery guns, which were towed by lorries and so confined to roads, the Royal Horse Artillery could travel cross-country. We travelled with the guns, in an office built on the back of a half track vehicle, which had been converted from a troop carrier It was pretty confined standing room only with the TAs, their drawing boards and site ranging equipment, a sergeant in charge and the battery officer. The observation post moved in fast light armoured vehicles, mainly tanks, and provided us with the grid reference for the enemy whilst our troop surveyor gave us the grid reference for our own position. The settings would be passed to the Number One gun layer; setting the gun to our specifications was the most skilled job on the gun. The sergeant would give the READY and the officer in charge who was in contact with the OP would give the FIRE. Immediately the OP would report back where the shell had landed and we would then plot to straddle the target. If the first shell had landed 200yds to the left then the next calculation would be 400yds to the right. We would probably need to plot about 3 straddles plus lowering or raising the elevation before No.1 gun had the range and then all of the other guns which had been adjusting but not firing at the same time were ready too.

Picture the scene. There we are out in the middle of nowhere, surrounded by hundreds of square miles of desolate heath, with pine forests, heathers, scrub, small villages out of bounds scattered about us. In all probability the gunners freezing half to death for the winters are bitterly cold and schemes were known to be stopped when men got frostbite. We work out the co-ordinates, factor in a head-wind of thirty-five miles an hour, and then wait for the big moment, the gunners stamping their feet on the icy ground. When everything is in order, at last, comes the command - the booming voice of our Sergeant.

"FI-IRE!" This is immediately followed by a grunt as the Gunner pulls the lanyard, a click from the firing mechanism… and then the voice of a less than enthusiastic Gunner:

"BANG!!!"

As usual, there's no live ammo. Fire, fire, fire! Bang, bang, bang! Day after day. Today they'd call it virtual firing. We called it a bloody waste of time. Live ammo was a precious commodity reserved for exercises in front of top brass, and of course the eventuality of a Russian invasion; we were close to the borders and we were still in the throes of the Cold War.

Our first three months out there we were always in uniform and didn't venture far from base; but we did make the odd foray along the road into our local village. Hohne was 3 or 4 kms and we walked there for a beer or even better Speigelei mit Kartoffel (egg and chips!). We were in the middle of a potato growing area and for the first time I tasted saute potatoes and thought they were wonderful If you weren't content with Hohne and had the money then you could take the three-tonner for the twenty miles into Celle every Saturday. Some chaps spent their free time lying on their beds and reading comics, counting down the time until they could go home.

We didn't go to the other local hamlet which was opposite the regimental gates. Belsen! We'd heard about the place, of course. Everyone had. It was abandoned to the weather by the time we were there. Liberated nine years previously, it still had an atmosphere of utter desolation about it. When we visited it seemed quite ghostly, the sort of place where you instinctively didn't want to raise your voice, partly out of respect, partly out of awe. The low concrete blocks where so many met their death or awaited it were windowless and silent; weeds sprouted from gutters, and in the open spaces between the buildings scattered trees were taking hold. Here and there were low mounds of earth labelled "1100 bodies buried here", or "1,000" or "4,000". There were monuments, obelisks, put up by the families of survivors who had come to see, to remember and to commemorate. It was a sobering experience; you never knew what to say about it without appearing either disrespectful or insensitive. I don't know how the ordinary British

soldiers who found this at the end of the war could cope with it –
dealing with it without training or counselling.

Back in camp we tackled some of the civilian employees around the place. There were hundreds of Germans working amongst us: barbers, tailors, cleaners, cooks, NAAFI staff, even rounds-men delivering our milk. The response was always the same: "We know nothing."

After three months we could send for our own clothes. They had to be inspected as being suitable by our Sergeant Major and we certainly couldn't wear them in barracks. As National Servicemen we weren't strictly allowed internal leave in Germany – just two home leaves to Britain in the two years – but if you played the game with the army they would treat you well. Stuart Fox who I met in our battery became a great friend and we both wanted to travel so instead of using the Naafi we'd pinch bread from the cookhouse at mealtimes and buy sandwich fillers from the Naafi shop to supplement our army rations and save a lot of cash. We had a good library so he got me reading; Steinbeck; C.S.Lewis; Dickens etc. We went to evening classes for woodwork. He was an artist from London and later worked in advertising in the City.

Colibri Ruf 42 61 65

das Kabarett der Sonderklasse
Hamburg - St. Pauli, Große Freiheit **34**

Immer noch einmalig für Deutschland:
Odette Byrill im **Schaumbad!**

Stuart was in the group of us who explored the delights of Hamburg. At that stage the Germans were really trying hard to rebuild their lives and their cities and work went on twenty four hours a day and seven days a week. We'd all heard of the Rieperbahn where the attractions of a red light district were on open display – if you could afford them. You might see girls wrestling in mud and I still have the brochure of a topless girl coming out of a champagne glass at the Colibri Club.

Compared with the entertainment on today's licentious Rieperbahn, where you are offered live sex acts of every gender, it was very tame but it was a magnet for any soldier with a leave pass and a few quid saved up, and it certainly didn't take much to get a gang together to go and investigate. We got our leave passes, signed out at the guardhouse, picked up our army-issue Durex, and headed for the bright lights, all done up in our best clothes. Smart sports jacket, collar and tie, creases in our trousers and polished shoes. Our Sergeant Major had no sloppy civilians in his Battery.. We weren't allowed into a place like the Rieperbahn in uniform. It had to be civvies.

In those days the brothels were housed in the Winkelstrasse which was screened off by two overlapping corrugated iron barriers with just enough space to pass between but making it impossible to see down the street. You couldn't wander in there by accident, but if you did go in you had a pretty good idea what to expect. You certainly couldn't complain that you were shocked. The girls worked from government run brothels and were well looked after and I sometimes think it would be easier if the same thing happened here now. However we lads were, understandably, staggered by the beautiful girls on display in the windows each with their name on show, and we knew - just knew – that we had to sample the wares. Trouble was, when we went and knocked on the door and asked for the name of a girl, we discovered that they were much more expensive than we'd imagined. We retired to a bar and, soldiers being what they are, we decided we'd pool our available funds, and at least allow one of us to have a night to remember. At that time we were all on about twenty eight shillings or 17 marks a week. We reckoned we could raise fifty or sixty marks between us, enough for a session with one of the girls but certainly not the best. How did we decide who would have the pleasure? The usual way: broken matches. And who drew the unbroken one? Why I did of course!

From an album of drawings by Stu' Fox

The only one we could afford was not exactly a beauty! And the truth is, it was an awful experience. There was nothing in the way of intimacy, no cuddling and absolutely no kissing. That was *verboten*. What we had was a business transaction, pure and simple and she more or less told me to get on with it.

The lads, naturally, wanted to hear a good story. So I just had to make one up for them, I could hardly say I'd spent their money on a horrid experience. Young men can be pretty crude when they're together and we were no exception. The wider their eyes, the bigger the lies I told them. One way or another they got their money's worth.

When we got back to barracks there was the usual ritual: you signed back in, entered the little room where you'd picked up the condoms, washed yourself with carbolic soap, and put your name in the book. You had to do this. Catching V.D., as we knew it then, was a chargeable offence. Her Majesty's Armed Forces had made available the means to avoid infection, and if you declined the offer you were in for a stretch in the glasshouse. On one occasion three of our mates, drivers, went out for a night on the town. They all went with the same woman, but upon their return only one of them took the trouble to clean himself up and sign the register. It turned out they'd all got the clap, but only the two who hadn't signed were charged. They spent twenty-eight days inside – not in the comparative comfort of our barracks, surrounded by friendly faces, but twenty or thirty miles away at Bielefeld, amongst total strangers in the army prison.

When Jan and I went back to Hohne and Hamburg in 1989 on our way to knock down a bit of the Berlin Wall I walked down the Winkelstrasse again. The barriers were still across the ends of the street with no women or minors allowed and the girls were still in the windows. But now instead of young beauties the windows were full of leather clad harridans with every type of perversion available, repulsive creatures reflecting the dissolute nature of the nearby Rieperbahn. First of all I asked Jan to wait for me at the end of the street but when she spotted the girls on duty her side of the barriers she declined and I had to take her back to the restaurant for another coffee. She then gave me precisely seven minutes to get there and back. She need not have worried, the attraction had gone completely!

We'd also managed to get into my old barracks with, of all things, a photo album I'd bought there thirty five years previously. The snapshot of me standing outside of my block convinced the guard we were genuine and we were allowed to wander around my old rooms and the NAAFI. We found the Scots Guards in residence and although still relatively well kept, Tom, our Sergeant Major, would have had a fit. You can't apply bullshit to regulars like you could to National Servicemen. By 1989 Celle was a major tourist attraction with tours out onto Luneberg Heath in horse drawn carriages and Belsen was a sanitised museum. When we crossed over into East Germany along the Berlin corridor it was for me more reminiscent of the Hohne and Celle I had known than the tourist trap behind us. Helping to knock down the Wall was an emotional experience in itself and we carried home from it great chunks of the painted concrete.

In '55 our leisure activities weren't all drinking and girls, not by any stretch of the imagination. Stuart, as I mentioned, had got me reading, and apart from the English classics he introduced me to the writings of C S Lewis, the great thinker on matters of the soul. As a lad I used to go with mum to Bromham church and later take girl friends to the evening service. I was actually quite religious at this time in my life and went on two or three religious courses at Church House near Hanover – mainly I must admit for the good standard of living there and being treated more as a student than a soldier, although I was confirmed by the Bishop of Salisbury in Hohne. If you had committed a minor misdemeanour and were put on Sunday morning fatigues – mainly scrubbing floors – you could escape by going to the church service.

Stuart and I visited Copenhagen, not so very far to the north of us and watched Eartha Kitt perform live in the Tivoli Gardens before we went on to visit the Carlsberg brewery. The ferry ride to Malmo in Sweden was an eye-opener, seeing the fantastic array of open sandwiches they served on board, and the smorgasbord of raw herrings, shellfish, beautifully cooked beef sliced wafer thin, exotic cheeses and those gorgeous sweet pastries. For Sweden, not being in the war meant there was no food rationing and of course at home there was still a shortage of almost everything.

One of the great things about Army life was the sporting facilities and the ready availability of all kinds of equipment. We could just grab a tent, blankets and stoves from the Quartermaster's Stores and take off for the weekend and by now there were seven or eight of us getting about together. Sometimes we were in too much of hurry, like the warm summer evening when we dashed off to Steinhuder Meer, a lake resort barely thirty miles away. We arrived there all hot and sweaty, ran to the end of the wooden jetty and dived into the lake. We landed, not in the clear sparkling water we had been fantasising about, but in thick, evil-smelling mud. The jetty, we discovered too late, was for the fishermen who gathered the rich harvest of eels that lived in the dark slime lurking below the foot of water..

Our regiment had a ski-team, and Stuart was a natural for that. I was a little less accomplished, but after a few lessons was proficient enough to enjoy several trips to the Harz Mountains, way down in the southern part of the country and I acquired a taste for skiing which means we still go to the Alps every year.

Army life was all about routine. I was keen, and I relished the challenge of learning the way the Army worked. As time went on and I got first one stripe, then a second, I came under a bit of pressure from my commanding officer to sign on for another five years. It was tempting: the money was much better for a regular soldier, and with your accommodation and food provided, even most of your clothing, you could save plenty. But I had no interest. I wanted to get back to the business I knew. Having said that, the last few months of my time were pretty comfortable. Once we'd completed the required eighteen months' National Service, we had to do an extra six, on account of the Korean War situation. For this we were paid as regulars. In my case, having been promoted to Bombardier, the weekly wage amounted to fourteen pounds, more than many a skilled man was making in Civvy Street. Although I carried on saving, I was able to splash out and fly home from Hamburg for Christmas 1955.

I'd already had one spell of home leave in the previous summer and had a great time dating lots of girls. Girls were rare in our part of Germany and I took full advantage of being on home ground. I managed to take out a different girl every day and on one particular day even managed two. I didn't pretend they were the only ones, they all knew what I was like and about the other girls I was taking to the pictures, out for a walk on the hills, for a drink in the local pub or to tea with mother sometimes. They were all lovely girls but some of them could be a bit naughty!

Home leave and a different girl every day – these aren't the naughty ones!

Despite this I also found time for another climbing escapade. A line of giant electric pylons was being installed across the county and had reached just down the road from us at Durlett. They hadn't yet been connected to the national grid so there were no electric cables nor barbed wire guards on the legs. They were somehow just waiting to be climbed but there would be little point in scaling one if there was nothing left as evidence. What would make people really sit up and take notice? I had the very idea, I'd make a dummy to hang from it!

They were somehow It was two o'clock in the morning and both Bernard Smart and I had had a few drinks in Swindon. We'd been to a dance there and still had the 'body' in the back of the car. We were almost home and passing the pylon nearest the road.

"What do you think Bernie? Should we do it?"
"Not we! should you do it you mean you daft bugger"

69

That settled it. Bernie helped lash the dummy to my back, both of us fumbling and giggling in the moonlight until it was secure and I was on my way. Up.

"Watch out in case anyone comes Bernie. Keep Cave"

I carried on, the first climb was easy for me and I was soon nearing the top and ready to clamber out onto one of the arms. This was a bit more tricky. I needed to concentrate now. I could hear Bernard calling up to me but couldn't quite make out what he was saying. Surely there wasn't anybody about but if he kept shouting like this there soon would be.

"What? What's wrong? Can't hear you"
"I'm going to sit in the car"
"What?"

He was yelling now.
"I'm going to sit in the car because if you fall you might fall on me!"

The miserable rotten sod, I thought, if I was intending to fall I wouldn't have got up here in the first place. But the prospect of falling never entered my head and I carried on to the tip of the arm. I sat, my legs swinging in space and wrestled the body from my back, tying its 'neck' firmly to the end of the arm. The whole countryside was swathed in silver light, really breathtaking. But probably time to get back down and get to bed.

"Ban-bon ban-bon! Ban-bon ban-bon!" the noise of the sirens woke me. An ambulance and a fire engine going past the house. Surely to God they don't think it's a real body – it was a joke anyone could see that. I dressed quickly and jumped in a van. "I'll collect the milk this morning from Farmer Carey. Won't be long" No! There was even a police car there too. I could be in trouble this time. Norman Carey was watching the action through his binoculars when I arrived.

"Look at this Fred, some-one's been an' 'ung their self from that new pylon. There's firemen aclimbin' up there now to tek 'ee down"

"No Norman, it was me last night but it was only meant as a joke, it's not a real body, it's a dummy I made. Don't say anything about it though, I could be in trouble again"

I thought I'd got away with it until the local paper came out. Was it, they wondered, the same person who had put the wellington boot on the church spire three years ago? They knew but by then I was safely back in Germany.

I was promoted Lance Bombardier after 13 months and was a bit proud of it. I had a photo taken showing my one stripe and put it in my photo album with the caption 'Fred gets Stripe'. It had gone to my head and very soon a caption appeared under my own, 'Stripe gets Fred'. Aah I thought – calm down you aren't a general yet. I was a keen solider and one month later I was promoted to Full Bombardier, I was paid more money and was obviously trusted but I now had to do guard duty. Until I became a bombardier in charge of the guard I had never done a guard duty at the barracks. Each night seven men were chosen for guard duty which required only six men. The smartest soldier of the seven was excused duty and I had always been determined to be that soldier.

One night when I was acting Sergeant in charge of the regular guard I went to close the NAAFI at ten o'clock, as per orders. I found the usual bunch of German cleaning women having a natter in the kitchen, and of course I couldn't resist shouting the odds, telling them to buck their ideas up so that I could lock up and get back to the guardroom for a cuppa. So they did buck up their ideas. They grabbed hold of me, lifted me off my feet and hoisted me above the big sink full of soapy hot water. I didn't think they would dare to do it. I thought it was just a joke but no, they dunked my feet straight in it. My uniform trousers survived wet to the knees, but my lovingly shined boots were just about wrecked, although the severest injury was sustained by my pride.

By the time I came to be demobbed I was commanding enough authority to order a three-tonner to take our group to Hohne for a celebration. We took a load of cheap booze from the NAAFI and arrived there in fancy dress. Naturally we were all getting well tanked up when we discovered that some of our full bottles had disappeared. We found them outside in the carrier of a German's bike. We were not well pleased and as we left we flung the bike, minus the full bottles, into the truck. Half way back to barracks we hurled it unceremoniously out onto the road. Several days later the powers that be caught up with us but by then I was out of the army and although I was requested to pay my share of the damage I refused. He was the one who had pinched our booze!

I must admit I have never been fond of the Germans as a nation. In 1969, driving through Karlsruhe in torrential rain, a group of us were forced to stop and find accommodation. It was getting dark and had been raining for most of the day. We were in open vintage cars and completely soaked to the skin but a hot shower and a change of clothes soon found us in the bar, sitting alongside a crowd of garrulous Germans.

"Ha ha. You English drive the old timers"
"Yes"
"Ha ha. You have no hoods"
"No"
"Ha ha. You dumbkof" – a rough translation of which is thickie
Silence.
"Ha ha. Today you get wet. In Germany it rains. "

The German put his hand into the water jug standing on the table between us and flicked water casually over our faces.

"No," I reply "it not rain. It pisses down"

And I upend the full jug of water over his head.

I do find that the Germans often have a sense of humour failure when the jokes are on them and this was no exception. The room erupted and I was saved by the height and bulk of fellow traveller Jack Eaton who slowly stood to his full six feet and glowered at the now dripping German. "You have problem?" "No. Is OK" Later that same evening we were invited to join a 21st birthday celebration where the boy's drunken father tried to buy Jan for the evening and wouldn't take no for an answer. Jack came to the rescue once again!

But my Army career, in retrospect, was routine, and fairly successful. The last entry in my Army pay-book, written by my Commanding Officer Colonel Goddard, reads, "*Here is a first class worker, one whom we are sorry to see leave, for he is the type the Regular Army needs. Quick to learn, he has been employed in a technical job which he has grasped well. Conscientious, willing and efficient he has been given responsibility right from the beginning and this he has shouldered well.*" But I had no intention of staying. I was going to go back and contribute whole-heartedly to our family business.

After two years, it was all over. We rode the train to the Hook of Holland, boarded the ferry, returned our kit to the barracks at Woolwich – everything except our boots – and then went our separate ways. By half-past two on the 3rd of August 1956 I was back home, and by half-past three I was in the dairy, in my wellies, helping to load the day's empties into the bottle-washers. Back to normality, two years older with a hundred and twenty pounds in the bank and on my feet a pair of not very shiny boots, which I wore out within the next few months.

Although I was now home I was, officially, on standby in case the Suez crisis flared up into extended warfare. Mercifully, that never happened, and I was able to concentrate on the business. The firm now consisted of five rounds, five vehicles, all emblazoned with "Hawk Street Dairy", and driven by Frank, John, Den Hard, Phyllis's husband, and myself. Phyllis had never got around to following her G.I. husband back to the States, and after a while an old boyfriend, Ken Parkinson, came calling. They were married and he was welcomed into the family firm. Father worked in the dairy mornings, scrubbing up and sterilising milk churns and working on the butter, which was quite a good earner for us. By this time, I'm afraid to admit, that often involved his buying in factory-produced stuff at wholesale prices, unwrapping it, re-moulding it between fancy wooden butter-pats, and selling it as local produce – which, in a way, I suppose it was. Another new development at this time came in the wake of the polio scare. Nobody seemed to know where this crippling disease came from. Sales of untreated milk plummeted as rumours spread that this might be a cause. We couldn't afford to put in our own pasteurising plant and we had to settle for buying in bottled supplies which meant less dairy work and more time to develop the rounds.

Just like Frank, I'd come home from the Army full of enthusiasm and with a few ideas of my own for modernising the business. I'd looked at two dairies in Germany and I saw my round as my own little empire and fully expected to develop it. But of course I had to set out any ideas for change before the old man, and he resisted them fiercely. The business needed re-organising so we could have a day off each week but no, father wanted to extend selling on Sundays and I kicked. My ideas were dismissed out of hand. It was as if father never ever listened to me, only to Frank. Here I was, fresh out of the Forces, where I'd been good enough at my job to earn two promotions, where I'd taken on responsibilities and grown up to be a man, yet at home I was treated as if I counted for nothing. Just another pair of hands.

Not surprising then that I was tempted by the only offer of a job I've ever had in my life. One of the leading auction houses head hunted me. They thought I had the makings of an auctioneer and wanted me to be articled to them. Auctioneers were looked up to in the community and obviously did well for themselves and their families and they certainly didn't work seven days a week. I was interested but it meant that father would have to put up the money for my articles, which would then be paid back to me as wages until I qualified. He wouldn't even contemplate such a proposition. This would cost him hundreds of pounds and furthermore he would have to employ an outside rounds-man and pay him a proper wage rather than a son for £4 a week. He was probably right. I could never imagine myself as a 'professional' man, bound by political convention and every other strait jacket of modern society in order to maintain my status.

I was having a great time socially, mixing with young middle-class men and women. I joined the Young Conservatives, caught up with the Young Farmers, where I found a lot of extremely attractive girls, some even with their own motor car but all bored witless by farmers' sons who couldn't find much to talk about apart from the state of their cattle's health, or the weather. I was a big hit with them. I'd been about a bit, seen something of the world; I was self-confident too, maybe big-headed, and took a pride in my appearance. I was often being invited home for tea or supper by one farmer's daughter or another.

Among the girls I met at this time was Rosemary Isaac, whose people had a lovely house out at Sutton Benger, just outside Chippenham. Her father was a highly successful dairy farmer, and her home was a complete contrast to mine: relaxed, informal, with everyone seeming to have time for a bit of fun. It wasn't all work, work, work over there. Theirs was a lived-in, comfy home. Where we had hard wooden seats they had settees and plump cushions. Where our smart sitting room had a grandfather clock that never worked, an office desk under the window, and was only ever opened at Christmas or maybe on a Sunday afternoon, theirs was always in use, with family and guests sprawled around a huge log fire, laughing and enjoying a drink. Their kitchen was centred around an Aga and a big scrubbed pine table. It was a traditional Wiltshire-Gloucestershire lifestyle, and I was in love with it. I wasn't in love with Rosemary yet, but I did take her out for a while much later before she left home and took a job as a catering manager at a college over in Gloucester.

So, one way or another, I led a hectic social life. I tried to ration myself to going out four nights a week: Wednesday, Friday, Saturday and Sunday. And despite the late nights I always managed to get up when the old man banged on the floor by the side of his bed with his stick at six o'clock and shouted his usual "Get up, you buggers!"

In the end, though, the lack of sleep caught up with me. At Christmas, at a Young Farmers bash, I was busy dancing the night away when I started to feel decidedly wobbly. It wasn't the drink, just sheer fatigue. I slumped into a seat completely out of it. I couldn't get up and go on. A friend, John Naish, took me home early. It must have been about midnight. Next morning, of course, I was up and out on the rounds again as if nothing had happened. It was our busiest time of year, with orders of cream and butter to add to all the extra milk people wanted. We'd bought in a load of poultry, as usual, and were praying for cold weather so that the meat would keep. The walk in fridges couldn't take all of the milk and the poultry so some had to be hung in the coolest places we could find. We had two or three hundred chickens, turkeys and geese to pluck, dress and sell. This time our luck didn't hold. The weather turned mild and the meat began to turn. It was tinted a pale green, so we did what father had taught us to do: rubbed flour into the skin to whiten it. And just to make it look nicer we stuffed fat sprigs of parsley around the body. We always had a big patch of that growing in the garden.

With Christmas morning deliveries over we were able to enjoy a dinner around the table and a few hours off before it all started again. Maybe it was then that I started flipping through the notebook I was keeping of ideas for the business. By now John had disappeared. He and I didn't get on and he took off to Canada with the intention of becoming a lumberjack. Frank had this huge round which he was making grow. Maybe we should split it between the two of us, even things up. It could have been then that I tried to raise the issue of reorganisation. Maybe it was later. But whenever it was the old man wouldn't hear of it. I should just get on with my round and leave him to worry about such things. But I couldn't help myself. I had another bee in my bonnet around this time. I wanted us to sell vegetables on the round. And I didn't mean just ordinary vegetables as they came from the fields. What I had in mind was buying up a stock of carrots, say, off the smallholders, scrubbing and dicing them, and selling them that way. I'd worked out the margins, the weights, the costs, the prices, and of course the sales pitch. I'd taken it to two growers in the village who thought it a good idea. Convenience. It was the modern buzz-word; the future. All I got from the old man was "Don't be so bloody stupid!" Looking back, I can see that Fred's Mad Idea wasn't all that mad, just a bit ahead of its time.

I soon felt my anger reaching boiling point and on New Year's Eve I sat down and put my thoughts on paper in the form of a letter addressed to father. There had been some sort of argument that day; I can't remember what it was about, but it was symptomatic of the rising tension as I chafed and he refused to listen. I don't know how many times I drafted the letter, but I put a lot of time into it. I tried to keep it impersonal, strictly business. I told him I was writing as if I were addressing my employer not my father, and that as an employee of four years' standing I felt we just weren't hitting it off. As a result of today's argument, I told him, I was giving two weeks' notice – unless he, Frank and I could get together and discuss such points as staffing, money and a policy for expansion. The letter was written in anger; no doubt about that. My big mistake was in threatening to leave. That put father in the position of having to call my bluff or back down, and there was only going to be one way out of that.

His response, a hand delivered letter, was swift and harsh. I could quit the firm, pack, up my belongings and leave the house, within the period of my notice. I was dumbfounded. I'd hoped to provoke a discussion, to get us together so that we could clear the air. As far as I was concerned you could solve every problem by discussing it. But father didn't subscribe to that view. He ran the family the way he ran the business. His word was law. I didn't have much time to feel sorry for myself. While the work carried on as usual, I had fourteen days in the dead of winter to find myself a place to live and think up a strategy for my future.

So on January 13th 1957, after finishing my milk round, I put all of my clothes into a suitcase and tied it to the back of my bike. I felt incredibly lonely. I didn't want to leave home; I'd just spent two years away not from choice and I desperately wanted to stay with my family. Safe. Secure with what I had known for 20 years.

Father came across from the dairy towards me as I stood by the side of the house, trembling a little both from the freezing wind and from my emotional state. For a moment I thought he was coming to tell me I needn't leave but then I saw the stern set look on his face I knew so well. He held out his hand to me. I hesitated and then took it holding back the tears.

"You think I'm a mean beggar don't you? Just remember I'm doing this for your own benefit. I'll see you when you've made good". He shook my hand and let it go. "Now bugger off" he said.

And with that I pedalled off towards Bromham. I had the hundred and twenty pounds I'd saved up in the Army, and that was it. I had found digs in a council house in the village and I needed to find a job. But I was also exhausted. I'd collapsed twice in the past few months, I'd been burning the candle at both ends, and I'd had the huge upset of being given marching orders from my own home. Guy Mitchell was top of the hit parade – 'I've never felt more like singing the blues'- it had to be my theme tune for a week or so.

Top Hats and Red Pianos

I couldn't live off my savings forever. The Labour Exchange in Devizes had nothing. I found a job in the newspaper – an assistant to an electrical retailer – but I didn't get that. Back in my room I sat on the bed, thinking. How did I end up here? What the hell can I do now? When I thought about it I realised I had no proper skills at all. What was I good at? Working a milk round, I supposed. What good was that?

Realising I would at least need a few references or testimonials I asked two of the most well known people in the area to give me a character reference. Everyone on my rounds had wished me well, but after two weeks I was getting nowhere, and I was nibbling into my savings. For that first fortnight I was willing to do anything and thanks to the kindness of my ex-milk customers I hung wall paper, scrubbed floors, dug a trench for a soak-away and did anything to earn money. Then I had a brain-wave. I'd been well aware that many of my old customers used to complain about never being able to get hold of a chimney-sweep. Or a window-cleaner for that matter. Maybe there was an opening for me there.

I wasn't scared of heights – my climb up the church steeple had proved that – not to mention the electric pylon, and it wouldn't need much equipment to start up a round. A ladder or two, a couple of buckets and some cloths. I could probably afford to buy a van out of my savings. I'd need to advertise – or maybe I could use my old milk-round as a basis, deliver a few flyers to my former customers. But what if I didn't get enough work to keep me going? As I sat there on the edge of my bed the idea took shape. Why not marry up window cleaning with chimney sweeping? It didn't really appeal to me at first. We'd had a sweep come round when I was at home and I always associated him with blackened overalls and a face covered in soot; having the sweep was a major operation for the housewife because all of the furniture had to be covered. Then I went to see Pat Garrett and talked to him about it and from him I found out about vacuum sweeps. Pat had set up in Bromham with a small workshop where he repaired and painted cars and vans and he had carried out all the alterations for the milk vans. He was good with his hands and he had a soft spot for me. Vacuum sweeps still swept the chimney with brushes but before they started they taped a cloth to the outside of the fireplace. As the soot fell it was sucked up and so was the dust filled air. Once the brushes were down, the cloth was taken away and the remaining soot cleaned up. And I'd seen sweeps in Germany. I noticed they swept the chimney from the roof down and their badge of trade was a top hat. Easy. I would be a clean sweep and I would stand out from the crowd by wearing white overalls, a flower in my buttonhole and a top hat!

And so with the supreme confidence of youth I got my business cards printed "F. Giles, The Clean Sweep" and went out on the road in my distinctive outfit. I'd bought a pair of ladders from the hardware shop, and then set about trying to get hold of an industrial vacuum cleaner. What I needed was something bigger and more powerful than a domestic vacuum but light enough for me to carry in and out of houses, but where could I get one from? There were no *Yellow Pages* in those days, and any innovation was regarded with suspicion. Pat said let's build one.

I went and bought myself a Ford Eight van for £80. It comfortably accommodated all my gear, and every Saturday I scrubbed it out thoroughly. It had bench seats in the front. If I went out with a girl in the evening all I had to do was reach behind me, lift a length of galvanised pipe, drop the back of the seat, and hey presto – a passion wagon but it still smelt of soot! I had some fun times in the van, mostly in a horizontal position, and always remembering Den's advice about being forgiven for being too fast.

By the time I'd got the van sorted out my friend Pat Garrett had rigged up a sort of home-made industrial vacuum. I was determined my idea would work. I put one ad in the local paper,

Pat's home made vacuum cleaner and my first van

but otherwise I relied on knocking on doors. Pat's contraption was fairly awkward – Ted thought it was just a huge joke - but I used it for two weeks before I found an industrial vacuum and changed over to that. I was known around the neighbourhood, I was personable, and I was supremely confident – at least at first. A lot of people were keen to give me work, so I got off to a decent start. They knew me as honest; as a hard worker; and as my father's son I was considered totally trustworthy. My father may have had a reputation as a hard task-master but he was also known as being scrupulous about paying his bills on time and giving the customers what they wanted, also on time. I've tried to do the same ever since.

I devised a system, a sort of timetable. I knocked on doors and offered my services. Whether people wanted them or not I would leave a card telling them when I'd next be back in the area. They could fill in the back of it stating when they would like me to call, and post it to me. That way, over a period, I managed to get all my week's work in the same area, and cut down on the travelling. There were good days and bad days. On the bad ones I would call at maybe twenty houses, not get so much as a nibble, and have a rest in the van before starting all over again. I found cold calling very difficult and sometimes I had to literally talk myself into going back out and trying again.

I did a good job, I was reliable, and I was efficient. Well, most of the time. One of my early jobs was at Rosemary Isaac's home out at Sutton Benger. It may well be that her parents hired me out of pity. They must have thought it was a bit harsh for my father to throw me out of the home the way he did, although they never said anything.

The Isaacs' house was a good couple of hundred years old, but the fireplace in their afternoon room had been modernised at some stage and now had a tiled surround. I unrolled my black-out curtains, taped them onto the glossy façade, poked my brush through the little opening I'd left, and started attaching my sectional rods. Of course, I hadn't yet learned to go outside to gauge the height of the chimney and to have a fair idea how many rods it would take to reach the top. The trouble was, after I'd fed a lot through there was no indication that my brush was coming out the other end. In fact, it seemed to be obstructed in some way. I was having to push harder and harder. What I didn't realise was that the new fire-surround hid a much larger, older stone fireplace with an inglenook. That was where my brush was stuck, and as I shoved more rods through they were just doubling over. Finally, the tension forced the brush back. It came spearing through the curtains, showering me and the entire room in a dense black cloud of soot. The beautifully upholstered settee, the easy chairs, the polished coffee tables, the parquet floor, the ornaments, the clock, the light fittings, the deep pile carpet, everything, not to mention yours truly, was coated in black, and all of it stank.

The Isaacs were very gracious about the whole thing. No, it wasn't my fault at all, and yes, if I cleared up the worst of it they would finish the cleaning. I was mortified.

Working for my father I'd been paid four pounds a week. At my new enterprise, I was astonished to find, I could take between forty and fifty on very good weeks. That was a fantastic amount of money in those days, even though I was now running a van and paying for my keep. Actually, within three months of being shown the door, I was allowed back home. My father never said a word, but mother arranged for me to come back on 20th March, my twenty-first birthday. Whatever kind of test the old man had in mind for me, I had clearly passed it, not that he ever allowed me to mention business under his roof. When we did talk, I told him I'd never work for him again. No worries there: he wouldn't have me, was the reply.

With all this money coming in I was down at the bank on a regular basis. At this time I had my account at the same branch of Lloyds in Devizes as father had used ever since he set up in business. Not for much longer, though. Arriving there one Saturday morning in my soiled overalls and brandishing a paying in book with a fistful of blackened pound notes and ten-bob notes, I was greeted with a rather supercilious "Can I help?"

"Yes, I've come to deposit my week's takings."
The clerk looked over the top of her glasses at my slightly dirty hands and the paying in book with my notes and coins.
"Oh, I'm not taking that. It's far too dirty."

I couldn't be bothered to argue. I reached in through the glass screen and picked up my money. I turned on my heel, walked across the square to the Midland, and went inside.

"Can we help you?"

"Yes, I'd like to open an account to deposit my takings. Lloyds don't seem to want my business because both I and my money are too dirty for them so do you want it?"

Yes please was the answer. Of course both Lloyds and Midland Banks knew who I was. There were not that many men in Devizes wearing top hats and whitish overalls.

I had an excellent first year in business for myself. Contracts such as a three-week stint at the mental hospital in Devizes, or the school windows during the holidays all helped. And, just as I'd been managing to do since that first naked photo of me was circulated amongst the villagers, I found ways to get my name in the papers. I was, and always have been, a bit of a show-off, and any publicity was good publicity as far as I was concerned. If I was going to make my mark in the world, the sooner people got to know who I was the better.

One Thursday afternoon about 4 o'clock I was just finishing work when the Bear Hotel in the centre of Devizes Market Place sent for me urgently. Their fireplace in the bar was smoking like the devil and driving customers out. I realised looking up at the lack of smoke outside that the top must be blocked. The central heating system also vented into the chimney which meant that fumes, as well as smoke from the fire in the inglenook, were causing the greatest problem.

I told Mr Earl, the owner, that I would have to go onto the roof and get to the top of the chimney and clean it from there. I'd seen it done often enough in Germany after all. I decided I'd better get on with it and did so but Earl had other ideas. He went along to the Gazette Office – the local newspaper for the area – to tell them. *Fred Giles, the climber, was going 60 feet up onto the top of his chimney.*

I really didn't think too much about it. I climbed out onto a balcony at the front of the hotel with my ½ ladder and propped it up as far as the gutter. Once at gutter level I could lay the ½ ladder along the roof as far as the ridge where there was a small ledge. I pulled the ladder up behind me and leaned it against the chimney which was itself 10 feet tall. Now I could get down to the job in hand. I inched my way up this final ladder, the wind now swaying me slightly, and from the top rung I could just reach the top of the chimney. I stood for a moment looking down at what should have been the opening then I kneeled on top of the chimney – still of course in my white overalls and top hat – and with my big knife which I always carried I began to chip away at the crusted wood oils which were blocking it. As they fell down the chimney and the fumes and smoke were released at the top I began to relax a little. Then I noticed them. The crowd in the Market Place some 60 feet below. Their upturned faces watching my every move. I hadn't realised they were there as I was concentrating too hard and quite honestly getting up and down was enough to think about. The following week there was a photograph in the local paper of me on top of the chimney which obviously did my business a lot of good but it also meant that I was becoming personally recognised about the town.

About this time I acquired a special walking stick. At the back door of a cottage in Heddington I had seen several walking sticks and I commented on this very unusual hazel stick. The old boy who lived there said that if I liked it I could sweep his chimney and take it as payment. For some reason I called this stick Hercules; it went with me everywhere socially. I was now also sporting a bowler which I had named the Duke and always wore a flower in my buttonhole. I had a lot of fun saying I was going out with the Duke and Hercules and I stood out from the crowd. This too did my business good – and most of the girls loved it as well.

Meanwhile I was broadening my social horizons and had started spending time with the art college crowd over at Corsham, just outside Bath. I'd met them through going to the Pack Horse Inn, a favourite haunt of theirs opposite their academy at Corsham Court.

This was a whole new world to me, and it was pure heaven: lots of beautiful girls with independent minds and free spirits who were far more adventurous when it came to relationships with boys than any of the girls I'd met at the Young Farmers. They were more confident, and had far more sense of style. They weren't exactly Bohemians, or even beatniks, but they wore their hair long, dressed in Flamenco-style dresses, smoked French cigarettes and drank beer. They thought that my being a chimney sweep was really quite romantic. Mind you, I had to scrub myself up pretty thoroughly after a long week poking my head up other people's flues before driving over there.

Before long I was regularly going to college parties, staying over at the halls of residence, eating breakfast with the students on some mornings, and being treated by most of the catering staff as if I was one of the residents. In years to come my artistically talented friends would be a great help to me in my businesses. I suppose it was odd that we got along so well. My aim in life then was to make money and develop a business; I was very focussed on that. They, on the other hand, were determinedly un-materialistic. Life for them was about art, not money. We would celebrate the Solstice with a big party: twenty gallons of cider, a lot of student friends, all of us driving over to Stonehenge, partying the night away and then watching the sun rise with the Druids - and a crowd of perhaps two hundred assorted enthusiasts. For me this was a liberating free time. We might drive over to Hartham Mill with a wind up gramophone and a pile of jazz records. We'd swim and drink and stay there all night partying for this was the age of free love amongst the art students and they had a totally different view to the narrow attitudes I had found elsewhere. I joined in all of the activities with gusto. These halcyon days were about to change.

So far it was only the arty crowd who were so free-thinking and liberal; The mid '50s was the start of a whole new era for young people, pre-runner to the swinging '60s. Not only were coffee-bars new, the music we heard there was revolutionary too. Elvis Presley, Tommy Steele; it seemed incredibly noisy and totally unlike the crooners we'd been used to. The night which was to change my whole career, I'd given a talk on chimney sweeping as part of a public speaking contest with Young Conservatives; I hadn't won but we all decided to go for a coffee afterwards in the 'Salamander', a new coffee-bar, the first in the area, which had opened above Woolworths in Chippenham. There was quite a crowd in, and as we emptied our cups the waitress had to come and take them away. There must have been eight or ten on the table. Instead of stacking them neatly she popped them into a plastic bucket. Very handy for her, but I found it rather amateurish. This was at a time when Freddie the Chimney Sweep was very much the show off around town, with my buttonhole, my bowler and my walking stick Hercules. I thought the bucket was poor form, and said so, probably loudly.

"If you're so bloody clever, Freddie Giles, why don't you open a coffee-bar yourself!"

.

Next morning, as I remembered what Jill Lemm had said, it was as if a cartoon light-bulb popped on in my head. That's it, I thought. That's what I'll do. I'll open a coffee-bar. I can do that. My mother always said I should be a little girl because I was so good around the house.

Coffee-bars were already big in London and had become associated with teddy boys and skiffle. And I did have a good friend in London, my old Army mate Stu' Fox. He was obviously the man to show me around. I only went up to town for a day, but what I saw with him during a whistle-stop tour of Piccadilly and Soho convinced me that there was money to be made – and fun to be had, certainly more fun than I was having climbing up and down ladders all day. These places weren't just street-corner cafes. They were a bit posh, and even the basic equipment was up-market. The image was tropical, with bamboo curtains, rush matting and actual palm-trees in pots. The tables were Formica-topped, but that was in the days before Formica became naff. Fifty years ago the rage was for anything that was modern, clean, simple. The colours were gaudy, with bright blues, yellow and reds. The clientele were stylish, and so were the staff. Being the show-off I was, I made up my mind that my place, when I got it off the ground, would be the talk of the town. Devizes might just be a little town nobody had ever heard of, tucked away in rural Wiltshire, but by golly it was going to have the most stunning new coffee-bar the county had seen.

It wasn't going to be easy to find business premises which would do the job. More than that, of course, was the fact that I was a fresh-faced twenty-one-year-old chimney sweep. What chance that I could find someone to rent me somewhere to open a coffee-bar? I just needed a bit of luck when I bumped into a friend of my father's, Sid Loveridge, who had a jeweller's shop in Devizes. He'd heard I was looking and he had an empty property down a passage-way off the Market Place, right behind a pie shop. Did I know it? Of course I did. It had been the old post-office sorting room and was where Bernard Smart and I had our first dancing lessons only a few years ago.

By God it was miserable. An empty shell; dark; dank; dismal; the covered passage-way too was just as shabby as I remembered. I didn't really know anything about building and decorating and that was probably just as well else I may never have taken it on. What could I do with this cheerless space? Besides the hall, whose only assets were a fireplace and what finally turned into a rather nice wood block floor, there was a poky kitchen and store-room and some rudimentary toilets round the back. The pie-shop was thriving, so at least there was the appetising smell of fresh baking.

This was going to be a lot of work but I was very confident in those days; I knew I could do it. Right from the start I could see what it would look like finished, with people in it, laughing and joking, telling their friends they just had to come and see for themselves. I quickly realised that you didn't actually need to know how to do a place up; you just needed to know someone else who did. My first move was to contact my old scout patrol leader

Roger Davies. He and his mate Jack Frewen had both been apprenticed carpenters at Gaiger Bros of Devizes. I soon sold them the idea of being involved in what was to be an exciting new development. We found an architect who drew up the plans and with Jack's father on board as a brickie we had the basis of a team. We were all young, we got on together splendidly, and best of all we were all totally enthusiastic. We needed to be because we were all holding down full time jobs. I certainly couldn't afford to give up the chimney sweeping and window cleaning – how else would I pay for this bright idea. No, this venture would have to take shape evenings and weekends.

Slowly things fell into place. Roger and Jack would arrive after work with their carpentry tools and set about making counters, booths around the walls to house the elegant tables Pat Garrett was making for me. He made the legs from tubular steel – ultra modern – and stools to match; two-seater stools, shaped like two hearts, joined together point to point - we still use one in our bathroom at home! I was doing what I started to do with this first building project and have continued to do ever since. I was the go'fer. I made sure they had the materials to do the next part of the job so that no-one had to stand idle. I fetched it, ordered it, sent for it, held it, cleaned it, and finally I paid for it! Whenever anyone needed an extra pair of hands I was there.

I had a lovely girlfriend at the time, Pam Bulsom. She was a great looker and so good to me and she threw herself whole-heartedly into the scheme too. Most evenings and weekends she was there helping whenever she could and giving me moral support. And of course I had all my art college friends who came to help with the decoration and finishing touches, led by another great girl and good friend, Anne Wigmore. We papered walls with bamboo wall-paper. Pam helped me to line the booths with colourful cord; a swirling Egyptian design; which both softened the atmosphere and also deadened the noise of clacking heels because we had eventually restored the parquet floor to its former glory. We hung bamboo curtains behind the counter; we straddled bamboo poles around the seats. Anne organised the art team to paint huge murals on the walls; multi-coloured Egyptian figures; geometric borders and panels; bold and vibrant.

I'd made friends with father by now which was just as well because I needed him when I was putting the place together. The coffee making equipment we wanted was the best – Gaggia – but it cost £600 which I didn't have. Despite being brought up never to borrow money this time I had no choice and Ted agreed with me. It was quite an emotional moment when we sat together in the Bear Hotel and he signed as my guarantor for the hire purchase agreement.

We rescued the fireplace with blazing log fires and to make music we installed a bright red piano complete with African tom-tom stool! The 'Oasis Coffee-Bar' was stunning – exactly as I had imagined it and I was over the moon.

I could now sell my first business, which I did for £400 to Freddie Green. He took over the equipment and a full order book but not the A40 pick-up which had replaced the original soot smelling van. A good margin for a year's hard work and my original £120! I had even managed a holiday in that time, to Lyme Regis, where I stayed B&B with a super couple, Vera and Tom Hughes. They lived in a council house but had linen napkins at every meal, an idea I soon copied. I was to go back there several times, usually when I had collapsed from over-work and needed a week's rest and recuperation.

The new business opened its doors on Monday 13 January 1958, one year to the day after father had thrown me out, 36 years to the day since father had bought his own business in 1922. We'd had a practice the previous Saturday night, a sort of press preview. I'd got the Wiltshire Carnival Queen along to make the first cup of coffee for the proprietor – me! I got the photographer from the *Wiltshire Gazette* along, simply by walking into their office and explaining to them that something big was about to happen in sleepy old Devizes, and they shouldn't miss it at any price. Then I gathered enough friends and acquaintances to make sure that there was a fantastic atmosphere: plenty of pretty young girls, art students, my friends from Young Farmers and Young Conservatives; and of course my family. Catering for that lot gave both me and my brand new staff some much-needed practice in banging out coffees in double quick time. Naturally too there was plenty of drink – it would hardly be a party if it was a totally dry do!

We opened from ten in the morning until ten thirty at night, Monday to Saturday. We were an instant hit. My first customer was a sailor in uniform and I was so nervous that I hid in the kitchen. So did the girl on duty with me but I was more scared than she was and I made her go out and serve him and that broke the ice.

We served all and sundry of Devizes; a real cross section of the community. Not even mainly young people. Lots of middle aged people came to see and they liked it too. Before long we had people queuing in the passage to be allowed in. 'Titch', a Pays Corps chap from the barracks came and played the red piano every evening, we hadn't yet gone down the road of the juke box which was associated with rowdy youths and loud music, so it was always lively.

I was on the premises the whole opening time I just couldn't leave it, it was a big learning curve, and for an hour or two after we closed there was clearing up, re-stocking and so on. I had a couple of full timers and one or two younger girls part-time, and I needed them. I wouldn't be allowed to do it now but I made a point of always choosing pretty girls and they were all lovely. Other people just wanted to be involved and to help too. And of course always the current girlfriend Pam Bulsom whose father was the electrical retailer who had not given me a job when I left home. We were part of the 'in' group and everyone wanted to be identified with something so new and different.

I've always been more than confident, but here I started to learn that there were some areas in which I was clueless. It wasn't until I had my first vegetarian in, for example, that I realised I hadn't the faintest idea how to poach an egg. "Well we need a poaching pan" said one of the girls. What was a poaching pan? With Mr Sercombe waiting for his egg on toast I ran down the road to Burt's Hardware store and bought a pan. It took a long time but strangely enough there was no complaint from my customer!.

There was no freezer: everything we served had to be made fresh. Neither were there any fryers, so no ready chips. No paninis or baguettes just different things on toast and rolls and sandwiches. Kunzle cakes were big sellers and hot pork pies, which we heated by putting the steaming spout from the espresso machine into the middle of the cold pie. The pie fitted the stainless steel milk jugs perfectly and gave us a hot pie in seconds. All those years ago we were making cappuccino, latte, espresso, americano but we didn't have the fancy names. Black coffee, frothy coffee, rich hot chocolate frothed on top and sprinkled with cocoa powder - delicious. We were incredibly popular and sometimes we simply couldn't cope, and mother would come in and do some washing up. I was everywhere. That's difficult to understand if you've never had staff to look after, to direct, and when it's your own business and your livelihood depends on yourself. There's an inbuilt instinct which enables you to see and hear what is happening in several places at once; while you are serving one customer you also notice that another needs attention; no-one has noticed them and you need to redirect staff their way to help. "With you in a minute" as you spot a new customer through the door or that tables need clearing quickly. "Whistle and ride" was another favoured expression when the girls started to chat too much; that came from father in the dairy; you can talk by all means but don't stop working while you do!

The idea of the place, of course, was to imitate the trendy coffee-bars I'd seen up in London, but although we served a lot of youngsters and servicemen – especially in the evenings – we had a lot of older customers in the daytime. We had several elderly and rather genteel ladies who'd come in on a regular basis and drink a pot of tea while they read the paper and waited for it to stop raining. One lady, Izzie, brought in flowers every week through the spring and summer, fresh from her garden, and popped them in vases. I think she just liked the place and wanted it to be as bright and welcoming as possible. Either that or she enjoyed the free coffee I always gave her or possibly the company of Dick Webb – a good friend and much younger than she was! Dick came to live with us later when we had the Central Café in Melksham. Goodness knows why but he later did away with himself. (I am fond of the bookcase he made for me; it's in our bedroom at home.)

Devizes was, and still is, quite a small town, but for hundreds of years it had been a garrison town. With National Service still going strong, it was full of squaddies who came in night after night for a few pints and a bit of action. With thirty-three pubs turning hordes of them out at ten o'clock during the week, the Oasis was their natural port of call – and we cashed in. Of course, we couldn't accommodate them all, and they had to form an orderly queue in the passage-way. Easier said than done. Sometimes it took a firm hand – namely my brother Frank who had been a boxing champion in the Navy. He would dare anyone to cause problems but of course they still did and there were, from time to time, fights which broke out.

It was quite stressful but very good business - and the town's constabulary seemed to be tolerant when we had to call them out. But after a week or two I had a visit from the sergeant. I sat him down, made him a coffee, and asked him how I could be of assistance.

"You've got to stop this."
"Stop what?"
"Serving coffee after the pubs turn out."
"But we're doing great. I do a huge amount of business after ten o'clock."
"That's as may be, but you're straining my resources to the limit. I can't be sending my men down here night after night to -"
"But you've only been two or three times and isn't that what we pay our rates for?"
The Sergeant sipped his coffee, looked me right in the eye, and spelled it out. "Okay, let's say you refuse to close at ten. Let me explain what'll happen – off the record. It's Friday night. Some drunken soldier starts a punch-up. You call me. Oh, dear me, I say, I'd like to help but all my men are out in the country on a case. Maybe in an hour or two."

It hurt, but in a way being forced to close early saved the Oasis' reputation around town. Locals who'd been worried about letting their teenage children call in now felt a little bit easier about it. We were in any case busy all evening, to the point where people who thought they could just order a coffee and hang out for an hour or two were having to be asked to order again or leave. At that time there was nothing else open in towns like Devizes at night. There were the pubs – and many of our customers were under the legal age for drinking alcohol but neither could they get a decent soft drink like coca cola there– and there was the fish and chip shop. That was it.

I was off to a flying start. My first month I had few bills to pay. Groceries, soft drinks from Wadworths Brewery, crisps, sweets, milk – all my suppliers allowed me a month's credit. They knew father's reputation as a prompt payer, and expected the same reliability from me. They got it too, when the time came. I banked my cash daily; I had no till as such, just a drawer under the counter; I kept no record of transactions. If any records were needed - for tax purposes, for example - they were kept by Mrs Bryant, who did father's books. She came every Thursday evening and did the book-keeping and worked out the wages. When my first bills came, on 1st February, I did what father did: sat down on the 24th, wrote out the cheques and posted them. It became the rule of my lifetime.

Things were going so well that I was soon opening seven days a week, and getting more or less swamped by the work involved. Here I was, only a year or so since I'd left the work-house that was home, and I was back at it: working seven days a week, fourteen hours a day and more. I was still dating Pam and although I was enjoying seeing her still that too was sapping my energy. Only the euphoria of my success was glossing over the fact that I was more or less out on my feet.

I've always been an impulsive sort of person, and I was about to leap into something that would have a profound effect on my life.

On my 22nd birthday, barely two months after the Oasis had opened its doors, I received a card from Rosemary Isaac. Rosemary and I had been an item for a short time until she moved to Gloucester but I hadn't seen her since: looking back it seems odd that a separation of a mere sixty miles should bring our romance to an end but at that time sixty miles was simply too far for me. There were so many other lovely girls in the world that I simply couldn't resist and I hadn't realised at that point that she meant so much to me. Combined with the pressure of work and the fact that any long conversation in a phone box was unsatisfactory, it was inevitable.

I'd got the card from Rosemary in the morning post. It had made me smile as I drove into Devizes and opened up the Oasis. Part-way through the morning, already wilting under the rush of orders, reps wanting to speak to me, a trip to the bank, and one of my girls calling in to say she had to go to the dentist, I suddenly found myself thinking of Rosemary again. "This is the girl I need!" I thought. Five minutes later I was on the pay-phone in the coffee-bar, finding the number of the college she worked at in Gloucester.

I really can't remember the conversation but somehow I asked her to marry me.

After I'd put the phone down I looked at my staff and saw they were staring at me. Had their ears deceived them? No, I told them, I was going to get married. As soon as the lunchtime rush had died down I hopped in the pickup, drove to Gloucester, and that evening Rosemary and I were formally engaged. We went out for a drink – not supper, and talked things through. She loved me and I was in love with her but had got tied up in business and hadn't really thought about it. It wasn't a sexual relationship as Rosemary was saving herself for marriage. That night Pam Bulsom went to mother and cried her eyes out; what had she done wrong? Mother had no idea what I was up to and she couldn't understand it anymore than Pam. They both knew I was a fairly wild card.

I went to Gloucester once a week and stayed over in a B&B some times. One night though I came home late and picked up five sailors who were hitching in uniform, Men were allowed to wear uniforms in those days because it meant they got lifts more easily. They were trying to get to Portsmouth and I realised that from just outside Cirencester they didn't have a hope in hell of getting there that night. I piled them into the back of the pickup and bedded them down in the dairy. I left a note for Ted who would be up earlier than me; God knows what he thought I was up to now for all it said was "5 sailors in the dairy". Ted and Frank being in the Navy and Mum's generosity meant they'd be looked after and Ted even took them to Westbury and put them on a train for Portsmouth.

Rosemary and I hadn't planned a wedding but just got engaged. Even so this was hot news. Within a month Michael Noad an agricultural auctioneer had told me about a property he had in Melksham, the old Central Café. The lease was for sale. We could live there upstairs, and work out a plan for the shop and café premises when we had got ourselves sorted. We took the lease on Midsummer's Day, 21 June 1958, three days after our wedding. That took place on the 18th, Waterloo Day, at the village church, barely two hundred yards from Rosemary's home. It was a lovely day, and we had a beautiful reception at the house. Rosemary looked a picture in the dress she'd made herself. My main recollection was my father's brother Uncle Bert, looking at me, and looking at Rosemary, and saying in his broad Wiltshire accent, "Ah boy, 'oping thee assn't met tha' Waterloo." I had no idea what he meant as we set off on honeymoon to Lyme Regis in her father Dennis's car.

The lease on the Central Café was a "full repair lease". We had to look after every aspect of it, and return it to the landlord after twenty-one years in good shape. It cost us £600 that first year: £300 to sign, and a first annual payment of £300 and it was to remain without any increase for the next 20 years. We didn't have the money, but our respective parents did, and that was their wedding gift to us. It would turn out to be one of the best deals I ever struck, that lease. With property prices sky-rocketing through the 1960s and `70s, we ended up sub-letting the property for a good rent. That lease was valid from when I was 22 to 43 years old. The only way out of it if you made a mistake would be bankruptcy as leases then were so binding. Unlike modern leases it was just two pages long and written in simple language.

The flat above the shop was a mess: filthy, draughty, not fit to live in. We got Roger and Jack in again to help us out; they'd done such a great job on the Oasis they had gone into full time partnership together and also done some work for my father at the dairy. They stripped and papered and painted, plumbed, re-wired and got the flat into generally decent shape. It had two rooms – a bedroom and a lounge – plus a bathroom. It was on the stairs that went from the shops to the flat that they encountered the biggest problem. Taking up the coconut matting one afternoon they left the dust where it fell. When Rosemary and I returned next morning we found it covered in the unmistakeable footprints of… rats. We put poison down, which soon saw the rats off, but we were then left with the hideous stench of rotting bodies which rendered the place uninhabitable for several weeks. When Roger and Jack took up the floorboards they found the electric cables gnawed through in several places. We could now see why the landlord was so pleased to be rid of the previous tenants. Meanwhile we moved in with Rosemary's parents at Sutton Benger.

I loved the place and it still seemed to me to epitomise a life of gentility and ease. But the only time we could take any ease was on a Sunday morning, that being the one time the cafes were closed. Rosemary's mother, bless her, did everything she could to make us comfortable as we enjoyed a morning's lie-in. At nine o'clock as we lay snuggled under the blankets doing what newly-weds do on a Sunday morning, she sauntered into the bedroom, and sat herself on the edge of the bed. What could she want? We soon found out. Leaning forward and rustling a brown paper bag in our faces she asked, as serenely as if she were sitting beside us in the car on an afternoon's ride in the country, "Would you like a sugared almond, children?" But then she was a rather naïve lady. When Rosemary happened to mention that we hadn't been sleeping so well because the bed dipped and we always ended up squashed together in the middle, she told us not to worry. She'd sort it out. When we went up to bed that night, there was a stout bolster running from the pillows right down the middle of the bed to its bottom end.

Rosemary worked in the coffee-bar in Devizes while I helped with alterations prior to opening Melksham. Rosemary was used to hard work, and to preparing food to tight deadlines. We worked well together. We set up the new place as a proper restaurant on one side, the Rosemarie, and a coffee-bar on the other, another Oasis. They shared a kitchen – that sometimes confused us when we couldn't remember which side the food order was for!

Just a fortnight after the wedding I opened both. I wasn't very good at delegating and now, even though this was mainly Rosemary's concern, I found myself in an unknown environment of white linen tablecloths; luncheons and teas. I had got through two managers at Devizes, the first didn't fit in and the next robbed me blind, so I was running both coffee-bars myself.

So there we were, a married couple. My business was barely six months old and already I had three separate businesses on the go and a wife.

Melksham did fantastically well for us. There was a huge RAF camp outside of town, so there was a steady stream of young men with money to spend, looking for company and fun. Once again I always employed attractive girls, partly because I preferred them to men, but also because the airmen and soldiers preferred them too. I employed schoolgirls too. They were so willing, and because this was often their first job they had none of the bad habits that they might have picked up elsewhere and they actually wanted to work evenings in a very trendy place. After they'd finished work I'd drive them home. Their parents appreciated that, and it helped form a sort of trust between me and the older locals. They felt that the Oasis was a safe place for their teenage sons and daughters to hang out; and it was run by a decent young fellow. Much as young women interested me, I made it a point never under any circumstances to get involved with any of my staff. That was the road to big trouble.

As well as these young women, several RAF lads would come in for the evening and help out, just to be a part of what was happening – and pick up a bit of extra cash and a free coffee. People made friendships, found lovers, told us their problems. It was a home from home for many of them, but without any of the restrictions they might have had at their parents' place.

This was both full time work and our social life but I could still see more potential. We started to cater for wedding receptions downstairs in the converted chapel at the back of the coffee-bar; we had Saturday night hops upstairs using a twin turntable record player made for us by my good friend John Naish; John and I had been friends since our Young Farmers days, he is a well built chap and somehow he got me out of a lot of troubles in our early days; It was the boom time for rock 'n roll and we installed a hide-away juke box in the coffee-bar; we sold hula-hoops and held competitions which had the place in uproar. Half the population complained that this latest craze was leading to moral degeneracy and the other half complained that they couldn't get hold of one.

Barely a hundred yards from us was a milk bar, effectively the only other place in town that was open in the evening. Situated right opposite the Maxine Cinema, and with all those RAF lads still coming into town, it should have had a decent turnover. And, fair enough, it was quite an attractive set-up, if a little run-down. It had been kitted out in 1947 by Peter Simper as an American-style milk bar: chrome and Formica, with high stools at the counter, soda fountains – all of that. The current owner came to me. The Oasis had ruined his business and he wanted to sell. It was obvious to me that this was a good move – it was so much bigger than the little

Oasis coffee-bar. The only problem was the money. With so much activity within nine months of opening the first coffee-bar, the cost of the renovations and refurbishments needed would be more than we were making and I had to borrow.

I made tracks to the bank. They'd surely lend me a few thousand. But they didn't. For some reason they turned me down. Now, just a year or two after I'd stormed out of my first bank and taken my "dirty money" to the Midland, I was back at Lloyds. Would they lend me what I needed to take over the milk-bar? The manager there, Mr Wilfred Chapman, listened to me, and said yes. It was all done and dusted at one meeting, and sealed with a handshake. No forms, no applications, no references. He had seen the amount of business I was doing just down the road. He had seen me trotting over to the bank every day with our takings. He would arrange an overdraft.

Still I've never been fond of banks or bankers. Maybe it's a throwback to father hiding under the stairs from them; they were somehow ever so high and mighty; nearly church-like. Of course as I became a better customer I was occasionally invited to take a drink with the manager in his office. Those were the days when it was mainly businesses which used banks and the bank manger was always there for advice. He had the authority to extend your overdraft or not but they were not pushing you to get into debt or to buy their insurance or other pet schemes as they are today.

In the early '80s I had the privilege to be invited to the Guildhall at Bath to the Annual Bankers Dinner, a very grand affair. Jan delivered me so that I could have a drink and they certainly didn't stint it. The guest speaker was the Chairman of Stothert and Pitt; very large crane-makers based in Bath. He was making such a right-wing speech and slagging off the workers that I thought he was out of order. Getting to my feet I told him so and that without workers he didn't have a job and without him neither did they – it had to be a team effort. I'm sure it was rude to barrack him and so did the two stewards who offered to escort me out if I refused to sit down. I did sit down but after dinner various people came to have a go at me. I found a pay phone to call Jan.

"Pick me up now. I'm in trouble. I've interrupted the guest speaker"

The haranguing continued and I was waiting in reception, my back to the wall, rocking on my toes and under some pressure you might say from the two guys berating me when Jan appeared. She was wearing a very smart velvet suit, a peaked cap tucked under her arm and strode across the room towards us.

"Good evening Mr Giles" she said "I have your Porsche outside Sir"

It stopped the discussion there and then! The following day the newspapers found me and during the questioning I was asked which political party I belonged to. "None" was the reply as I have never been involved in politics. That evening the Bath & West Evening Chronicle carried the headline "Managing Director denies he is a Communist" Strictly speaking they were technically correct but the twist was typical of all newspaper stories. Within a few months Stothert and Pitt went bust – I wonder why!

I wasn't invited to the Guild Hall again but I was invited to the Lloyds bank regional lunch in Salisbury, this time being chauffeured by my bank manager. Wow this was living. Uniformed flunkies: endless gin and tonics: a wonderful old timbered building which spoke money. We were each given a name tag to wear and, as by this time it was just beginning to be "What's your number?" rather than your name, I wrote the number of a small account I had with Midland Bank. It certainly led to a few puzzled looks. That's not one of our numbers! The staff could tell the difference but I made my point.

It was a great lunch. Wonderful food and a different wine with each of four courses: brandy - "What type sir?" and coffee rounded off with large fat cigars. I hadn't smoked since father's pipe incident but brother Frank enjoyed a cigar from time to time and so I took one for him. Then the cigar cutter came round. I made sure that everyone on our table had used it and then slipped it into my pocket. Frank didn't have one and with a cigar this big you definitely needed it. Oh, the demon drink! The following week I had cause to go to the bank and the pretty teller told me that the bank manager wanted to see me, and I he to thank him. I went in thinking a glass of sherry might be the order of the day, not so. "Please sit down – you don't happen to have picked up a cigar cutter last week at the luncheon?" "Well yes, of course I did" explaining that my brother enjoyed a cigar but didn't have one. Well. It turned out that Head Office keep a check of all items used at functions and one plated cigar cutter was missing. At a cost of a few bob, bank managers over the whole area were to question their guests about such a trifling bauble. How stupid could they be? Would I get it so they could hand it back. "No! But we're off to France tomorrow – I'll post it from Dover with no explanation." "Excellent Freddie" Result: a happy bank manager and no more invitations!

On another occasion the bank manager and his wife were not so happy. I'm afraid that I may have upset them. Jan and I had been invited to dinner with Jem Marsh, the maker of Marcos Cars, to help impress his bank manager! A lovely dinner, good company and we'd said our goodnights to our hosts and were all walking together to our cars on this beautiful starry and very frosty night. Jem lived on a windswept hill in an old farmhouse some quarter a mile from the main road so I hadn't bothered to lock my car but, as you would expect, the methodical, steady bank manager had. I'm afraid the frost did for his lock. It would not undo and he didn't want to call out Jem. I, of course, being resourceful and prepared at all times like a Scout always has to be, said I could open it easily if he would like. "Yes please" Well the next part was easy. I simply relieved myself on the lock and hey presto the key worked instantly. I never did find out if Jem got his loan!

But in 1958 I had got mine. The milk bar owner had come to me in November. Early in the New Year, on 13 January 1959 – that date again! - I bought the lease. Our landlord was Arthur Poulsom, who ran a butcher's shop next door and had a slaughter-house out the back. He was kind to us, and took an almost paternal interest in me. It was quite early on in our acquaintance that he gave me a very sound piece of advice. "I can see you're doing well, Freddie," he told me. "You need to think about your future. Whenever you make a bit of money, go out and find a commercial property of some sort to buy. You won't look like a rich man now, but you'll be assured of a decent pension when you retire." It was one of the best pieces of advice I've ever had, and I took it. He told me about the first property "not on the market" and I went and bought it. Today we still own it and it's a thriving bookshop.

I could see that handling four businesses, even with Rosemary to help me, was going to be too much. Something had to go. So, having had it for barely two years, I sold the original Oasis to the family. My father, Frank and John all chipped in and bought the coffee-bar. Later on they bought the pie-shop on the front and remodelled the coffee-bar. I could never go back and look at it when it became the Ploughboy. It had been my first real business love and I couldn't bear to see it changed.

So now I had three businesses in Melksham, all thriving. I was always good at getting my face in the papers, always up for any stunt that would attract the press. We entered the carnival every year with a simple but topical float. I've always loved dressing up and I'm happy to make a fool of myself. I enjoy making other people laugh.

I was happy to enter the carnival Adonis competition which took place at the Blue Pool – the town's swimming pool – and even happier when the audience, a great many of whom were my customers, voted me the winner. I am ashamed to say it was not my perfect body which beat the only other competitor; my landlord Arthur Poulsom wore the original long striped bathing costume he had had since 1916 together with his socks and shoes! Pram races; wheelbarrow races; drinking and running competitions; anything for carnival fun. I used my first vintage Bentley in one carnival procession. I'd grown a beard and dressed up as an Arab and of course the car was loaded with beautiful girls, my "harem". On the back we put a rack and a baby's cot. One of the younger boys sat in this with a dummy and a notice pinned to him. "The Sheik's Mistake". A keen vintage man in the town, Dr Cardy grumbled at me for using a nice car in this frivolous manner.

The following year they couldn't get any entrants for the Carnival Queen Contest. Come on girls, I told my staff, who's going to enter? No reply. What's up with you? Don't you think you're up to it? Not good-looking enough? As far as I was concerned they were: I had a lot of very attractive girls working for me.

Then they put it to me: we will if you will.

You will what?

We'll enter if you will. Can't have us all dolled up and putting you to shame, can we Freddie?

Clearly my girls knew me. I was into it straight away. What a fantastic idea. The next week all my waitresses went down to the hairdressers and I went with them. They shaved my arms and legs, made up my face and sorted me out a long dark wig.

The judging was to take place in the Magistrates Court next to the Assembly Rooms and so I found myself lined up with a bevy of beauties waiting to appear before a panel at the very bench where I had received my fine for driving without due care and attention a few years previously. Each contestant was to read a piece, walk up and down, flutter their eyelids and generally display themselves. My appearance – which we all thought was extremely funny - went down like a lead balloon with the man on the door, one of the main organisers. In fact, he told the panel what he thought.

"You won't want Mr Giles, I think," he intoned solemnly as the girls around me all tittered and jostled each other.

"Oh yes we do." It was the boss of the United Dairies speaking, John Hutchinson, chairman of the judges. He knew Freddie Giles, Esq., man about town, and thought it was all delightfully amusing.

Over at the Assembly Rooms, where we were to be presented to a crowd of some 400 before the final selections were announced, I got a different reception altogether. As the line shuffled forward and I approached the door the same man put an arm across me, barring my entrance.

"You're not allowed."

"You're joking."

"No I'm not. We're not having your sort up there on the public stage."

"Why ever not?"

"Well, it -" that had him. He couldn't find any reasonable objection to a little harmless fun. Yes, I'd got him okay – why, there he was blushing as he looked down at his programme.
"It'll encourage…"
"What? What will it encourage?"
"Homosexuality!"

How ridiculous. All of my customers were inside waiting for me and this was simply huge carnival fun. What was the man thinking about? And with that the customers inside the hall began to barrack. "Where is Freddie? Where is Freddie". Too late I was on my way home where I ripped everything off in sheer bad temper. I learned the next day from my girls that my impeder, a teacher, was a constant pest, taking every opportunity to touch up the older girls and make a nuisance of himself.

Well, that was one stunt that failed, but I was not to be outdone. From somewhere came another idea. Around this time there was quite a craze for walking. I don't mean hiking for pleasure, but feats of endurance; a number of odd people around who promoted long-distance walking as a therapy of sorts. When Dr Barbara Moore wasn't plodding her way from John O'Groats to Land's End her exploits Down Under were being charted daily in the newspapers as she trekked across Australia. This was also an age of student rags - piling thirty undergraduates into a telephone box and so on - and we must have been talking about such exploits one evening when four of us somehow managed to convince each other that pushing a hospital bed to London would be a fun thing to attempt.

Well, the first thing is to get yourself a bed– which we did easily enough, from Melksham hospital. I don't know why they let us have one: we weren't raising money for any charity; we weren't seeking sponsorship; we were just four lads having a bit of a laugh. But those were comparatively innocent times, neither charity shops nor sponsorship had arrived. Of course, a hospital bed wasn't ideal for travelling up the A4. The wheels were too small. So we took our bed to the blacksmith who fitted three small bicycle wheels, two at the back and one up front so that we could steer it. People must have thought we were mad, but the press were at least tolerant – unlike the father of one of the lads, who refused point blank to let him go.

John Bright   Ronald Shephard   Tony Wilson   and myself

It was nine o'clock on a Saturday morning and I was wearing what the press described as a 'gay nightdress' – when gay still meant merry - and a top hat. We had a fantastic send off to the sound of the hunting horn, with hundreds of people turned out to line the streets of Melksham. Don't ask me why we undertook the trip on the fifth day of December. We weren't surprised then to run into bad weather that first evening but we certainly hadn't allowed for it. There we were, in our pyjamas, shoving the bed up the hills, riding it down the other side, with no lights, along the A4 on a cold, wet December night. Despite our hot water bottles and hot whisky flasks, by the time we staggered into Reading we were soaked, freezing, and starting to wonder why we hadn't bothered to arrange anywhere to stay the night. The bed was limping too, its front wheel having buckled under the strain. We came across a timber yard, however, climbed wearily over the fence, and at least found a little shelter from the gale amongst the piles of pine boards. It was too late for one of the lads. He was shaking like a leaf, clearly suffering from hypothermia. It was after all winter. We were now thoroughly demoralised. Not only soaked and hungry but frightened too. As unofficial expedition leader I decided I ought to go and seek help. I managed to find a phone box and called the police.

The police were wonderful. They showed up in a Black Maria and piled us all in, including the stricken bed which they trailed behind the open doors. They dried us off, gave us hot drinks, and put us in the cells overnight: one of them even fixed the wheel for us. As we set off for London at five o'clock next morning, ready for the road once more, we all agreed that your average British Bobby was a wonderful fellow indeed.

We'd managed mile after mile of the A4 through Wiltshire without lights, but as it got dark within sight of our target we were stopped by the law and made to continue our journey with torches wedged into the bedstead. We got to Marble Arch by teatime, 110 miles from Melksham and our only achievement was a new record for pushing a bed to London. That and a significant amount of publicity for the coffee-bars. Two to three days later saw both the bed and ourselves on board a rickety ferry crossing the River Severn and bound for the TV studios in Cardiff. This time though the bed was loaded on the roof of a Morris 1000 Traveller rather than being pushed. We even got a £25 fee for our trouble.

Life was still an enormous amount of fun.[2]

---

[2] Photographs and news cuttings courtesy of the Wiltshire Gazette

A Short Sharp Lesson – or two!

Things were going swimmingly – and moving on at a rapid pace. Rosemary was now pregnant, so it was time to find a permanent home. We bought a beautiful house half a mile out of town on Sandridge Road. Brick built at the turn of the century, detached, it had four bedrooms and two bathrooms – one of them a shower-room. A walled garden hung with peaches and grapes. It was by any stretch of the imagination, state of the art for Edwardian times. The original cooker, albeit having the ubiquitous blue glazed finish, was gas and on two levels, the oven sitting at the side of the hobs. No bending down to take the meat out at practically floor level, this was a split level job. How modern is that.

The shower, however, was idiosyncratic and so was the plumber who came to fix it. Mr Cutler was of the old school: thoughtful, deliberate, sage. He came on his bike with his tools in a front carrier. He went upstairs, looked at the shower, turned it on and off, and scratched his head. Then he went down to his bike, and returned with a length of rubber hose, maybe six feet long. We thought we'd leave him to it, but he was back downstairs within five minutes.

"Done that, boy."
"You were quick."
"Ar."
"Well, how much do we owe you?"
"Ten bob."
"Ten shillings? But you haven't been here ten minutes."
"Tain't what I do do boy; tis what I do know."

We'd been running a small B&B over our Melksham flat which we now closed up. I sold the blankets to some brothers who kept a pub in New Park Street, Devizes but try as I might I could not collect the money. Years later I was visiting one of our commercial properties, a car body repairs and spraying shop, when our tenant introduced me to a chap I half recognised. "This is the new owner of the business and he is taking over from me". Then I realised: he was one of the brothers who had never paid me when I could have really done with the money. "Ah! The Royal Oak in Devizes and you still owe me money if you recall for some blankets I sold you. If you think you're taking over this business you can forget it. I'm not assigning any lease to you and you are not doing any business in my property." He was dumbfounded but could do nothing. I really believe that if you treat people unfairly then it will catch up with you when you least expect it.

I was just 24 when our daughter Jill was born at a nursing home in Bradford on Avon on the 24th November 1960. While Rosemary was in there I somehow managed, by nefarious means, to get hold of a copy of the infamous *Lady Chatterley's Lover*, the novel by D H Lawrence that caused such a storm when the High Court debated whether it was liable to deprave and corrupt the reading public. The girls in hospital with Rosemary loved it. We all did. It was the first attempt to loosen the bonds that prevented my generation from exploring the world of sex and eroticism.

I couldn't sit still for a minute, and was always on the look-out for something new. Rosemary had a nanny and a gardener and was settled into our new home but on the business side, as ever, things moved forward. I think I had a sort of vision then of limitless wealth. If you'd asked me my ambition it would probably have been to become a multi-millionaire, a captain of industry. All I had to do was maintain this pace for a few more years and who knew what would happen? The sky was the limit.

Well, why not add outside catering to the restaurant? People needed food at various indoor and outdoor functions, and we had the equipment, the staff and the experience to provide it. It had started modestly enough when we picked up the contract for providing drinks and snacks at the newly built open-air swimming pool in Melksham. We bought a wooden shed, did a few alterations, and hey presto – a kiosk. Following that came the chance to bid for the contract at the town's Assembly Rooms, where we had danced to the big bands. This was still quite a hot spot, opening several nights a week for anything from Chamber of Commerce events to Paul's Pops, a series of early discos run by one of the RAF guys on a Monday night. He would have as many as 400 youngsters in there jiving the night away – or at least until 10:30 closing-time.

I was, of course, up to my neck in all this. Frantically busy, making good money, and loving every minute of it. I was the man about town, totally confident in my ability to expand the business indefinitely. The idea that I might one day bite off more than I could chew never entered my head.

The house was Rosemary's preserve. I was concentrating on work. I'd dropped most of my Young Conservative and Young Farmer activities by now, although a number of my old friends still popped into the coffee-bar for a bite and a natter. The outside catering was taking off, with weddings, dinners and receptions, even regular Young Farmers dos. We found ourselves catering at ever bigger functions – 500 for a Trade Union sit-down do in the Assembly Rooms and we were managing to turn a decent profit. In this respect I was lucky in having Arthur Poulsom the butcher to advise me. He had years of experience in costing and taught me how to work out menus which were easy to prepare; how to cost each item so that you could offer a selection of food and prices to the customer; how many people one girl could serve; how many girls each supervisor could look after; who would give the signal for one course to be cleared away and the next to be brought in. It saved me from learning it all the hard way.

The venture into outside catering, however, was destined to come to an unhappy conclusion. It was the annual Christmas dinner for 120 United Dairies employees in Melksham. We estimated that it would require thirty chickens, with each one being quartered. Simple maths. We'd use Arthur Poulsom's ovens to cook them. All was going smoothly. The poultry arrived in good time and was stored in our walk-in fridge at the Rosemarie until they went up the road to the butchers for cooking. The dinner had started, the first course was ready to be served, and it was time to fetch the chickens across, quarter and plate them. We had Mrs Davies, Roger's mother, together with her daughter Mary helping us. As she cut the birds, I was stacking the heated plates onto the trolleys. Suddenly she stopped cutting.

"We haven't got enough."
"What do you mean?"
"We haven't got enough. Look – twenty-eight plates left and I'm on my last bird."
"Well, that means we're missing six. We must have left them behind."

I dashed back to Poulsom's, shot through the shop, into the back and opened the oven doors.
"What are you looking for?"
"I'm short of six bloody chickens!"
"Well, they aren't here, Freddie."
"Shit!"

After the panic came the total embarrassment. First I had to go and apologise to the guests. Most of them were tucking into their dinner by now and were happy as Larry, but two full tables were sitting there wondering when their grub was going to arrive.

There was nothing for it but to come clean, apologise, and offer an alternative. I knew I had a large tin of ham and another of tongue back at the restaurant. Would that do? It had to. The guests were very decent about it all, and we got them fed, after a fashion, but the whole business took years off me. How the hell had something like this happened? Back at base, after the dust had settled, I found the answer to it. The delivery man had put most of my chickens on the floor of the walk-in fridge, all apart from one solitary box which he'd placed high up on a shelf, out of sight if you were concentrating on the floor. I still can't watch Fawlty Towers without getting hot under the collar when I think about it.

I learned one valuable lesson from that debacle. Well, two. One was that if you try to tackle too much at once mistakes will surely happen. The other was that outside catering was not for me. We then let the Rosemarie to John Spencer who was an excellent chef and also took over the outside catering, which had the added advantage of relieving Rosemary who before Jill was born had been heavily involved with both.

People would say I was lucky; to an extent I was but I took advantage of every bit of luck and found too that the harder I worked the luckier I got! The whole business was doing very well and we could now indulge ourselves, and that's what we did. Ever since I saw an old Bentley going around our village years ago I'd aspired to owning one. Well, the money was in the bank, so why not now? I was talking about it to a rep one day in the coffee bar. A Bentley, he said. I know just the place. You want the Halfway Garage, just the other side of Newbury. They have plenty. Plenty of pre-war Bentleys. He was right. I picked out a very early 3 litre model 1924 with a cone clutch. If you let the clutch in with a bang it would stick in and you just couldn't release it. As the car would be stuck in gear you had to switch off the engine, stop and then get underneath with a big hammer to free the clutch. This car was well worn out but it was great fun. It was a 4-seater and we would use it to go out for the evening with a crowd of friends. We had a nanny right from the start so babysitting was never a problem

As with cars, so with houses and businesses. I was never satisfied with what I had. I still thought that any expansion would benefit my family, hence the move to Street, which I'd sprung on Rosemary without really bothering to consult her. More would surely be better.

Street and Glastonbury were both quite affluent areas. There was very little unemployment, and most people were on decent wages.

Both were more or less one-company towns: at Street it was Clarks' shoes, at Glastonbury Moreland's sheepskin coats and slippers. They seemed to me good reasons to look for a business over that way.

Street was aptly named in those days, consisting as it did of one main thoroughfare. There weren't a great many businesses; there was only one pub and that was on the outskirts. There were still horses and carts to be seen during business hours. The town's only fish shop continued to stock salted and dried cod. It was no great surprise, when I found the property I was looking for, to discover that it had a covenant on it: no alcohol to be sold on the premises, ever. All properties in the town had the same covenant imposed by old man Clark in the 1800's and even the Clarks' Hotel; the Bear in the town centre was unlicensed. However, the 'Black Cat' was a busy little café with waitress service, selling sweets and tobacco at the front and with car-parking space at the back. Upstairs there were three bedrooms, with a sitting room downstairs behind the café.

If I was going to buy this business we had to move house, again. So we sold our nice house at Melksham for exactly the same price as we had bought it for. After paying off the mortgage for a year I found to my surprise that I'd made a loss and owed the bank more money than when I'd started. I decided there and then never to get another mortgage. From that moment on every property I bought I financed with a straight overdraft.

We moved into the flat behind and above the shop. I'd sold the Bentley; the nanny didn't come with us and we had no need of a gardener. The hand-over, I have to say, didn't augur well. The vendors were, to put it mildly, fussy. It would have been easy enough to estimate the contents of the large sweet jars. They weighed every last sweet from every last jar and computed the value of all of them to the last farthing. It took forever, and by the time we'd finished gone midnight I could cheerfully have throttled them. To add insult to injury, the buggers removed every light-bulb in the place before they left the premises.

This was the first time I'd taken over a thriving business and I should have just stood back to see how it worked. It was a simple system. Nothing was ever written down: the five waitresses just called the orders through to the three girls in the kitchen. "Two roast beef, one fried egg on toast, and one poached egg not hard." It was all very labour-intensive and I immediately decided to sort it out. As far as I was concerned it was simply old-fashioned.

I made a complete balls of it. First I started to lose staff, who clearly didn't like my methods. Then I found, to my surprise, that I simply couldn't deliver food to the tables as quickly as they'd been doing under the old system – or, more importantly, at their prices. Within three weeks I'd lost the business and had to close the place down. Up until now I'd only had success and so I had no experience of this new sensation. I'd moved my wife and baby into a miserable flat and paid a lot of money for the place. We were a long way from friends. But I was young and with plenty of energy and ideas. I needed to rethink quickly and I came out fighting to find the answer. So far this "Black Cat" hadn't brought us any luck but it would and the sign from it in the shape of a cat still hangs on the outside loo at Seend Park Farm.

Another lesson: never buy a successful concern. From now on I made it a point always to go for businesses with promise. Build them up and then sell while they're going strong – don't be greedy and leave something in for the new owners to make their living too.

The bank – forty-five miles away in Melksham - didn't know yet that I'd hit the buffers with this place. I had no intention of letting them know. Having shut the place down I now set up a crude counter, installed a cheap boiler rather than a coffee machine, and started afresh as a counter service café using only the front part of the premises. Then, over the next couple of months, I slowly converted it to a coffee-bar, installing a coffee machine and changing the decor but still calling it the 'Black Cat'. It was a far cry from what they'd done when I took it over, a step down effectively, but the people kept coming through the doors: it was, after all, more or less the only place in town.

Although Street was a bit backward, it was actually quite a busy little place. Throughout the year you could rely on an influx of visitors twice a week. That was on Tuesday and Thursdays when Clarks' seconds were sold, the pairs tied up with rough string and hung outside the town's several shoe-shops. People came from far and wide to snap up quality shoes at bargain prices – and after a hard afternoon traipsing from one outlet to the next, called in at the Black Cat for some refreshment. We had the staff from the factory in the evenings as a bonus.

Much more profitable to us, though, was the town's situation straddling the A361. The summer holiday traffic was heavy, slow-moving and frequently stationary. Tired of the annual crawl to Devon and Cornwall, many a family would set off from the London area or the North late on a Friday and complete their journey overnight. This was a golden opportunity and quite early on we started staying open until ten in the evening. It was an immediate success, and you didn't need a degree in Marketing to realise that there was an obvious demand for all-night opening. The succession of frustrated motorists banging on the door as we mopped the floors and counted the takings at gone ten o'clock was evidence enough.

For eight weekends of that summer we stayed opened from Friday morning right through until Sunday, and the bleary-eyed drivers, their wives and children trooped in to stoke themselves up on huge fried breakfasts and mugs of tea. The staff boosted their earnings with the extra hours and night-rate, and in no time we had the Melksham café benefiting from the same trade, opening up at four in the morning to catch the families we'd missed at Street.

Living above the shop in Street was a come-down from the rather elegant Edwardian villa in Melksham, but we coped. However, with Rosemary pregnant again, and Robert being born on 4 April 1962, I decided we needed to move once more, this time to a detached house in Glastonbury, about a mile and a half away. This was a pre-war house on the Roman Way, one of the very few hills on the Somerset Levels. Not only was it a fair climb up the hill, but from the road itself there were thirty-five steps to the front door: not exactly the ideal situation for a young mother with a stack of shopping, a toddler and a baby in a pram. However, at least the house was big enough to accommodate a nanny, so Rosemary had some company and assistance around the place.

I had put a manager into Melksham, Brian Chilcott, who in time had become a Director of the Company formed in 1961, The Oasis Coffee House Ltd. I got my first warning that all was not well when Brian took a fortnight's holiday. Standing in for him, I realised the full extent of the pilfering that was taking place – by customers more than staff. The stealing was largely due to the self-service arrangement whereby the customers helped themselves from the counter and paid at the till – except that they were pocketing certain items before they got there. Brian hadn't noticed but as soon as I spotted it I changed the whole system, having staff behind the counter and cutting down drastically the number of items that were within the customer's reach. Problem solved… until the manager came back from his holidays and saw what I'd done. Understandably, he was outraged that I'd acted in what he considered a high-handed way, he gave me his notice with immediate effect and left. I suspected that he was intending to seek new pastures in any case, but looking back I can see I should have consulted him before changing his whole system around. But that's how I was, how I'd always been. Blame my father, if you like. Anyway, I was right about my late manager: within weeks of leaving me he'd opened a place in Swindon and from what I heard he did all right at it.

But now I had to travel from the new house to Melksham one day a week to work in the old milk-bar. I'd found a new manager after Brian had left. Sid West was fine, but he had one request: he wanted a day off once a week to take his lady-friend out. It was more than a request: it was, in his words, an absolute stipulation and that meant me doing the job every Friday.

After its calamitous beginning, Street was now doing very nicely. Ever the empire-builder, I now started to look towards Yeovil, another fifteen to eighteen miles away. The Blackbird was set up in 1963, right in the middle of one of the worst winters Britain had known – worse even than 1947. Snow fell on Boxing Day and was still on the ground in the middle of March. For several consecutive days in January the temperature never got above freezing, day or night. Potatoes froze in their sacks and the costs sky rocketed.

I seemed to have gone from the devil may care attitude of my chimney sweeping days back to the workhouse situation that I had been so desperate to escape from. At the age of 26 I had a wife, children and work. The Bentley had been a way of escaping but I had sold that with the move to Street and I had quickly learned that business doesn't earn the same money under management. With a single shop you could devote yourself 100% but with four they didn't even get 25% each as the travelling between them took time too.

I was now doing a great deal of dashing about the Somerset countryside in my sturdy, much-travelled Austin Westminster. With interests in Street, Yeovil and Melksham it would surely make sense to find a base more or less equidistant from each. Frome seemed the ideal place. How could I think of moving again so soon?

There was snow piled up against the front door, and the inside was cold and draughty. Clink Farm. It was a huge old Somerset farmhouse, three storeys high and built of warm honey stone, albeit then flanked by a black tin shed which became my workshop, and facing a spacious farmyard bounded by low built stables and cowsheds. A walled garden led to the front door and the open hallway. The oldest part of the house was just one room deep with windows on both sides so that from the back you looked out over a huge garden, open fields, with views on fine days as far as Cley Hill eight miles away. The previous owners had built a further one room wide extension but at a slightly higher level so that to get from the kitchen to the sitting room you just navigated a path, first down a slope and then through every living room in the house. It was to prove exasperating at times, less than perfectly private, but it was full of character – and I was to have twenty-six very happy years there with my family.

That evening I went home and announced to Rosemary that I'd found us a dream home. There was one problem that needed to be overcome: could she live there? She suffered from asthma from time to time, and found that certain old buildings affected her quite badly. With John and Ann Naish we lit a fire in the empty house and bought fish and chips for lunch. Within weeks we moved into our fifth home in five years.

All this time, busy as I was, I'd kept close ties with my family back in Bromham. Whenever I was in Melksham I'd pop over and see my mother for lunch or tea. Father was fine with me: he treated me as much like a blood-brother as a son, but resolutely refused to talk business. If ever I brought up the subject of my work he'd cut me off in mid-sentence. He didn't want to know. Of course, he knew full well what I was up to: Frank would have told him, mother would have told him, his mates down at the Bell would have told him – and if he chose to turn a deaf ear to that lot he'd read about me in the paper.

The old man was always an enigma to me. At my wedding he'd been the life and soul of the party; at the opening of various cafes he'd been foul-tempered and unpleasant. Was he jealous of me? I have no idea, but I'd be dishonest if I said it didn't upset me that he got on so well with Frank. The two of them, and John, were doing

124

well with the family business now, buying up more and more rounds. John in particular was a brilliant milk man. His customers loved him and he loved them and couldn't do enough for them. They'd taken over my first café in Devizes and were making a success of that; they had grocery shops, and even a couple of pubs which they'd bought and refurbished. But could I have been a part of that enterprise? No. My brother reached forty before the old man let him sign a cheque for the business. That wouldn't do for me, at all.

We'd moved into Clink as the last of the winter's snows finally melted. Rosemary was already pregnant with our third child, Jonathan. And me? I was busy acquiring more interests, this time another café in Yeovil, The Bluebird and also in Yeovil a large private house, Woodside, which I started to run as a bed and breakfast place. Unfortunately I did this without worrying about planning permissions and was forced to sell. That didn't slow me down for I soon found another hotel in Warminster, bought that and moved the manageress from Yeovil there.

Back at Clink there was a lot of work to be done to get the place habitable and comfortable. But before I got too embroiled in that I set up an office there. I converted an old cow-shed and hired one full-timer, Yvonne Jones. She wasn't actually the first office manager: I'd had a couple of men running the place but each of them had failed. I realised around this time that I was always hiring mature women. If there was a pattern here it was probably deliberate, although I'm not sure I realised it at the time. I was learning that women who had raised families and run homes and reached their early forties were evidently mature, and likely to be highly motivated. Freed from the tyranny of domestic routine, they were ripe for a fresh challenge, and relished the opportunity to help build up a new enterprise and manage it. Managing a place gave them a sense of ownership, and they generally worked as if the business they ran really was their own. As time went by I found myself, every time I needed someone to run a new business, gravitating towards women of a certain age. I was hardly ever let down.

I can't believe now that I did it, but in this same year I bought yet another café, ex-milk-bar, this time in Chippenham. In diametrically the opposite direction from those in Street and Yeovil and stretching my lines of communication to the limit. I must have been getting dull; there was nothing in my life but work and my family; I had arrived full circle into another workhouse and I could see no escape.

Faster and Faster

"Fred. I'm sure I've seen that old car you used to like up at Pat Garrett's"

"Which one Mum? "

"The one you liked as a little boy, I think it was a Bentley wasn't it? Used to see it when we were up at Hawk Street"

I was sitting in the kitchen of my parents' new bungalow. They'd built it after father had suffered a heart attack in 1960, demolishing in the process a far more beautiful but less practical old timbered house which had been Ted's family home as a boy. They had finally escaped the workhouse which had taken such a toll on their health and now they were probably watching me do the same thing. I certainly don't think Alice expected me to have more than a passing interest in her comment.

But this was the 4.5 litre model I'd seen and admired so many times as a child in Bromham. It was owned by a family called the Moneykurls who lived just outside the village, in a big country house. I was in need of a diversion and mother was right. It was in Pat Garrett's garden, awaiting repairs. But there was evidently no rush: when I called by, there it was, with a broken windscreen, weeds growing up around it. I tracked Pat down in his workshop.

"Is that the car I think it is?"

"It is."

"Can I buy it?"

"You can try, Freddie, I'll give you their phone number."

John Naish and I went together, struck a deal with Mr Moneykurl, and a day or two later were able to drive her away. It had cost me £410, which even then wasn't a huge amount of money, but it seemed that nobody was really interested in old cars. They were too expensive to run, used a lot of fuel - and petrol, even at about six shillings a gallon (7p a litre!), was still a luxury item in an age when most people who could afford a car used it for family outings and holidays rather than the mundane commute to work. This was still very much the post-war world, when everyone wanted whatever was, and proclaimed itself to be, modern – on the assumption that what was modern was an improvement on what was old. Well, I was doing my bit to reverse the trend. I was about to restore a 1930 Bentley.

Rally in Ireland 1966

The car boiled over before we even made the fifteen miles home. The radiator, we discovered, was badly furred up. Getting that fixed would cost me half the purchase price. The bodywork – a wooden frame filled with horsehair stuffing, then shaped, covered in cloth and lacquered - needed some help too and that wasn't going to come cheap. No wonder everyone thought I was mad.

This was the real start of my love affair with motor-cars, and presaged what would in time be a change in the whole focus of my life. But I didn't realise that just yet. In the New Year 1964 I entered my first rally event. I had a maintenance engineer by this time to service all the catering equipment, Ray Stephens, who knew quite a bit about vintage cars. The first thing he insisted was that I join the Vintage Sports Car Club[3]; a whole new world. He persuaded me to enter my first competitive event, the Measham Rally, a 200-mile night time rally in the middle of Wales and in the middle of winter. "Come on Fred: I'll help you sort the car out and I know a chap in Trowbridge who's a brilliant navigator. We'll all do it together!"

So I entered the Measham – a virtual road race starting in the Welsh Borders. We'd stopped on the way up to tighten the wheels – we could hear them moving on their splines. In the Long Mynd Hotel at Church Stretton at minute intervals competitors collected their instructions one hour before their start time. 180 to 200 six-figure grid references to plot onto four 1" to 1 mile OS maps hopefully before their due start time – all of this in the first weekend in January.

A frenzy of forty teams getting their maps, plotting in the bad light, yet all plotting alone. We manage the snooker table; the route is drawn on the maps; hope it's correct; the route planners have tried to find ways of getting us lost or of not having quite the right road plotted. There will be code boards to note down; checks to see you have come the correct way, time controls to check into and secret passage controls too. Speed 'only' 28mph but this is total running time – not the fastest you can drive! We start on our minute. This is a big car. Heavy steering but once underway I am full of confidence. Down small Welsh roads – single tracked – crossing the late night drinkers from the pubs – no closing times apply here. This is so exciting.

---

[3] The VSCC

In the middle of the night we get a break – an hour's respite to refuel, grab a coffee and a sandwich before we are back in the car. On. On. On. The navigator is very good but starts to fall asleep so I give him one of my short-fused 'few sharp words' and he wakes up to concentrate again. We have time to make up and Ray wants a pee! "Piss over the side" I shout as the car flies up and down hills at full stretch. The result for Ray is fairly uncomfortable. Now there are early morning lights in farmhouses; milking parlours lit up; a new day. Time flies and we think we are OK – the finish is in sight. No time for tiredness now as we slide into the final control at the Long Mynd Hotel. Wow! What a night. Have I found something or what! Excitement: adrenalin: danger: it's over: what fun!

Winding down over breakfast and coffee we wait for the results. Yes, we figure – 3rd in class and best newcomer. Two silver plated ashtrays with the VSCC club badge. Didn't realise this could become addictive but I knew I wanted some more. Those two ashtrays with my name engraved are part of my most memorable trophies.

I couldn't wait for the next event and sent off for the entry forms right away. I signed the indemnity and dated the entry – January 13th 1964 – for the Pomeroy Trophy at Silverstone in March. This was an event to find the best overall sports car with an engine over 2 litres and included moderns. There would be tests for braking, fuel consumption, acceleration, steering, timed plug changing, speed and reliability on the circuit and all against the clock. The following day would be an 80 mile navigation route similar to the Measham. I just had to enter with John Naish as my navigator and pit crew.

We all stayed at Towcester and that night joined in a huge party and drank our share of the beer. John is a well built chap, 14 or 15 stone then, while I am a relative lightweight and was only just over 11 stone. In those days it wasn't the least unusual for two chaps to share a double bed if that's all there was on offer, nobody thought anything about it, and so that's where we ended up. But like lots of B&Bs the mattress was well and truly knackered and we ended up rolled together in the middle. Hardly conducive to a good night's sleep when you're hanging on to the bed irons to stop yourself from being squashed to death. No problem. We simply took the mattress and put it on the floor; except in order to have space to do that we had to take the old fashioned bedstead apart and lean it up against the wall. Really no problem for John the engineer! Of course we fully intended to put it all back together the next morning but unfortunately the lady of the house appeared in our room before we managed that, bearing on her tray two mugs of steaming tea. To say that she was not best pleased was an understatement. We didn't get the tea and I can't remember if we were given any breakfast.

I didn't do very well at the Pom, The Bentley is a bit of a big lump for a circuit like Silverstone, it weighs 35cwt and isn't exactly equipped with power steering. At slow speeds it's really hard to turn the wheel and the stopping and starting and reversing on the driving tests meant my time was inevitably slow. But it was a great event – the Bentley just wasn't the right car for it. It was all so new to me. I knew nothing about tuning or tweeking but I loved it. And I was given a valuable piece of advice!

"The way you drive Freddie Giles you don't want a Bentley. You need a Frazer Nash!"

"If we liked nice, safe, quiet lives, we wouldn't be driving our Nashes. Nashes are fun, stimulating, endearing, addictive, entertaining and even practical. But they are not nice (in the sense of 'naice'), nor are they safe (compared to a Volvo), nor are they quiet (compared to an XJ12). So we see no reason for Nash members (or anybody else for that matter) to suppose that anything connected with Nashes will be nice, safe and quiet. With Nashes, getting there includes heart-stopping moments. And sometimes you don't get there, which is heart-breaking. It's the contrast when it does all come right and you succeed in your objective which gives

rise to those moments of euphoria" from an editorial in the Chain Gang Gazette[4].

MV 1764; my favourite car. John helped me again. He and Ann and I picked it up and drove it home. The Frazer Nash Section[5] were agog, they'd never heard of me. Who is this idiot who had just paid £700 – no Frazer Nash had ever been so expensive. I loved her – she was like a young race horse and she still is! If you've never come across a Frazer Nash read the following extract written by Mike Gibbs[6] in 1983 telling of a day's competition in the mountains of France and you may begin to understand why I was so excited about the cars and the people.

A Day out with Blare Scringe – by Mike Gibbs

Blare Scringe sounds a bit Irish. In fact it's an apt euphemism to characterise the sound and effect of Martin Stretton's progress through France.

He was driving solo and his only (occasional) passengers were unsuspecting victims of circumstance, Within minutes all his passengers would be sitting bolt upright with glazed eyes, and develop instant symptoms of Parkinson's disease, or bouts of hysterical laughter and giggling. By Voiron his silencer had removed itself, so Blare (for this is his nick-name now) "scringed" and "blattered" boldly about town, single-handedly making more noise and drama than a Frazer Nash race. It was fun, and to varying degrees we Chain-Gangers do like to show off. The locals enjoyed it too. They adored the spectacle of Blare and Captain Smith urging small boys – and sometimes old women – to push the harder in order to start their engines (boy racers apparently eschew engine starters and reverse gears).

---

[4] The Chain Gang Gazette is the magazine of the Frazer Nash Car Club
[5] The Frazer Nash Section, which was part of the VSCC went on to become an autonomous club in 2005 – the Frazer Nash Car Club and is referred to as club from this point
[6] With thanks to Mike for letting me reproduce part of his article

Amazingly, Blare's tyres had almost worn away by the time he had got to Villard de Lans. In the dry they gripped well enough for him to beat all the other Chain-Gangers at the 4km hill climb in 245seconds – just 5 seconds slower than a 1951 Targa Florio Nash. We all looked forward with anticipation to Alpine Day. The rules were simple: start in own time – verifying time of departure and arrival, prove visit to controls and earn points for beating the bogey time – which was 8 hours to cover 410kms of passes.

Because my Frazer Nash cracked its chassis in Villard on Sunday, all Monday was spent, with Blare, in Grenoble having it repaired. By the time we got to Gap – late and wet – neither my car nor I were in the mood to race. Good news for Blare. Could he "borrow" my wheels and tyres? Better still, will I "navigate" for him and help him win? I remembered what his passengers all went through and I remembered returning to Villard after a reception at Autrans and being suddenly overtaken by Blare on a downhill stretch – he sideways in a full-powered over-steer. His intrepid passenger gritting his teeth, I aghast at his speed. No, I knew better. I like to drive, and besides, I am a poor passenger and a worse navigator. What's more I told him that I was already entitled to wear my Nash badge upside down. Blare persisted. "Could I really drive with my throbbing and bruised finger?" (hurt at Grenoble). By 1am it was all settled. Dick Smith and Janet Giles ministered to my "black" nail with a red hot darning needle: Blare fitted my wheels to his Nash. I was co-driving!

8.20 am and several Nashes have left. I am given the route card and clip board, collect my maps and hunt for all the paraphernalia required for a long cross-country trip. I jump in and before I'm settled, we're away to the main road. I tell Blare to follow the signs to "la Batie". Blare sees one to la Batie Vieille and I nod approvingly. Soon the road starts to narrow, and it dawns on me that it's not important enough to be coloured red on a Michelin map. We drive on across a farm yard and we slither past a hen coop. We stop and discover it's a white road and we are in the hills between Gap and la Batie Neuve – some three miles across the valley. No option but to press on. Blare is peeved. I feel uncomfortable.

The road we are not supposed to be on is a narrow windy pass over very steep grassy hills. Blare puts his foot down and the scenery comes up at me with an alarming rush. Up and over a crest, and we storm down the other side. About a third of a mile ahead is a hairpin. We are hurtling toward it. 4,000 in second: I'm impressed. 4,000 in third; I'm worried. He changes into top. AARGH. I close my eyes and grumble. The car bucks violently left and right and through blurred eyes I perceive that we've negotiated this obstacle, but are heading for more below. I try to hang on as Blare scringes down the hill and slews the car through successive bends. I feel very ill. I don't smoke, but yearn for a cigarette. Moreover I am alarmed to find that these French roads have no armco or barriers. I work out the best way to jump out and get ready to do so. Blare gets speed happy, we go faster still, and I realise that his 9/10ths are equal in scale to my 12/10ths. It's a bloody quick Nash, and the driver thinks he's Nuvolari incarnate. Always sideways we flick through bends and dips, and blatter up to another summit. Luckily the road is pointing in the direction we find ourselves, and we charge across the top at over 80. There is an ear-piercing scringe and I am thrown forward to find sheep in all directions. Luckily we haven't hit any, but we are in the middle of a very large flock, shepherded by a couple of tough looking types surveying us with curiosity.

All this stopping is obviously resented by the driver, who now blusters on at even more impossible speeds; I, bolt upright, trembling violently and wearing a glazed look, pray aloud for his axle to break. It's a cowardly thought, but I feel I cannot endure several hours of this, and worse still, I note we have only been on the road for 10 minutes or so. Now panic stricken, I shout URGH at each open bend, and AARGH every time we go airborne over the edge. I close my eyes, but feel a bigger coward, so pretend to read the maps instead. G-forces pull me this way and that. Head down I just hope that the road is clear ahead and trust we will survive. Another loud scringe , and we halt at a T junction. We're on the N94 at La Batie Neuve. Blare asks me to estimate time lost – I guess at 4 or 5 minutes. We turn right into main road traffic and speed along into the middle overtaking, without hesitation everything in sight. Everyone toots, waves and gesticulates. Are the natives hostile? We don't think they are, wave back and press on. We commence the ascent of the Col Lebraut; the first official pass.

By now I have severe cramp in my right hand which grips the bodywork behind the driver, and white knuckles show on my left hand holding the maps. To keep from falling out, I have braced my feet vertically against the bulk head, and my bottom is wedged firmly into the seat back. This posture keeps my legs dead straight, and therefore my knees can be "locked". I now realise it's the only possible way to sit but I can't always stop my knee-caps from clattering. We swoop through corners and dodge rock debris at sickening speed. The mountain is assailed with our noise and pollution. We rush the summit and Blare is scringing down the pass. This is unbelievable – it's a nightmare – the road cut into sheer rock cliffs, each corner blind. Sheer terror. My knuckles turn whiter – I trust Blare wants to live. With immense relief Blare always exits from these blind corners on his own side of the road. I am impressed. I gain more confidence and find myself becoming elated. This is an epic drive and I'm in brilliant hands.

The Nash seems only to have a passing acquaintance with the road surface as it skips and dances along the straights and slews in sickening slides through all the corners. I can drive my Nash like this but only for the thousand yards or so at Prescott or Shelsley. I can't believe this pace can be kept up for 250 miles.

How exciting was this car! How exciting were these drivers! How exciting have been the last 40 several years driving them!

With MV 1764 I had now found my way into another wild crowd, the Frazer Nash Car Club. These drivers were the equivalent of the arts crowd in the mid 50's and at only 28 I rediscovered part of my devil-may-care attitude. I could have fun and was in my element showing off because I'd discovered another skill. I was discovering I had the ability to drive well – or so I thought.

The Mountain Day in 1983
Mark Joseland and I are first home after an epic 250 mile race
From an original watercolour by Lionel Stretton

Ray and I once again tackled the Measham Rally in January '65. Ray was a strict vegetarian at home and relatively shy. We had been entertained by a boisterous crowd of Nash men before the event and both meat and drink had been taken. Ray was not at all used to meat but too polite to refuse the brawn, of all things, with the result that we had hardly got into our stride before he was violently sick and practically lost his teeth over the side. It was very icy and snow banks lined the narrow lanes and I stuffed the car into a bank and bent the axle before the mid-night break. I still hadn't learned how to handle the Nash in these conditions! Despite the oxyacetylene repairs it was too late to go on and it wasn't until the following year we made amends and won a 1st class award. By that time I had started to come to grips with this young race horse and her strange habits.

*MV's first race. Castle Combe Race Meeting 1965 in the sun with
no gloves or sleeves. H&S not yet invented.*

*Getting to grips with a hand-brake turn. Enstone Driving Tests
1969 in the wet!*

A rare sight – a Frazer Nash with the hood up. As there is no door on the driver's side, the contortions needed to get in and out of the car with the hood in position are extreme.
Photo courtesy of Agency Renel Mille Miglia Argentina 1997

With a cockpit only 32" wide, navigational rallies get very cosy and there is positively no room for luggage.

MV was made to slide around corners; in fact it is the only way that a Nash will corner with its solid back axle and both wheels having to travel the same distance. There is no differential – which would allow the inner wheel to travel less distance. There is no gear-box – a solid back axle with four sprockets fitted with chains effect a crude system of gear ratios. Lock to lock is very direct – just over half a turn of the steering-wheel and so you have to learn to steer on the accelerator. Set up a back end drift and keep it drifting by acceleration or you end up doing thruppenny bit cornering – the old fashioned octagonal sided ones. Of course it's easier said than done and in the wet you can execute a pirouette a ballet dancer would be proud of but any oncoming car would not be happy with. Can be scary. Even worse is approaching corners too fast and braking hard. You are now going straight on until you have the courage to release the brakes, flick the steering wheel and accelerate out of trouble. The clutch is superfluous except for starting and stopping. Your reactions have to be very fast, it would do 70mph in 3rd gear quite comfortably, and you definitely need a place to practice these things. I had never driven such a strange and quick car before.

My new found skills came at some cost to my pride; there is a certain corner in Westbury where the stone wall jumped out at me not once but twice but that didn't dent my enthusiasm despite the two very bent front axles. There were few moderns which could live with a Nash in the 60's and 70's and MV really was the ultimate pre-war small sports car. I was beginning to drive it over its limits but I had already started to love it!

In what was to become a repeated expedition we entered the first ever Frazer Nash Raid to the continent in 1965 and set off for Boulogne to   commemorate the anniversary of the Boulogne Races. The club was made up of a complete cross section and the evening before we sailed we stayed with Willie Court in a rather grand house with an equally grand dining room. Willie was extrovert beyond, his camp way of eating snails or his cartwheels in the middle of a conversation could have won him Oscars. He was also a hefty chap and I watched with fascination as, still in full spate, he sat on the end of the polished dining table which predictably tipped and the myriad of crystal wine glasses slid slowly and inexorably to a smashed heap on the floor. Not even his wife turned a hair.

Later in Boulogne the solidarity of the club became apparent. These were chaps well used to dining out in stylish restaurants, all so new to me. Part way through dinner it was so hot that I took off my jacket. The maitre d immediately came and asked me to put it on again. I pointed out that there were several what appeared to be rock stars in some very strange and unconventional garb and so I didn't see why I should. Well apparently if I wasn't willing to put my jacket on then there would be no dinner for me and I would have to leave. To a man the rest of the group all removed their jackets and hung them on the back of their chairs. I was so grateful and felt so welcomed and part of the group and my best friends still come from the club today. Of course I've never been quiet when enjoying myself and later in the year the club magazine – the Chain Gang Gazette – wrote up the event *"There was a moment's hush during the weekend whilst the other members went into quiet contemplation when Giles revealed he had two livelier brothers than he at home"*

I didn't neglect the Bentley and later in the year took part in a rally in Holland with John and Ann Naish, convoying with some-one who was to become another good friend Air Commodore Buckle and his wife Win. What a trip. Buckle was so full of fun and tricks and we laughed our way through the days – of course the breathalyser didn't exist. From Buckle we learned to tie twin beds together with a shoelace. I learned the number one lesson of long distance motoring; *at the end of the day, feed and bed down your horse.* In other words make sure your car is full of fuel; check the oil and water; look at any little rattles; and finally face the way you want to leave. No matter how you feel in the morning you're ready to go. I've tried to follow this rule in all my motoring especially

Around the World in 80 Days in 2000 – it was one of the secrets of winning the event.

We found ourselves caught up with both a dock strike and a bank strike in '66 when we went with Buckle on the International Rally to Ireland. Not many competitors got there and we were feted as one of 40 cars instead of the expected 400. Beamish Beers sponsored the event and we felt it would be rude not to help them drink as much of it as possible. I met another life-long friend Mike Wylie from Belfast being one of thirteen people in his Ford 8 on our way to a ball. When it was time for home Buckle was ready with his next tutorial. Although our ferry was booked from Dublin there was no boat. A single boat manned by British seamen not involved in the strike was the only one available but the queue was enormous – days of waiting loomed ahead. Buckle collected together all of the money we had left and he used it to bribe the dockers. As the last cars from England were lifted out of the hold – before the days of roll-on roll-off – our two cars were driven past the queue and lowered into the hold first. Then Buckle waited until the boat was almost fully loaded and reported to the ticket office. They went berserk but by then there was no possibility of the cars being unloaded – we were the bottom of the heap – and we were on our way. The kick came as they unloaded the Bentley, hoisting her out with a crane by using a net which went under the front and back wheels. As the crane swung the car precariously over the side of the boat the nets slipped. Thank God they went inwards as there was no insurance while the car was neither on land or sea! The wings were ripped off but at least we hadn't lost her!

By '65 however the Nash had become my new found love – maybe too much so. I had my first competition licence and had started racing the car. The VSCC organised more than 25 events a year; a whole new world for me. I was off racing at Silverstone, Oulton Park in Cheshire, Cadwell Park in Lincolnshire, Donnington. These have never been touring events; drivers need a medical and the car needs a safety check – scrutineering. Practice in the morning and some 10 to 11 races in the day – some scratch races and some handicaps - but with no money prizes and no sponsorship. Everyone is really trying hard with both race trophies and annual trophies to aim for. But despite the fierce competition on the circuit the race meetings were great fun. In the '60s a lot of beer was consumed before and after races. Great friends appeared at every meeting and with real sportsmanship all helped each other. The unwritten motto of the VSCC *'the right crowd and no crowding!'*

I discovered hill climbing all over the British Isles. Trying to drive as quickly as possible up steep, twisty, smoothly surfaced hills and where you are individually timed to 100th of a second and trying to beat everyone else in your class. Classes based on a combination of engine size and grouping between sports cars and racing cars. In the '70s and '80s I progressed from MV to own and race two single-seater racing cars both of Frazer Nash parentage and in which I was able to achieve some notable success, taking records at several venues throughout my thirties and forties.

Nigel Arnold-Forster became Captain of the Frazer Nash Club in December '65 and was to stand for three years. I was 29 and thought of him as a God – the way he and Pam, his wife, competed in everything using one 1926 Nash. I would watch in awe at trials – driving our cars as far as we could up steep, muddy stony tracks; across fields; up mountain sides; passing as many of the 20 marker posts as we were able without stopping; 8 to 10 hills in a day with no preview; no practice; driving on public roads between hills so we all needed to be fully road equipped and road-worthy. Nashes with their solid back axles are usually very good at this exercise and were frequent winners.

The VSCC also arranged driving tests, laying out a course on private land; an airfield; redundant parade grounds; nowadays at Brooklands race circuit or what remains of it. The tests are timed and often require great feats of memory to manoeuvre in and out of imaginary garages created by knee-high bollards or to skate through a figure of eight winding twice round the first bollard and three times around the second until both car and driver are giddy and disorientated. Some of the tests were very hard on the cars; trying to change gear between forward and reverse while the car is still moving; heavy braking and sudden changes of direction. To see Nigel AF performing was something I aspired to and in 1967 I managed to win the Archie Frazer Nash Cup – the winner overall of the year's events and I was needless to say utterly delighted.

Despite all this extra-curricular activity, I was still working hard. More than once I started to feel the strain, just as I had done when I lived at home and was out all hours chasing girls and delivering milk. My body told me that I'd been overdoing it. I collapsed. I knew we needed a proper break so Rosemary and I flew out to the Canaries for a fortnight in the sun. We went by De Havilland Comet, we went without the children, and we simply soaked up the restful atmosphere of a place that had yet to be discovered by the hordes of northern European holidaymakers. It was more than undeveloped: it was positively backward. There were very few tourists, just a floating population of ladies whose husbands sent them out there for the winter while they stayed in London or wherever they worked, and pulled in the income that allowed them such luxuries. Most of them – the wives, that is – had gigolos, handsome young local men who escorted them around the place, looked after their various needs. Nice work if you can get it. There were very few young women; and those that did go were warned quite explicitly not to display too much flesh on the beaches. Two-piece bathing costumes – bikinis, that is – were strictly against the rules and if you were bold enough to try it then you would be thrown off the beach by the police.

For a glorious fortnight, then, we were able to forget about work, but once it was over we went straight back to the same mad routine. Rosemary never complained. I don't know why she didn't, but there we are. In September 1965 she had our fourth child, Rachel. We had now racked up four children and five homes in as many years. I was working so hard in the week but making every effort to get home for teatime with the children, who were starting to grow up and take notice. They were quite a handful. Sundays would be a day off and I would invariably take the whole family out somewhere – I loved having the children with me. It would only be a local outing – a walk or a picnic or over to grandparents for tea. The last thing I wanted after dashing about all week was a long drive. That was part of the motivation behind putting in a swimming pool at Clink. We had a live-in nanny and a lovely couple who lived in the cottages opposite came in to help. Granny Cox as she became known helped in the house and her husband, another Fred helped me in the garden.. I did notice that other people in business would buy themselves a cottage by the sea, or take off on a cruise now and again. But I considered them to be lacking in ambition. I was driven: there was no doubt about it. I wouldn't have called it that then: to me it just seemed normal. You worked as hard as you could to provide for your family. The more business you got, the better. Simple as that. Besides, what would my staff think if they saw me taking time off? As well as driving myself on for my family's good, I felt I was setting a good example.

To add to my empire I'd bought an empty shop in Corsham, right next door to the Pack Horse where I'd first met my art student friends several years before. We set it up as a coffee-bar and tea-shop, and it took off. Everything was going smoothly until I put a new manager in, and then things started to slide. The figures were never quite what they should have been. I had a word with the manageress, and started doing weekly stock-takes, but still couldn't make the figures add up.

I don't think I was very good at management on my own. Yes, I was a man of action, but where does the ability to act end and the impulsive streak begin? If I saw a problem I'd weigh it up without talking to anyone, come to a decision as to what to do and then do it, and never mind the consequences. In this instance I knew that my manageress at Corsham was working a fiddle. I didn't know what it was but I'd had enough of it.

"Ray, grab a tin of whitewash. We need to go to Corsham"
"What's up?"
"I'll tell you as we're going along."

I looked through the window of the coffee-bar. Things were pretty quiet: we were in that lull between morning coffee and lunch. There were only a handful of customers in. We had to move one or two of them. "Sorry to disturb you, madam, but if you wouldn't mind taking a seat over there...."

At this point the manageress came out.
"What the hell's going on?"
"Well, Ray here is whitewashing your windows."
"I can see that."
"And as soon as this lady has drunk her tea I'm closing the place down."
"Closing it down?"
"Yes – and then I'm firing you."

The woman had been working a clever fiddle. At the end of the day when she cashed up the till she decided how much of it she wanted for herself. Then she would make a whole new till roll but leaving off the last few sales. The money she paid into the bank always agreed with the new till roll. Tills weren't so sophisticated in those days; they didn't tell you the time and date! But neither did they come out of the ark. Every time the till was cleared ready for cashing up, it registered on a counter. Where she slipped up was in not realising that the till counted the number of times it was zeroed and printed it at the end of the roll.

Well, I'd sorted it out in spectacular fashion, but I now had a business shut down, minus a manager. This particular incident didn't necessarily improve my managerial skills, but it did persuade me to tighten up on security by employing a useful little practice – keeping a spare drawer with every cash register. The spare would be ready loaded with a change float, always a fixed amount and this enabled us to whip out the cash drawer at any time of day and do a spot-check on takings, merely totalling and clearing the till and substituting the spare without disturbing the running of the coffee-bar. In the middle of a manager's shift I could walk in, tell them we were checking the money, and see whether they'd be pulling the old trick of charging a customer eighty pence for an item, ringing up sixty, and pocketing the difference at the end of the day. Why not pocket the difference there and then? Well if you are running a fiddle you need to wait until there is no-one around, neither customers nor other staff, if you want to open a till and take money out. It's too risky for a small amount and of course every time the till is opened without a sale then that is recorded on the till roll too. No, much easier to wait until you've done it five times and you can take out a £1 note. Don't get too greedy and it won't be noticed. If someone was on the fiddle, this sort of spot check would steady them up. It helped the honest staff too. If a customer claimed to have offered a £1 note rather than a ten shilling note it was an easy thing to change the till drawer, total the till and count the takings to see if they tallied. Tills were never exact but the difference was usually a small amount. If they became exact day after day then there was definitely a fiddle going on.

However, the fact remained that I was running this whole business by the seat of my pants. I didn't understand management skills, nor the sort of book-keeping system that I should have had in place. We'd managed without it at home; we reckoned up our income by counting out the cash on the kitchen table; the till was a drawer that went ding! Still, I had set up the office at Clink, turning part of the old cowsheds into three small offices. You had to mind your head as you went through the door into the main office, with a small office on the side for me and a cigarette store/ money counting room on the other side and I'd got a good person in Yvonne Jones doing the wages, paying the bills, and keeping records. But then one day I had a visit from a couple of chaps calling themselves business consultants. Their sales pitch was simple enough: they'd put my business on a sound footing, make me more efficient and profitable and earn themselves a fee, which would be considerable, and payable in advance. I was decidedly impressed with these chaps. They were highly trained at selling themselves and I thought they were good news. Without much hesitation I decided to hire them. I distinctly remember calling Yvonne into my office

"Bring the cheque-book with you."
"Why do I need the cheque-book?"
"Well to give these chaps the go-ahead. They're going to sort us out and make sure we are well-organized. We'll end up making more money if we do it their way!"
"You don't need them, Freddie."
"Yes I do."
"I don't think so."
"I'm right. I know I am. You wait and see."

She wrote out the cheque, and slammed the book on the table for me to sign. "You bloody fool!" she said and walked out slamming the door behind her. I went after her.
"What's wrong?"
"Can't you see they're ripping you off?"

I'd left these chaps in my office but Yvonne convinced me and I suddenly realised I was wrong so I went back in to them to say I wasn't doing business. They were very tenacious and I had a hell of a job to get them to leave but leave they finally did and empty handed.

Some time later, I was obliged to attend a course with the Hotel and Catering Industry Training Board, a government body, set up to help train staff in the industry. Over a certain size you paid an obligatory two percent of your takings – not your profits – to the HCITB and they in return spent most of it on administration and a small proportion on training courses. After my experience with the consultants I was wary about being taught how to run my business by anybody, let alone a couple of youngsters who looked as though they would struggle to make a picnic for a family of four. I was less than impressed by what they were telling us, so I asked the question that was on everybody's mind.

"Have you ever actually run a restaurant?"
"Oh, yes. We ran one together."
"Are you still doing it?"
"No. Not any more."
"What happened?"
"Well, it went bankrupt."
"And you're here telling us how to run restaurants and hotels?"
It was both insulting and galling but we had no choice in how our contribution was taken or wasted

My role now, with seven separate premises to care for, was less hands-on, although I did get to most of my cafes once or twice a week; and I always carried a clean apron with me. I liked to get stuck in, and I think my staff appreciated it. I prided myself on always boosting the takings when I relieved a manager for her day off or her holidays. And I liked to show the other staff how it was done. It was little things, generally; simple things. "Egg and chips, is it, sir? Certainly, and would you like some bread and butter with that?" Invariably the answer was yes. Old-fashioned salesmanship, as taught me by my father.

Since we had settled in Frome I always said that I wouldn't buy another business on my doorstep, as it were. It would be too easy to get dragged into popping in after hours, or being called on because I lived just around the corner. With a growing family I wanted to spend more time at home. Nevertheless, in 1964 I became interested in a place in the town centre. I don't recall what its background was, but a chap had bought it as a café and tried to move it up-market, way up-market. He had changed it to a steak-house. He'd kitted it out beautifully, with an all-singing all-dancing till, plush seating, deep-pile carpets, and some really fancy cutlery.

As far as I could see he had done everything right – but he wasn't making money. I suspect that he was simply ahead of his time. Steak-houses had barely taken off in London at this time and the rural West Country certainly wasn't used to the concept of eating out at night with a glass of wine. But to give the guy his due, he had tried everything he could think of to promote the place. It just hadn't worked. Now he applied his mind to getting the best price for it. According to the reports we heard, when he had potential buyers in he'd round up as many of his mates as possible, give them a free dinner and try to make the place look as though it was doing a roaring trade. By asking around, I found out that he had finally sold to a man who was borrowing to stay afloat, and paying something like 22% interest. The new owner was in trouble. So much so that the place was up for auction.

Somehow, I was getting interested. Intrigued would be more like it. So I went and had a look around the place. The chap had evidently gone bankrupt and the moneylenders were doing the selling. The electricity was cut off, the restaurant closed down; I found out that he'd been running a card school there at nights until the police found out and put a stop to it. But my overriding impression was that the place was way too plush and up-market for Frome. That was where they'd gone wrong. When it finally came up for auction one Thursday afternoon in the George Hotel, I decided I might as well pop along. After all, it was only on my doorstep.

There were, as I recall, five other people there. One was asleep, another was an old farmer George Davis, who showed up at every auction and never bought a thing. The others looked as though they had popped through from the lounge bar out of curiosity. There was one lady, and I knew her quite well. Nancy Moore. She owned a café and bakery in town.

"Hello," I said. "What are you doing here?"
"Oh, just having a look."
"Not many in."
"No, I can't understand it, nice property like that."

"Listen, would you like £200 in notes?"

"I beg your pardon?"

For a moment I swear she thought that a young man of 28 was propositioning her.

"I'd like you to do me a favour."

"Go on."

"Promise me you'll sit here with your hands under your seat and not say a word."

"You mean if I don't buy it…?"

"Exactly."

The auctioneer tried to get things started.

"Who'll bid me five thousand?"

The room was silent.

"Well, how about two? Two thousand anybody?"

Nothing.

"Come along, ladies and gentlemen. A thousand."

He eventually got started at five hundred.

"Five hundred I'm bid. A thousand, anyone?"

Nancy was still sitting on her hands. He tried to raise it by a hundred, then fifty, finally accepting advances of twenty-five pounds. Slowly the bidding crept up to £775 and, after a pause, to £800. By this time I'd decided it was worth having, but not if I had to pay much more than that. So I whacked in a bid, and the opposition just melted away. I'd got the business, lock stock and barrel for £850, with an eighteen-year lease at £300 a year and no review, plus the sum I paid Nancy, in cash, in a paper bag. She used the money to buy two paintings. The last time I spoke to Nancy, the young artist had become more than sought after and her 'investments' were worth thousands!

The property repaid me half my investment within no time. The state-of-the-art cash register I sold immediately for £400, and the cutlery –well, we're still using it in our house forty years on. As to the actual restaurant premises, they were of course in excellent shape and didn't need a huge amount of work to convert them to a café-cum-coffee-bar and it was a phenomenal success.

I had a great deal of help from George Philip, a Londoner, a cabinet-maker, a superb interior designer, and a life long friend. George was the key to training my eye and brain in designing and shaping practical solutions in cafes, pubs, shoe shops and homes. I'd met George via my maintenance man, Ray. They'd both been professional racing cyclists when they were younger and then both became interested in vintage cars and kept up their friendship. As well as our common interests we hit it off big time. We did a lot of work together in the 60's and the early 1970s, and then he moved to France, returning from time to time to work on various renovations. He wasn't a businessman at all, but a wonderful craftsman and designer. At one time he had worked with Sir Hugh Casson at the Academy of Design, and later on with Terence Conran, the founder of Habitat. He certainly had the credentials. George was to have a huge influence and to figure largely in the interior design of future properties.

I was already in danger of having taken on more than I could handle. I'd just turned 30 when I bought a leasehold café in Chippenham. At the same time I acquired another shop and premises in Melksham, one of my first forays into commercial property. With four children already, all these businesses, and a growing interest in vintage cars, there weren't always enough hours in the day. With George Philip I also embarked on another scheme that took up huge amounts of energy and time. This was bringing all our coffee bars and cafes under a single umbrella name. You didn't hear the term "branding" in those days, but this is what we were now doing, using the name Farmer Giles for all our branches. Well, my name was Giles and I lived on a farm. It made sense to me. It also meant that George and I had to re-fit all the coffee bars, milk bars, restaurants and cafes, nine of them by now, so that they shared the same basic café style, décor, furnishings and menus.

Leading young people astray

Does Mr. Giles honestly believe the installation of a contraceptive machine in his Melksham milk bar is justified because one poor misguided mother of seven thanked him for saving her husband the embarrassment of buying contraceptives from shops?

Does Mr. Giles really believe his machine would help to stop the spread of venereal disease?

Or is the real motive to rake in the silver coins?

True, many such machines are selling in many like places and it's about time all decent folk cried out with righteous indignation.

And Melksham should shout from its roof tops.

Control

I have for many months been corresponding with firstly a Member of Parliament, and secondly with the Secretary of State seeking to outlaw the machines from toilets, where the temptations are made only too obvious especially to young people.

It is time legislation was introduced to control this source of further damning not the lives alone but the very souls of the younger generation.

J. Meaker

Wolverlands
South Barrow
Somerset

We were in the middle of the swinging sixties and as part of the refit at Melksham I installed a contraceptive machine in the gents toilets. That certainly landed me in trouble. I was thrown out of the Chamber of Commerce in Melksham by the chairman, a local chemist, who claimed "this is a morally bad thing", despite selling them himself. He had talked to the local schoolmaster who 'took a dim view of the machine' and urged members to press for its removal and to tell the local church authorities about it! I was adamant and certainly didn't intend to take it out, convinced it would both stop the spread of venereal diseases and prevent unwanted babies. On the contrary I threatened to install them in my other cafes as well! My goodness how things have changed.

Just getting round to see every café once a week was becoming a logistical nightmare, but I was determined not to miss any of them out. They were my babies, and I cared for them. It helped that I always made one of my calls at lunchtime, and so was able to grab a bite to eat, and on the last call of the day I'd often bring home any sandwiches left. That was a bit of a standing joke, but I had been raised not to waste food, and if a café had a spare roll or two, well, that would go towards our family tea at home. I called it good housekeeping.

Added to this we weren't knocking out bacon sandwiches any more: we were cooking prime cuts of beef and lamb. We would have two- or three-hour sessions at Clink Farm, in the kitchen, going over the procedures and techniques, with the cooks passing their know-how on to the other staff. I had a relief manager cum training officer by now, Mike Sharpe. Our training methods weren't that sophisticated, and somewhere along the line the messages were getting blurred. The managers who had been running their branches perfectly well were suddenly being bombarded with different ideas. There was unrest in the camp all round.

I had no idea that it was going to go bang.

All this time, of course, Rosemary was running the house, and then dealing with a human dynamo when I got home at night. Somehow I never tired of talking business, and on the occasions when I brought George home with me we were like a pair of machine guns, chattering incessantly, firing ideas off each other, and generally maintaining a fever-pitch of creative output. On top of this I was now going away at least once a month on various motoring events and when we were at home our social life was hectic. I don't suppose I gave too much thought either to what Rosemary was going through, but I should have done. In 1968 she sent me a Valentine's Day card with a slightly enigmatic message in it. "Can our love get any stronger?" To this day I'm not sure what she meant, but I'm certain she was trying to tell me something, even if it was simply, "We need to talk." We'd been married less than ten years.

A few weeks later, at the beginning of April, I returned home from racing at Silverstone about ten o'clock on a Saturday night. I walked into the kitchen, half expecting to find Rosemary there, but it was empty. Maybe she was watching a bit of television before going up to bed, but no, the lounge was empty. She must have had an early night; couldn't blame her for that: she had her hands full with four children. The nanny was certainly in bed: I'd seen her light go out as I parked the car outside. It was only when I wandered back into the kitchen that I saw the envelope. What was this? A note? Yes, it was a note, very short, and very clear. "I've left. With Rachel."

I didn't even know where she had gone. Certainly not to her parents; I remember driving around the Somerset countryside in a frenzy of worry. I couldn't think straight. I was absolutely numb with shock. To me it had come out of the blue. I thought we were happy.

But then I hadn't thought very hard about it. In hindsight – the blessed virtue of already knowing the future – I can see that I was totally unfair. Rosemary had been brought up as a lady. She wasn't used to arguing her corner, standing up for herself, telling me I might have it wrong. I was too strong for her and she couldn't fight me. I didn't think about it and she never said. Friends could tell me afterwards that the children were completely out of control and ran rings around her. I never saw this. Whenever I was home they were well behaved; bright, energetic children who loved doing things. Despite the domestic help in the house, they were helping to wear her out, as I was myself.

She wouldn't come back. She had no idea what she was planning to do right now, but she was quite certain she wasn't coming back, ever.

And now, just to twist the knife in the wound, the nanny was not allowed to sleep in the house. She came during the day but her parents, quite reasonably, didn't want a sixteen-year-old sleeping in a house with a single man twice her age. I was 32 years old. I had four lively children under eight and a growing, demanding business. What I needed right now was something akin to a miracle - and lo and behold, that's what I got. I stuck an advertisement in the *Daily Telegraph*. I can't even remember what I put, but I must have conveyed a sense of desperation, I must have mentioned that I had four children, and I must have put my address. I don't think I would do that today, but things were a little different in 1968.

A day or two after the ad appeared, a little old lady – well, she was sixty-plus and seemed old to me – appeared on my doorstep with a suitcase. I'd like to say that she had a rolled umbrella too, like Mary Poppins, but I doubt it. Her name was Violet Smith. She said she had read the advertisement, had got on a train, and here she was. She'd come from London, a single retired schoolteacher who could see I was in trouble. She'd come to stay until such time as I found someone permanent. And that's what she did, filling in for the next couple of months while I tried to get back to my work.

Rachel at 35. She grew up with her brothers and sister.

I sent for Rachel. I loved my children dearly and I was determined to keep the family together. Rosemary offered no resistance. I thought it was better for the children to have each other for company and support. We couldn't have the baby growing up as an only child. Jill was by this time seven, Rob barely six, John four and Rachel two; Rosemary was still living with her sister and brother-in-law. She'd come over every week or two and take the children out, which seemed perfectly reasonable at first, until I realised that she was basically turning her visits into extended treats. I thought she was in danger of spoiling them, and said so. It seemed to me there was a real risk that they'd start seeing me as the parent who imposed discipline and provided the food, whereas Rosemary would become a sort of fairy godmother who descended every so often and sprinkled stardust on them. I put it to her that she should either come back and be a full-time mother, doing some of the un-glamorous parenting that I had to do, or maintain a bit of a distance. She opted for the latter course, and soon afterwards flew out to New Zealand where she remarried and stayed for ten years.

A Red Hot Socialist

The first housekeeper didn't last long. She lived in, as I expected her to, and she brought with her a little boy. It became fairly obvious that she was looking for a new husband, and she certainly had me in her sights. She made a huge play for me and I sent her on her way; simple as that. A relative found me a lovely girl, a very attractive blonde. We took the children on holiday to Majorca and I have to admit I couldn't resist her. She was a student on vacation, only with us for a few weeks and she went on her way too.

Her successor, Mrs Norris, lives in my memory still. She made a huge impression, even though she was only with us about six months. At first Mrs Norris seemed fine. She was well spoken, deferential, and seemed to know how to run a household. She had friends in Frome, and she kept a horse in stables somewhere close to town. If I had to sum her up in a few words I'd call her pseudo fallen gentry with a horse. She was kind to the children and appeared to be a model of diligence. She had a son away at public school.

Around the time of Mrs Norris' arrival, the most amazing thing happened to me, this time as a result of my interest in vintage cars. I had two very good friends up in Bewdley, in Worcestershire, Keith and Jane Hill. They invited me and the children up to their place for a party. It was late September, but we drove, all five of us, in my 1926 bull-nosed Morris. It had a bench seat in the front and a rumble- or dickey-seat in the back. It was a coupe, so of course we had the hood up. Even so, it was bloody freezing, but the children loved riding in the car, so there were no complaints. Okay, the battery went flat at Gloucester, but we got there in the end, albeit more like teatime than lunchtime.

After we'd eaten it was already time to be putting the children to bed. I went up to run a bath for them, and took with me Susan, my host's daughter. She was about five, I should think. There I was, in the bathroom on my hands and knees, blowing bubbles and generally amusing a tub full of giggling children when the door opened and a young woman came in. Nice figure. Intelligent looking and an immediate sense of fun. "I've been sent to help you," she said. "Fine," I replied. "I'll wash, you dry." Then we put the children to bed and started nattering.

We were still nattering when I asked her to come to the pub with me to get some booze for the evening, still nattering as I set to in the kitchen and made up a bowl of my killer punch, based on lashings of cider and plenty of gin. We were still nattering when everyone else went to bed boozed as coots on just a couple of glasses of the punch and left us alone. I made several attempts to seduce her, but she was having none of it, and that made me all the more interested. I wasn't used to not getting my own way. The fact that she was a rabid Socialist made our conversations all the spicier.

Jan had grown up in Wolverhampton, and had gone back there to live. Her parents, Lily and Sid Swann, were a solid working class couple who had worked their socks off to get her through grammar school and send her to university. She told me that after she passed her eleven-plus they'd had a visit from her headmaster. He told her parents that they wouldn't possibly be able to afford for her to go to the High School for Girls, the most elite school amongst the four grammar schools in the area. Her father, after all, was only an engineer in the aircraft industry. "Is that so?" he'd replied. "Well, we'll see whether I bloody well can." And they did, working extra hours to pay for her uniform, books and bus fares. After graduating from Cardiff University with a degree in languages, Jan had first of all worked for an American based company carrying out a Transportation study. She had taken the first job that came up to pay off her student overdraft but within three weeks had been promoted to head of their home interview department with forty women working for her. They had given her a lot of computer training and a few months later she landed a job with West

Bromwich Council, putting their electoral roll onto a computer. This was ground-breaking work: only one other local authority in the British Isles had yet attempted such a task. When I met her she was working for a large firm of civil engineers, Freeman Fox, who had just moved her back from their London office to Birmingham.

Jan had made a huge impression on me that Saturday night. On the way home on the Sunday we stopped off at Frank's house in Devizes. "I've met the girl I want to marry," I announced to his wife Rosemary while helping her with the washing up. "You must be mad, Freddie." was her reply.

I didn't see Jan again for a week, but I thought about her a great deal. That next weekend John Naish and I had entered the Welsh Trial, again in my bull-nose Morris. At that time, before the start of the event, the cars lined up in number order along Station Road in Presteigne. Jan had met Keith and Jane through vintage motoring and was great friends with them so I knew she would be there. I walked back along the line of cars and sure enough there she was in the back of an Alvis with Keith, Jane in the front with the driver Brian Sismey. There wasn't any time to waste, the cars were being set off at one minute intervals and John and I were an early number.

"You're coming with me, quick"
"How can I do that, I'm bouncing for Brian and Jane. Anyway you're in a two-seater and you already have a passenger"
"You're definitely coming with me; we can sort the seats out later"

It was John who persuaded her to squeeze into the front seat where she perched on his knee for the whole day and I think he quite enjoyed it. The bull-nose misbehaved all day. We didn't even manage to get up some of the approach hills let alone the steep, muddy, rock-strewn sections above them to compete. The sun shone. The autumn leaves were in full colour and I was happy.

It wasn't long before Jan was coming home and we were meeting every weekend. She would drive down from Birmingham after work on Friday evenings in her grey mini and back again on Monday morning leaving before dawn to be there for an 8:30 start. Or we would meet in the Midlands, often at the George at Bewdley where we were later to commit deliberate and technical adultery so that Rosemary might divorce me. There were motoring weekends too but being winter not so frequently as the summer. We were made for each other and I loved it. We were though both quite fiery people and by Sunday evening would end up having monumental rows where neither of us would give in. One Sunday in Bewdley Jan threw her clothes into a case in an argument about something.

"I wouldn't marry you if you were the last bloody man on earth"
"That's fine" I replied "because I haven't bloody well asked you!"

A week or so later, one winter's night in February, Jan was driving the bull nose Morris to a pub meeting at Woolverton. I opened the passenger door and climbed out onto the precarious running board. She was only doing about 45 to 50 but it suddenly felt much faster.

"I'm asking you now" I called "Marry me else I'll throw myself into the road"
"OK" she said "but I'm not slowing down so get back inside"

We could have no date in mind. I was still married and Jan had a first class job but next day we celebrated, choosing a ring and taking morning coffee in the elegant Pump Room at Bath to the sound of Chamber Music. But now I had to meet her mum and dad!

We went to Wolverhampton with some trepidation. Her parents lived in a modest but very attractive terraced house in a tree-lined street with a pub, a chippy and a post office just down the road. They treated me well, and didn't ask any embarrassing questions; but at bed-time they pulled out a camp-bed which we erected on the front room floor. That was where I was sleeping. There wasn't going to be any hanky panky in their house. She hadn't told them yet we were engaged – not until I'd left the next morning.

Jan had already met my family and been totally accepted by them. The first time I took her to meet Alice and Ted we went for tea with all four children. I hadn't told mum about how I felt so she was not to realise who Jan was by October '68. Their bungalow had a sun room where the children used to play and as Jan came in with our four Granny Giles was her usual kind self. "Hello my dear" she said after welcoming the children, "if you would all like to go down to the sun room to play we shall have tea later" By the time I had sorted out the car and dog they had all disappeared. I wondered where they all were but with no particular hurry. I chatted to mum and it was some time before I realised Jan was missing. "Where is everyone?" I asked. "Well I've sent the children to play with their new nanny!" Poor mum was so embarrassed but from then on made Jan totally welcome.

I had started to have doubts about my housekeeper. Nothing I could put my finger on, but I suspected that things were going missing. Food, cutlery, odds and ends. Nothing was ever quite where it should be, but I never had time to work out what was happening. And then a very strange thing happened. Jan and I were taking the children for a Sunday out at Corfe Castle. The night before we'd had a buffet party in the house and there was lots of food left over. I asked Mrs Norris to make a picnic, and left her to get on with it. We set off for the coast, parked the car, found ourselves a nice spot in the castle grounds, took the hamper out and opened it up. It contained a lump of cheese, a loaf of bread, a bottle of milk, and nothing else. It was quite, quite bizarre, and I was very, very angry.

When the dust had settled we went home. The fridge was empty of any remains of the previous night's party and Mrs Norris was out. I sat and waited for her. Jan put the children to bed, and I sat waiting some more. She finally showed up at around midnight. She offered no explanation, merely stared at me with a supercilious expression and continued to do so while I fired her.

"Thank you so much Mr Giles" she said at once "I'll leave in the morning. I'll be out by eleven". Fine. But I was back to square one with a houseful of children and several businesses to run. With no domestic help what now?

On the Monday morning, Jan provided the answer. "It's quite simple," she said. "I'll move in here and take over."
"What, the house, the children, everything?"
"Yes, everything."
"But what about your job?"
"That I can sort out but before then we have something far more important. The children"

The children had been thrown into turmoil when Rosemary left us all and they were just beginning to settle down again. Jan insisted we make a pact. No matter how we felt about each other in the future, if we fell out, there would be no way that we would split up before the children were grown up and had left home. We couldn't subject them to a second abandonment under any circumstances. Jan decided that it would be unfair too if we had any children between us. It would make for jealousies and favourites and we had quite enough to do without that. I still find it incredibly brave of her. She loved the children as her own from the beginning and seemed to have no problem with discipline or any of the physical organisation it takes to manage a household of six. Right from the start she never tried to bribe or cajole: she would give them as much time as they wanted and either they liked her as she was or they didn't. I couldn't believe my luck.

Jan moved in April '69. It was obviously a massive decision for her. In teaming up with me she was effectively sacrificing a promising career and taking a leap into the unknown. Here she was, throwing up a good job which she'd got after years of education at great cost to her and her family, 'living in sin' with a married man and taking on his four children.

Jan and I were now partners, and we complemented each other perfectly: as the saying goes in our family, she could read and write, I could add up. As well as running the house she took over the office almost as soon as she arrived and very quickly learned how the business worked. She was soon helping me physically, stepping in for management relief when needed. One of our managers Gay Baker was kind enough to take Jan under her wing and show her the ropes before she was needed to help in this way. It meant that she knew how all the equipment worked, how the customers were served and how the tills were cashed up from the beginning. Before some of the less kind employees could take her to task for making public mistakes. Some of the staff and several of my female friends were more than a little jealous of Jan when she moved in with me, perhaps they thought without a partner I may have been 'available'!

Jan was already interested in motoring; now she became deeply involved. Before we lived together we competed in the Measham Rally – the same competition I had first entered in the Bentley with Ray, but now again in my favourite Frazer Nash. It was a fearsome cold and the chicken sandwiches her mum had packed for half way through the night froze solid. Whenever we hit any standing water on the narrow lanes the spray turned instantly to ice across the small screen and I was forced to strain in my seat to see over the top. Jan was a natural navigator and timekeeper and we were doing really well. We had managed to plot all of the route at the Long Mynd Hotel before we set off which meant we could concentrate on the timekeeping. We had lost no time into the controls and we hadn't yet lost our way. The road is always narrow and winding; the cockpit is cramped and the magnifying light distorts the detailed scale maps – kilometre maps had not yet arrived and expanded the scale by 25%.

"I'm sorry but I feel sick"
"Don't worry darling I'll stop in that gateway"

Jan got out of the car and after a moment was violently sick. Five minutes later we were back on the road but I had to drive really hard to try and catch up and we lost a little time at the next control. I didn't mind. We won a first class award. A year later, after we were living together the same thing happened again, with one crucial difference.

"I'm sorry but I feel sick"
"Well I can't stop; we don't have enough time in hand. Just lean over the side, you'll be fine!"

Jan with passenger June Richmond competing in driving tests in Italy

Jan loved the Nash as much as I did. Together in '68 we organised the Nash Christmas Party to have music and games for the first time. In previous years there had been no dancing after the annual dinner and prize-giving; the chaps had simply retired to the bar to talk about cars and left the girls to their own devices. We organised a disco; 'Lily the Pink' was hot in the hit parade and almost the whole club joined in the spirited dancing it provoked. Go-Go girls were all the rage with their mini skirts and swinging tassels and we had them dancing on the tables; a group of us staged a shadow show behind a huge white sheet; Peter Still 'performed' operations, extracting great lengths of chain from an unfortunate body; I put on a mock striptease – again behind the sheet and I've obviously got good legs because some of the chaps thought it was one of the go-go girls! To be fair we got a considerable accolade for the party – it was voted as the best ever. The committee had been in a complete dither about having music at all but finally they thanked me as "the kinetic energy that Freddie built up carried the discotheque through to success".

At that party David Thirlby, a Frazer Nash man of long standing, gave us the run down on what was to be the most exciting foreign trip the club has ever organised. 40 cars were going to try and drive to Bolzano in Northern Italy and 12 of us would be selected to take part in the International Mendola Hill climb. An adventure we couldn't afford to miss!

You have to remember back in '68 not many people ventured abroad for holidays and to think of taking a vintage car across the continent was ground breaking stuff. By the summer of '69 Mr Wilson, our esteemed Prime Minister, had imposed, amongst other things, a limit to the amount of cash which could be taken out of the country. It was £50 per head and for this you were expected to pay for all of your transport costs, hotel bills and entertainment. No-one had credit cards or foreign bank accounts. Still when you could get dinner bed and breakfast for £2.50 in the best hotel in Innsbruck it wasn't so bad. The Italians were so keen to have tourism that they issued us with free petrol coupons too.

We planned a convoy. Keith and Jane Hill – the friends who had introduced us - would drive our Volvo with a trailer and some spares. Five Nashes would then drive across Europe looking after each other and contributing to the breakdown facility. In wanton excess of the allowances we stuffed pound notes into the lining of the Volvo in case of emergency and set off for Crystal Palace – the big send off. One of our group, Bob Upston, blew up his engine on the way there but no-one was being left behind and we bundled Bob, Margaret and their minimal luggage into the back of the Volvo. The next casualty in the group was at Ostend where Mike Gibb's car broke down spewing oil everywhere. We managed to sort that out but at the overnight stop Mike left his suitcase behind and for the rest of the trip was in borrowed clothes – lucky really as they ended up saturated with oil. Adelaide, his gorgeous wife, was travelling in an avant-garde, body hugging, silver leather motor cycle suit and wrapped herself in fresh rolls of wall paper before getting into the car, peeling off the sodden pulp at each stop – stuffing the waste into the back of the Nash. By the time we reached the hills overlooking Innsbruck they had enough for a spectacular bonfire which brought out the local fire teams!

If we had never seen anything like it, neither had Austria or Italy. We paraded through the streets of Innsbruck like gods, young girls in national costume handing us bunches of mountain dried flowers, our snake-like convoy waving and hooting at the crowds as we headed for the Brenner Pass. Until that is the convoy came to a sudden and unscheduled stop. Our victorious leader, David Thirlby, had, of all the ignominies, run out of petrol!

The streets of Vipiteno are narrow and cobbled and barely one car wide and the convoy assembled at the edge of town. An oomphah band struck up and the sousaphone players belched out a rousing march. The lederhosen clad musicians lead the 40 strong convoy triumphantly into the heart of the village, jetted buildings hanging over the cars as bumper to bumper we edged our way along the crowd lined route. Hoping that this slow progress won't be for too long or we'll all boil like mad! I had never seen so much drink left behind! Crates of whiskey and gin, campari oranges still not drunk, beer by the gallon. The tiny wooden framed town hall is awash with it but the club has had more than enough and the noise level reflected our ebullient mood.

Into the cars and with a roar the engines fired into life, the sound ricocheting off the surrounding buildings as we headed to the Giova and our first mountain pass ever! We were all inebriated with the drink, the adulation and the excitement of throwing the cars sideways around blind hairpin bends. Fortunately the Italian police had anticipated this and had given us outriders on motorbikes to lead the way and clear the road in front of us, waving down the odd local driver with uncompromising gestures. The thing is they'd been at the same party and they'd probably had as many Camparis as we'd had so when Dick Smith and I pushed their speed up a little they didn't seem to mind. Up hill is apparently OK. We got the lecture at the top! Down the mountain "Qui va piano va sano e va lontano"! These would be the first of many motorcycle police who would lead us through Italy – and indeed for me the first of many years of following police outriders in raids and rallies. We learned from this first adventure. In Venice, in Rome, as the rally cars heading for a city time control bunch up in traffic, you can spot the outrider coming through on the outside and can pull out making a third lane right behind him, knowing full well he will stop all traffic at the next junction to let you through – but now you are ahead of the queue!

As a first it was also Mike Gibbs' birthday, June 19th. Adelaide decided that she would like to present him with a personal strip tease show and I was roped in to help. She had the most stunning red hair – and it was all natural!! About thirty of us were drinking after supper in Bolzano when Adelaide explained what she proposed to do. "Get people to hum or sing The Stripper and then when I've finished I want to do a handstand and you can hold me up. The only problem is Freddie......um....er... it's the wrong week". "And?" "And I've got a tail showing". "Well, just tuck it in and go for it!" What a display. The noise; the chanting; the laughter. It was so typical of Adelaide and she carried it through with no problems and swept the curtain around herself as a finale. Fantastic! What a girl. The older members were amazed. Wow! Virtually every time we did big raids it was Mike's birthday and she would always perform – but never on this scale again.

It was a wild fortnight the high point of which was a formal dinner in the garden of the Park Hotel Laurin in the middle of Bolzano. *"The delight of the Italian Brass at that "formal reception" when Freddie Giles presented a bouquet of roses to Helga Frass. The roses were so obviously stolen from the garden of the Hotel and wrapped so tastefully in one of the Hotel's napkins. Colonel Christofoletti said it was one of the funniest things he had ever seen and only the "verve" of the English could have carried it through"*[7]

It was a warm evening and the hospitality bar was generous and was more than well supported by all of us. After the official speeches we could do no more than issue the universal cry of "last one in the pool's a sissy" but we didn't need much goading except for Jenks[8] who was seen flying through the air fully clothed after exhibiting a little reluctance to jump himself. We found a delivery bike with its ample wicker basket in front and rode this round for a while until Mike Gibbs and I were dared to ride it into the pool which of course we did without hesitation. We extracted the machine by dint of tying our ties together to form a rescue line but the bike was a little worse for wear and necessitated a whip round the following morning to compensate the unfortunate owner. As we left the reception we tried vainly to follow in each other's

---

[7] From the Chain Gang Gazette

[8] Denis Jenkinson, Regular correspondent of Motor Sport Magazine and friend of the Nash Club. Jenks was navigator to Stirling Moss when together they won the Mille Miglia in Italy in 1955. They averaged just under 100 miles an hour for a thousand miles – and set an all time speed record for the event..

footsteps through the hotel foyer – being reasonable and trying to keep the water dripping from us to a minimum but the owner was also a reasonable man. How can I complain he said, after all it's my water! This was one evening when we were clean – driving in a Nash can make you incredibly dirty and it was reported that never in the history of Italy had so many receptions been given to such a dirty lot of people.

The competitive element in this raid was the Mendola Hill Climb which had an unexpected result. The hill takes about 12 minutes to climb at full speed and with the road closed. Some of us couldn't resist a little unofficial practice before the event and after a bit of trouble with a non-competing Opel I suddenly found myself looking into the face of an extremely stroppy policeman who had taken a dislike to my enthusiastic motoring. He suggested a little more piano and a bit less forte but waved us on our way nevertheless.

From Kaltern the Mendola begins innocently enough but you soon find yourself in a series of tortuous bends with the rock face bearing down on your right and the low stone wall protecting the drop on your left and not much width of road in between. There is no leeway for mistakes on the narrow hairpins and you arrive at the top dry mouthed and breathless. Well you should do but sadly for me during the race itself MV was in sight of the top when her whole gear change linkage got out of control and she stopped. I mended the car and finally made the top but in 57 minutes rather than the bogey 12. As the hill is closed for the whole of race day, the way down is a circuitous route through several villages and many more miles than the upward trek. The natural thing to do is to visit what was then the only bar at the top of the hill. The natural thing was that several other Nash men found the same bar. We were straight away greeted by a jovial sud tiroler, wearing his traditional blue apron and a wide grin, who offered us a glass of wine. "Mamma mia Madonna be Donna! This is my friend," he said introducing us to a corpulent German. "I call him Hermann the German, the illegitimate son of Mussolini". And so we met Hubert who became a life long friend despite my lack of Italian or German (his native tongue) and his lack of English. There was a chemical reaction between us which superseded language.

Hubert took us back to his house and opened up his cellar which contained a store of home made wine and racks of home made grappa both of which he served to us in vast quantities accompanied by raw speck and turnip. It was the first of many such evenings. In '69 we met on about three occasions and didn't stay in touch but 10 years later when we were all there doing the same again Hubert was found by one of our gang wandering amongst them showing anyone who would look a photo of me in the car and asking "Is this man here this time?"

A small group of us visited the historic cellar and then walked to Hubert's cantina where we had more to eat and drink. The Sud Tirol was alight with beacons all round the mountainside protesting for its independence, having been annexed by Italy in WW1 and Italianised against their will. Hubert had been made to change his name to Huberto and it was forbidden to speak German with the result that the children went to Italian school during the day and German school hidden in the cellars each evening. In the cantina the locals began singing, they sang well, we tried to sing and failed dismally until I had a brain-wave and got everyone on the floor for the hokey kokey – they didn't know what to make of that but joined in enthusiastically. I think I must have got hot because shortly afterwards I went outside to look once more at the beacons and fell into a horse trough filled with water.

That evening cemented our relationship with Hubert and his wife Maria and we visited them whenever we found ourselves anywhere near the Dolomites, staying as their guests in their beautiful house surrounded by peach and apple trees. I would help him in his orchards which were his livelihood and we would walk back in warm sun and companionable silence still unable to communicate with language. Their daughter Petra, who was about Jon's age, came to live with us for a while to learn English and later a good friend of Petra's, Jimmy, also came to live and work with us for a few months. I have a photo of us in 1989 having lunch at the top of the Mendola at Hubert's weekend hut. Jonathan, Fletch, Petra, Hubert, Maria and ourselves. Within 10 years both Petra and Fletch would be dead and when we visit now there is a sadness to our meeting.

*1ier Rallye Neige
et Glaces
Alpe d'Huez*

But in '69 it certainly set Jan and I on the road to continental adventures in the Nash. The following winter we set off to compete in a snow and ice rally at Alpe d'Huez – a really 'free' weekend rally if you discounted the cost of the ferry crossing and the 600 mile journey to get there. I remember going to the Isle of Man too on a virtually free weekend taking my single-seater racing car, Salome. The accommodation was hardly four star – our boarding house on the promenade prohibited going to the front door in curlers, taking a bath more than once a week and when our next door neighbour said her prayers we were able to join in the amens. But the crowd and the motoring was pure pleasure. I managed to lose the convoy escorting us from the parc ferme to the hill climb venue and was forced to drive the length and breadth of Douglas promenade twice at great speed and noise (Salome wasn't silenced in those halcyon days) much to my enjoyment and the distress of the marshals.

We must have been a bit of a rag bag lot back in late '68 early '69 when Jan took us over. Jill aged seven and Rob aged six were at Junior School in Frome with some 400 youngsters and really not making any progress and Jon at only four was due to go there after a C of E infants school. What could we do? Though I had lived at Clink for several years we had only just found out that about a mile and half away in the hamlet of Berkley, next to the church and the big house, was a tiny 'school in the woods' with just over 20 pupils. Why not give it a try? They were delighted. Our three would take them over 25 pupils and prevent them from being closed down. It was in cycling distance on very quiet lanes and they quickly settled down there. Jill and Jon made good progress but poor Robert wasn't getting it at all until Miss Morgan, the

Head Teacher had a bright idea. Robert could be the tea monitor for the staff. Of course at home they had to do so much for themselves and he quickly and easily coped with these duties; they may have taken him away from the class room a little but he now had a responsible job which he could succeed at; his confidence immediately improved and also his attitude to learning. Like me he was slow to start reading and he and Jan would sit for hours on end in the dining room going over and over his words. Now you can't keep his nose out of a book. But not so then and not so his nose which continually ran to the degree that he just accepted it, didn't notice it anymore. Jan decided this needed dealing with and pushed to get the small operation done. Suddenly we had a lad that was lovely to look at again and, although he was never destined to be an academic, he could enjoy school enough to channel his personality and his intelligence into developing a very bright and astute business sense.

We were married a year after Jan came to live with us
Photo courtesy of Peter Lawry

Finally by 1970 Rachel was ready for the little school in the woods and Jill at eight was designated to ride to school every day on an adult's bike with her sister in a carrier on the back. Jan was really coming to grips with our family and sorting us all out and was on her way to becoming a much loved mum - and has been ever since. We are so lucky. I don't know what would have happened to either myself or our family if Jan and I had not met. I don't believe that I would have coped with looking after the children and a business, which could easily have gone to pot. No matter how much money I earned or spent I could never have bought the fantastic amount of love which Jan gave to all of us and carries on giving every day.

Being a mile and a half from the town centre meant the kids could walk or cycle to school, scouts, guides or wherever they wanted to go. We never had to become taxi drivers for them, they were very independent. We were still in the country and they were able to ramble the lanes and the fields just as I had done in my own childhood.

As the children went on to secondary school – comprehensives were just being introduced – there were great and heated debates at home about their education. I thought that public schools might be the answer and we went to look at a couple in our area where they took weekly boarders and occasionally day pupils, but the latter were discouraged in the main. We were horrified by the lack of manners shown by the kids and for a moment I considered full time boarding schools further away. It didn't last long. Some of Jan's socialism had rubbed off on me by now and she was dead set against them being sent away from home at all. "If anyone's going to influence their morals, help them with their transition into adolescence it's going to be us" was Jan's argument. While she believed Jon's pragmatic approach to life might enable him to cope she thought Rob was far too vulnerable and would be desperately unhappy away from his family. She wouldn't even consider letting the girls go. Jan was happy to spend the time helping with home-work, encouraging them to read and listening to their tales for hours on end until they finally arrived at the questions they hadn't

known how to ask at the start of the chat. And I was happy to
spend time helping them acquire physical skills, making, mending,
scouting, woodwork, metalwork – all the things I'd enjoyed as a
boy.

*Photo courtesy
Neill Bruce*

Rob seemed always to be in the wars; on one occasion he knocked out a front tooth in a hotel near Silverstone whilst standing on a home-made stool which collapsed under him. He had first class treatment from the race course doctor and an ophthalmic surgeon – both racing with me the following day – but the local dentist wouldn't turn out and although they planted the tooth back it wouldn't take. I confiscated the stool – as evidence – and asked the hotel for compensation for the expensive dental charges. We finished up in a Registrar's Court where the opposing solicitors told the judge that they had come to an amicable agreement. They were sent out of the room and told not to come back until they had at least tripled their suggested figure. "Don't you realise" the judge told them, "this boy's smile is his open window to the world." I was really impressed but Robert had to have a lot of dental work so that his 'open window' can now reflect his happy nature.

As he got older he was often getting into scrapes with motor bikes or cars. On one particular occasion a crowd of young lads were in the town centre with their motor bikes and didn't realise I was about. I knew that they had only just got their first licences and that Rob was one of them. I watched in horror as they all took off together, spread across the whole width of the road, forcing oncoming traffic to stop. Was I angry! I went home and into my workshop where I found my largest engineering hammer. Then I went and poured myself a large whiskey and waited until he came home. He arrived safe and sound thank God but I took my hammer into the yard and smashed the aluminium front wheel on his motor bike to pieces. I told him he was loved too much to trash his life. It took several weeks to get a new wheel which I paid for but those boys learned a valuable lesson. He still loves his big bikes now though I am secretly pleased he has stopped racing them.

By the mid-80s both he and Jonathan were competing in motor sport and already getting into tricky situations. For some reason one year, probably work related, Jan and I couldn't get to the Lake District in November for a regular VSCC trial so Jon and Rob borrowed the Nash. These are the Northern Lakes, Buttermere, Crummock Water, and by November there were then no remnant of meandering tourists.

It used to be one of the highlights of our year; fantastic Lakeland scenery; empty swooping roads; spectacular colours of the late autumn trees; an exciting days sport using roads and tracks through the National forest or storming up quarry roads wet and slippery with slate; the inevitable noisy party on Saturday night where we drank too much and shouted ourselves hoarse in a bid to be heard; the cold, long, often wet drive home down past Windermere and the never-ending M6 to Spaghetti Junction when we thought we were nearly there with only 100 miles left.

This year, true to tradition, after driving the 300 miles on Friday afternoon, Jon and Rob decided that evening to go for a drink. Jon had an exhilarating ride with a friend in a very quick Nash while Rob enjoyed a lift with Dick Smith's son Andrew in a mini-scamp for the 15 or so miles to Buttermere. The non-drivers at least appear to have consumed their share of alcohol in the local pub and they swapped cars for the return journey. It transpired that the Nash had failed to negotiate the bend on the wet leaves – nothing to do with speed – and rolled via the bank, trapping Rob underneath. Despite this the driver had with superhuman strength lifted it to let Rob out and together they pulled it off the public highway – so as not to annoy the neighbours. Andrew and Jon gave them a lift home but as soon as Dick discovered there were only superficial injuries he gave them a jolly good rousting and sent them back out to get the car.

Avoiding the markers on a Lakeland Trial with Rosemary Smith as passenger

One of many car rolls for poor Rob; an MGB on a dark night heading for a girlfriend's to deliver a secret box of Black Magic! T-boned in a racing car at Cadwell Park; and probably many more I don't know about?

The children all learned to ride motor bikes with Sunday morning lessons. In fact Jill was top of her class and her instructor, Andy Westlake, had taken a shine to her and took her on the back of his new '78 MV Augusta on the National Rally, a 600 mile 24 hour ride around the country. He went on to teach the other three and we thought no more of this until in 1999, the 21st anniversary, he wrote to me enquiring if he could write to Jill and invite her to do it again or at least have her photograph taken for the local paper. He knew

she was married and so he rightly wanted to know what her husband's attitude might be. In fact her marriage was at an extremely low ebb with divorce in motion. "Yes, write to her" was my reply. Andy was still a bachelor but that changed relatively quickly after that and they were married in 2001, a very happy occasion with her first husband at the wedding, wishing them every happiness. Jill's two children Moon and Mishka are very happy which is brilliant and long may Andy have a grin from ear to ear and Jill continue to be the happy caring and loving girl she has become again.

Another pupil at the school in the woods was John Fletcher. John or Fletch for short was the son of an old motoring friend, Bob, who lived at Frome. In fact John's sister Claire married our younger son, Jonathan and they now have three lovely boys but I digress. Bob was a professor of mathematics at Bath University and had his family relatively late in life. Despite spending the war in motor torpedo boats operating in the English Channel he couldn't understand how his lovely son could want so much excitement or be so wild. He knew that I always ran a Saturday boy in the workshop at home, starting them off on cleaning and putting away tools, sweeping up and gradually becoming a very useful pair of hands with my vintage cars. The boys usually started when they were about 14 and they either left after a couple of weeks or lasted years and became not just Saturday boys but evenings and Sundays too, doing jobs for themselves as they acquired the skills. One lad, Chris, made for his A-level metal work a weather cockerel which still tells me daily where the wind is from. He left me to join the Navy as an engineer, becoming involved with the fish wars with Iceland in the '70s, but came back regularly to visit as they all did.

Bob knew this and wondered if I could employ John and try and get some sense into him. Bob couldn't control him. Yes, I'd love to help and a boy from a vintage background would at least know something about cars. He was only just 13 and he loved the job, he was so willing, and although a little younger than Jon they soon became great mates. Although John never had a motor bike he could ride a push bike at dangerous speeds. He virtually became another son and spent a huge amount of time with us. Jon was the first of the pair to buy a three-wheeled Messerschmitt and start his own collection of old cars but Fletch was soon to follow with an Isetta bubble car. The Messerschmitt is a strange style of car; very narrow with the passenger seat directly behind the driver and a Perspex dome over the pair of them – just like a Spitfire. With two little wheels to the front and one at the back it's quite sporty. One night they came in the car together to a VSCC pub meeting only three or four miles from home. They had a few beers as young men do and took to the lanes to drive home except they were a trifle over exuberant and rolled it, falling straight through the Perspex dome. One of them staggered to the main road where we found them on our way home, all bloody and knocked about but looking out for us to come past. Sugar butties, what sort of mess were we to find now? They weren't too bad by the time A&E had sorted them out and our modern had picked up the car – and the pieces. Bob and his wife Marion weren't to know about this for several years despite the fact that the accident happened 200yds from their home.

Jonathan and Fletch prepare the Beetle at Silverstone

After university Fletch went on to join a company building ocean going sailing boats and spent a lot of time at sea in some very exciting races. He and I had planned to do the Peking to Paris Rally together in 1997, with the car bought and sorted. But then early in 1996, a day or so before my 60th birthday, he was given the chance to test drive a demonstrator, a very powerful TVR sports car. He wrecked the car and himself and died ten days later. What a terrible waste. He left behind a lovely girl, Lindsay, with whom he had lived for eight years and was due to marry in a few months. Fletch we miss you but you did ride the roundabout fast!

*Jon and Fletch in their twenties at the end of a rally in the Beetle
and covered with oil and glory*

The rag bag lot on holiday in Majorca 1969

School holidays in the summer meant the sea-side. Our friends in the Midlands had discovered a beautiful beach near a hamlet of no more than a dozen houses and farms on the north coast of North Wales, the Lleyn Peninsula. No pub, no shops, no car park but miles of wonderful sandy safe beach arrived at after a half mile trek across the fields and down a cliff. You could more easily reach the beach by boat but the harbour, half a mile along the coast, was just a small opening in the rocks with no place to moor permanently and nowhere to leave a car. Alternatively, courtesy of the local farmer Gareint, you could just about get there by tractor and trailer at low tide, taking all of your holiday gear, Mirror dinghy, small sailing boat, fishing gear, wet suits and snorkels, chairs, windbreaks and whatever was needed and leaving it all on the beach for a week or a month. No thieves, no great unwashed, no ice-cream bells, candy floss or anything to spend money on. Paradise.

The Joselands, Mark, Whit and Sarah their daughter; the Strettons, Belinda, Robin and their four children were Frazer Nash people to the core and all had cottages or caravans there. Come and join us in this children's paradise. Naturally I include the men under this heading as Llangwnaddl brought out the children in all of us. We could spend the whole day damming a stream or building a raft, hours after the true children had got bored and found a new project. It really was totally unspoilt. We started by renting part of a farm for our first holiday and took with us Ron and Elsie Footitt, very close Nash friends. Ron was the funniest child of the lot but the holiday didn't start well. The house was for six people so we reckoned four adults and the girls in the house and the two boys in a tent in the garden. The farmer's wife was a blowsy blonde – and English in the centre of a very Welsh community. She wasn't having any of it. "You're not stopping here and that's flat" was her reaction when she saw how many we were. "Not only are you not camping on the lawn I'm not even allowing more than six people in the house at any time so you can go now." After driving the Bentley with trailer, boats and sundries and with four small children in the back of this open car for 200 miles we were not ready for this. Jan waded in with a logical argument. Yes we were wrong to assume that two children in a bivouac didn't count but now that we are here perhaps we could offer you more money. The argument quickly degenerated into a full scale row. It was the August holidays, everywhere was fully booked and we'd all had enough so what now? We had specifically been asked to pay in cash and when I noticed the farmer lurking in the background whilst the dispute was going on I went and found him. I told him that we were leaving but as he wanted the rent in cash then presumably he wasn't showing it on his books and my first call on Monday when I got home would be to the tax man. What a change in attitude. A few quiet words with his wife and the doors were open to us. But no camping so only to ourselves and the children. Poor Ron and Elsie had to find less than basic bed and breakfast in a small cottage down the road and walk up to us for meals. Everyday when we were out the wife came in and 'inspected' so we made sure she was never able to find fault. We didn't stop with them again!

It became our annual two week holiday and usually coincided with the Joselands, the Strettons and Ron and Elsie and sometimes we would be joined by other Nash friends and their families. With at least nine children and three grown up male children to feed and look after the girls were kept quite busy in the mornings, making sandwiches for picnics, shopping six miles away for supper. We children were sent to play.

The first thing to do would be to get the fishing nets in. These nets, no longer allowed, were 100' long and 6' high with weights on the bottom which just skirted the sand and had floats on the top to keep the curtain perpendicular. The net was clear nylon and once fish swam into it they would normally be caught up. We hauled in the nets twice a day, early and late if the weather allowed, and usually within 24 hours we would be catching enough fish to live off; cod; pollock; a few crabs or lobsters; huge dog fish – sometimes so many you had to take the net ashore to get them all out and sort out the net itself. Great fun and very Robinson Crusoe.

The next task was to motor along just off the shore with the Mirror dinghy and the vintage Seagull engine to land at various little beaches and coves gathering up washed up timber. We would drag this back to our own beach to assemble a huge raft which could be floated out and anchored off shore. Then we could swim out to it and practice our diving. The raft entailed borrowing empty five gallon chemical drums, preferably not round ones, from the farmer and after several timber trips, lashing them all together with used baler twine. After this it would be time to look at the nets again if the weather held. Mackerel fishing every day, fresh out of the sea and eaten within the hour. Jonathan was our gutting man, he loved fishing and spent hours and nights with Grandad Swann teaching him. Give him a sharp knife and cleaning mackerel and he was as happy as were the gulls that he fed with the innards! One time when the nets were not yielding much Jon went fishing. Jan was about to make a shark pie as a last resort when Jon arrived home out of breath and carrying a three or four pound cod. Wonderful. Fresh fish as fresh as you can get. How would the children like it? Battered with chips of course! It melted in the mouth like butter.

We finally bought a holiday house there, Muriau, when business was so intense and we needed to escape from the general public.

We tried to get up there once a month and I bought a new boat for fishing, a Dory with twin hulls and a fairly flat bottom and twin drop keels. On almost its' first outing a friend and I tried to sail around the point with the tide in full spate and the wind against us. We were soon in trouble and up and over it went. It was Easter with the sea at its coldest but we were determined to rescue the boat. It's amazing what country folk see and Pierce Thomas was quick up to Muriau to tell Jan of our trouble. "There's stupid, see. With the wind and the tide in opposite directions and trying to go round the point, bound to happen isn't it?" Of course he was right but he hadn't volunteered to help us. Jan was soon with us and wading fully clothed about the treacherous rocks off the point, one minute up to her chest height in water and next climbing onto the ridges of the rocks. We saved the boat but little else and my reputation of being a non-thinking, stupid, careless, daft sailor had increased 100%.

The nets were out and the weather was a bit rough but not bad enough to stop us one time when brother Frank and Rosemary were staying with us. Out we went, lifted the first net and retrieved our catch, throwing the net back in as the wind and the sea were rising. I thought we were close enough to the other net to check it. Wrong. We had just pulled it in when over the back of us a wave broke and put the engine out. It would not restart. Shit. The wind was now pushing us ashore to a remote rocky area and I tied the net to the boat and pushed it overboard to act as a sea anchor. Frank sat very quiet in the front while I was taking out the plug to clean it and not really noticing the boat's movement. I glanced at Frank, his hands tightly clasped together; he was having a silent prayer. Oh dear. I redoubled my efforts to get underway. The plug had furred up under the 2-stroke tick-over. It would be nice to think that after a dozen pulls on the starter cord it roared into life but no, rubbish, it so so slowly put-putted into life before it picked up, keeping us on tenterhooks until we had power again. While I kept the engine going Frank scrabbled the net aboard as fast as possible and then we pushed the little 50cc motor back to the harbour. Frank clambered ashore wet through and ashen faced to where Jan was waiting for us, very worried as we were long overdue. "I'll take Frank up home now, jump in the car Frank". "No thanks, I want to walk and thank God that I can feel the earth under my feet". I hadn't really thought it was dangerous, it was

186

only a little hiccup to deal with. The only time Frank and Rosemary have been in a boat with us since was in a pedalo on our river when we took fishing rods and a picnic spending an idyllic afternoon not a quarter of a mile from the house. He was safe there.

We had some spectacular weekend parties at the house – mainly with Frazer Nash friends. On one occasion, after a great deal of wine had been taken, an argument started between two friends, one accusing a mutual acquaintance of being a crook. No-one, replied the other, in the Frazer Nash Car Club is a crook so take back that remark. When the retraction was refused the good member decided that he must leave, with his wife and dog. Where he thought he might be going in the dead of night and full of booze no-one was sure but he was calmed down and the accuser apologised. Sort of. Having said several times how sorry he was he finished sotto voice "but he's still a crook" and the whole tempestuous argument began again. More wine was taken and the quarrel subsided when it was finally time for bed – for the defendant, his wife and the dog. Failing miserably to remove the good lady's undergarments – he wasn't too sure how they all fitted together – but having safely established her in bed fully clothed, he decided to come back downstairs to seek advice from any remaining females. Unfortunately he tripped on the first step and landed in a noisy crumpled heap at the bottom of the stairs. We rushed to his aid of course asking if he was alright. "That's a bloody stupid question. You didn't ask me how I was at the top of the stairs so why ask now?" he riposted obviously thinking he was exhibiting a high degree of wit. He was of course quite unhurt and was sent back to his wife with detailed instructions.

Ron and Elsie were staying with us one weekend and somehow late at night we fell out, I think it was about religion, Elsie was very religious and in some ways I envied her belief it was so strong. But I couldn't see this God, which allowed children to die so young and having lost Sarah Joseland to cancer at only eighteen, as a God of Love. Plus all of the horrific natural disasters. Couldn't

God stop the destruction caused by tsunamis or the earthquakes in Pakistan? Be that as it may we fell out and Ron ordered Elsie against her will to pack their things, they were leaving. We begged them to stay and mend the fence even to the extent of standing in front of his MGB but no, he'd drive into me if I didn't move and into the night they went. Oh bugger. Such good friends. I rang when we got back to Frome and Ron answered in his usual way. "Silly buggers we are, we drove to Nefyn to stay in the Nanhoran Arms. They were closed so we knocked them up and found they were full. We had no petrol in the car!" You had to be a bit careful in North Wales especially on a Sunday. No pubs, no shops, no petrol. They slept in the car, too proud to drive the six miles back to us, and then in the morning had to find some-one to let them have enough petrol to get to Portmadoc. They were brilliant friends for over thirty years and we are so sorry to have lost them to whichever God they went to.

Choirboy and Jezebel
Ron and Elsie at a 'vicars and tarts' party at Clink Farm

Ron was also very good at making bullets which I would fire. After a particularly good party one Midsummer's Eve at Clink we decided rather than go to bed we'd all go out to Stonehenge for the summer solstice. It was a lovely night. We arrived as the stars faded and the light woke some of the sleeping campers, and people began milling around, waiting for the dawn and the sun on the stones. The Druids appeared but still nothing happened and a feeling of restlessness pervaded the crowd. "They're waiting for virgins" said Ron, "so they can start the ceremony". We wandered away from the stones and came upon a line of sleeping bags, their occupants obviously female, still coiled in drowsy sleep. "Here they are" he said, "go and ask them which one is a virgin so we can start". And with this he began to nudge the end of their sleeping bags with his foot so that they sat up – and then he faded into the crowd leaving me to pose the question. A foolish question indeed! I never realised possible virgins could be quite so vitriolic in the early morning or that they had such a command of Anglo-Saxon before I made a timely escape.

Dance of the Seven Veils

Ron, Mark Joseland and Lionel Stretton were partners in a Frazer Nash Garage at Cleobury Mortimer, rebuilding, repairing, making new parts and of course making Nashes go faster. It was a Mecca for us Frazer Nash boys in the '60s especially a new one like me. One of the unwritten rules of owning a Nash was 'if you needed a service manual then you shouldn't own one of these rather special cars.' Frazer Nash also includes GN's which were very early chain-drive cars made by Godfrey and Nash. They split in the early '20s; Ron Godfrey going on to make HRGs and Archie Frazer Nash obviously making Frazer Nashes until the late '20s when he sold out to the Aldington brothers who continued making to AFN's designs until the mid '30s. Only 300 odd were ever made but the survival rate is tremendous, they were so exciting and still are.

I met up with Ron via his business and his very competitive GN with its 6 cylinder 2-litre engine rather than the usual air-cooled V-twin. Somehow he and I hit it off and yet he was so quiet, so dour, a fag hanging from his lips, 15 years older, an engineer to his fingertips and very funny. A contrast to myself, noisy, brash, know all, who knew little about engineering. Thank goodness for John Naish who had a natural ability in all things mechanical and very much kept the Nash on the road. But I met Ron early on – when I needed the two new front axles both of which I'd bent in learning to handle my skittish thoroughbred. Maybe we got on because we'd both been in the 7th Armoured Brigade – except Ron had fought in North Africa and then gone on to the Italian front finishing as a major in REME whereas I was only a peacetime bombardier. Ron loved our kids, in fact knew Jan before I did and he and Elsie soon became part of our family life weekends and holidays.

When we went camping with the Bentley they would take bed and breakfast nearby and join us during the day. Every evening Ron would say he had to get back to his "hot and cold running carpets"

190

leaving us to our Spartan tents. Despite the dreadful first holiday they always joined us at Llangwnadl and Jan loved going out in the rowing boat with him. I couldn't understand this as Jan normally hates boats, big or small, won't go on a cruise, but yes please with Ron. It took me some time to twig it: he had a very old pair of swimming trunks in which the lining was worn out so when he rowed facing Jan his bits dropped out. He didn't care and they were rather large bits; the old sod but we all loved him.

He knew he was well endowed. One weekend in Lyme Regis, he and I had been mackerel fishing and met the girls for lunch in the outside courtyard of the Royal Albion next to the Cobb (perhaps courtyard is an exaggeration for what in those days was simply an open yard enclosed by white painted walls). Jan had bought me a pair of trendy denim shorts and was anxious that I try them on so that she could take them back if they didn't fit. There was an outside loo in the yard and I dutifully went and tried on the shorts. Yes I thought they were great; they were approved by the girls and I changed back into my rolled up sailing trousers. The shorts were once again held up for inspection and now it was Ron's turn. "Go on Ron, you need some new shorts and they look super on Freddie" said Elsie. "Don't be bloody stupid; we're different shapes." And so we were for Ron had a big chest, narrow hips and absolutely no tummy. But Elsie insisted and Ron traipsed slowly across to the loo picking his way through the tables which by this time had filled up for lunch in the sun. And then he traipsed just as slowly back through the crowd wearing the new shorts. They didn't fit at all and of course he accentuated this by pulling them as high as they would go and leaving a good two inches on show down his left leg. "Told you they wouldn't f****** fit" he said in his broadest Manchester accent. I'm not sure which was more comical, Ron coming from the loo or Ron making his way slowly back to the loo in the offending shorts and, at the insistence of Elsie, a small ineffectual towel wrapped around the front of him like a Roman Centurion.

He had no hang ups about his body in public or private. We would often stay at the home of June and Vic Butler who had a huge Victorian house not too far from Prescott Hill Climb. Stables, tennis courts, croquet, housekeeper, billiard room, the lot plus a large bathroom with nothing but a huge cast iron bath on lion legs and a service bell. Ron and I would do our Saturday practice runs at the hill climb and then head there for an evening's party and being hot and August we needed a bath first. It could have been the days of saving water as we took our bath together in the huge bath and having noticed the service bell we had to try it out. It was answered by Pauline Hingley, wife of Phil another Nash man, who put her head round the door and enquired what we wanted. "Two gin and tonics please" "I'll speak to June" and off she went. We knew that June, who was rather dishy, a lovely body and full of fun would return with our drinks, she had to. There was a knock at the door. "Come in" we called in unison and as the door opened and June came in we both stood up. As gentlemen we had always been told to stand when a lady entered the room but she was gorgeous and it showed! She loved it, what a joke! June and I got quite close sometimes after this and naturally I kept this to myself or so I thought. It wasn't until my 50th secret birthday party which Jan threw for me that I found the clever girl knew about my wandering ways and had invited June. No domestic. No fuss. Just saying you can't hide anything from me!

Our friendship with Ron and Elsie was so lovely and easy; he was more and more successful with his GN racing car, the COGNAC, and he asked me to drive it on many occasions. An early drive was a race meeting at Thruxton, which is a very fast circuit. At this time he had a modern oil pump with a belt drive on the engine. I was leading the big race when the belt let go but I hadn't time to notice the oil pressure just disappear and suddenly there was a huge bang. The power had gone; oil and metal bits like shrapnel flew past me; the two big Bentleys hot on my heels had blow outs as pieces of engine pierced their tyres; two gallons of oil spread over 100yds of track; red flags – means STOP; The race was stopped and my, or rather Ron's, engine was cut in half. "No matter" he said. "I've got plenty of engines but I won't try belt drive oil pumps again!"

But the après-racing could be just as exciting as the event itself. In the party room above the Red Lion in Cleobury Mortimer, a favourite venue after a Shelsley Walsh weekend, the décor was nothing but swords and antique guns and one night, a motoring party in full swing, Ron and I somehow got into a sword fight. As the 'fight' developed we found ourselves cutting and thrusting on top of the trestle tables where we had all had supper. It was good stuff, Errol Flynn would have been proud of us. The matronly lady whose lap I fell into was not so proud nor was she very amused. She hadn't approved of us beforehand and the coffee spilt on her dress did nothing to change her mind so we both had to effect a serious charm offensive – a regular occurrence when we'd goaded each other on to go over the top . The girls either got used to Frazer Nash parties and all was forgiven or they were never asked again..

Another such sword episode took place in Normandy when we were competing in the Paris-Deauville with MV. One of our friends was being enrolled as a "Knight of the Tripe" which is pretty serious stuff in the region even to the extent of tripe broth for breakfast with eau de vie chasers. The evening event took place in the Knights own Meeting House and all were dressed in red ermine trimmed cloaks, knee breeches and swords. Wonderful dinner with as much wine as you could consume and champagne for the ceremony. Swords were very much part of the official proceedings and of course afterwards they just had to be used. We tried to emulate the graceful upward swing of the sommelier removing the champagne cork in a single stroke and failed. We tried to knight our own nominees, naturally in fun, but it got close to getting out of hand with a few bad tempers as the swords were confiscated. We all thought it was hilarious except for the real Knights. They were serious; it was a genuine tradition and fellowship.

Kitchen knives had to suffice for a do in Bratton at the village hall. A mock horse racing evening with six lanes and horses and a throw of the dice to move them forward – petty gambling – drinks and much hilarity. Sandy Forbes (whose lovely wife Jill had a position of 'authority' at this do) and myself fell to in the kitchen to help - until I found in the dresser drawer four or five carving knives. Sandy was wearing his kilt – in the traditional manner – and we took it upon our two good selves to entertain the relaxing gamblers during the supper interval with a little sword dance. With the carvers as swords and a rousing highland fling on the record player we prepared our dance. As Sandy was already correctly dressed I was told that I had to harmonize with him and the only way to do this was to perform in nothing but a shirt. What could I do? The locals may have been a little shocked but they seemed to be enjoying the entertainment until Jill appeared from the kitchen and we were severely admonished. At least I think that's the correct word! There was suddenly an awful lot of washing up to be done as a punishment.

But if its not swords I'm in trouble with, its guns. I always used to have a gun or two about but since the very strict licence system I have only the 12 bore for vermin on the farm. It seems that as I get older the less I want to shoot but as a boy all of us were into it. The army – the pot – the skill; it was natural and to a degree I passed it on to our own boys. In the sandpit they would organise battles with model soldiers and equipment, the Germans against the Brits, and from the flat roof of the workshop above they would take it in turns with an air pistol and an air gun to fire into the sand. Lots of their friends joined in and we never worried about it. It was great fun with only one rule – never point a gun at anybody, unloaded or not. Rachel had rats in her stable and Jon was patient enough to sit and wait to let fly with a 410 shot gun with some success. We experimented with two or three black powder guns which I had, great fun and very nice and gentle to use. Place half a tea spoon of black powder in a saucer either at home or in the pub. Put a match to it and it would whoosh up like an atom bomb cloud and spread across the ceiling before minutes later dropping all over the room.

You might need both a drink and a very understanding host before carrying this out and wives can't see the funny side at all!.

The last time I really upset anyone with an explosion was at Jon and Claire's engagement party in the house, a full family gathering for a splendid lunch. Jill with her two young children – Mishka was in a carry cot still – left in a great storm after I gave Robert a thunder-flash and persuaded him to light it in the hall. Wow! What a BANG, the house shook bits of plaster, dust everywhere. As my brother Frank said at the time "Silly bugger, just restored the house and now trying to blow it up". I must admit on a scale of stupidity it was over half way up.

~~~~~~~~~~~~~~~~

'Salome' came into my life quite by accident. In '69 I was advertising for a vintage engine – it was an ABC flat twin air-cooled I needed for another chain drive car that Big John and I had built up from GN parts. The engine that we had used had been driving a saw bench in Chippenham for years before we bought it. It was quite successful but heavy footed Fred had blown it apart hence an advert in Exchange and Mart. "Yes" said a man on Easter Sunday in reply and "Yes" he was in tomorrow. Where? Scotch Corner! Well, they were like hens teeth – better go and get it. Jan and I set off early on Bank Holiday Monday and we'd bought the engine as soon as we'd seen it. We were busy paying the chap when he asked "Don't you want the old car with it?" What old car, where? Out the back, amongst the stinging nettles. We couldn't quite believe it but there was a little single seater racing car with a Morgan 3-wheeler chassis married to the back axle of a GN. Complete but sad, it had obviously been outside for some length of time. You could just discern 'Salome' sign-written on the bonnet. We didn't get over-excited, we'd never heard of it, but for a little money we bought it.

We were in a modern tank – a Volvo estate with a drop down tail gate. Naturally I had my tool kit, which I always carried: always repairing little things in the cafes and of course you needed a good tool kit to take with you in a vintage car: so I proceeded to take the back axle off the car and put it in the back of the Volvo, followed shortly after by the body of the little green racing car. It fitted a treat; we couldn't put the rear window down properly but fine. Home again home again jiggerty jig; very pleased!

I rang the VSCC office the following morning to ask if they'd heard of 'Salome'. There was great excitement. "Have you found it?" "Yes and bought it!" "Great stuff; been missing for years!" It had been built by Jan Bryer for racing on dirt in the early thirties in the CAPA races and then used for hill climbs and sprints until it disappeared. When she was assembled pre-war she had no vestige of body panels or 'clothes', hence her name, but by now she had doffed her seven veils and sported a light weight body. What a lucky boy I was to have her albeit not with her proper engine; she should have had a JAP V twin of the '20s and so she was put to one side while John and I fitted the ABC engine to the 'Beetle' as the GN had now been named; it wasn't to last long because we then found a 1000cc HRD V twin which would be brilliant.

We fitted the ABC in haste before a Frazer Nash Race Meeting at Castle Combe. The Beetle was flying at 6000revs when suddenly – bang. I had a very hard thump in the rear end and the car came to a sudden halt. We were towed in and took up the floor boards to discover that the prop shaft, made from seamed tube, was out of balance and at 6000revs had let go in the biggest possible way and torn the clutch apart. Back to the drawing board. Now we had time to concentrate on 'Salome'. About this time Alan Cherrett found and sold me a KTOR 1000cc V twin that was perfect for her. She was another flyer but not always reliable and despite persevering for some years we couldn't attain the holy grail of reliability which continued to elude us.

Overleaf: Tony Coles and Cherry with a paddock rebuild of the KTOR

In 1979 Cadwell Park Race Meeting was the last of the season. The circuit is in Lincolnshire just 10 miles from Louth. It's not flat like the ex-airfield circuits of Thruxton, Silverstone, Castle Combe, where there's acres of space to go off on a very wide course. Cadwell is built into folds of a very hilly little area and it's very narrow. Bike racing there is wonderful to watch and to drive a racing car there is something else; there's no room for mistakes. I was going to sell the car that winter; I'd got a bit fed up with her. She didn't have a starter and required a push start every time. There wasn't too much space to push and it meant commandeering any strong body you could see to help. If a handicap race didn't start quickly after a warm up lap then she would overheat on the start line. It could then be a bugger to start at the 3 minute signal. If she failed I had to sit with my arms in the air indicating to the cars behind that I wasn't going to move, hoping they would see me and not drive into the back of me. Then when I'd let all the cars go we could try to push start her again but of course by then the field had gone. If all went well, especially on scratch races where we all started together, you could let the engine run.

Our practice times often put us on the front of the grid and we
would hope then that the race would start quickly. Salome only had
two gears; a very high 1st gear and then top. I would slip the clutch
and coax her, losing 150yds until she would get going and I could
wind her up. Because Cadwell is so narrow and twisty it meant that
I now had to drive like stink to get past the cars who'd started
behind me. Along the finish-start straight; up the right-hander hill;
swoop down a little then climb again fast; a long right hander and
into the Goose Neck. Salome corners fantastically, she's only three
inches off the road and wouldn't roll, but the Goose Neck is a very
fast area and one year when Robert was racing her an Austin 7 lost
control and hit Salome side on, flipping her over. Robert didn't
come out and slid down the tarmac on his back ending up for two
weeks in Louth hospital. "Motor Racing is Dangerous". Racing
cars pre-1960 never had roll-over bars and still don't and we don't
wear seat belts – better to be thrown out! After the Goose Neck is a
left hander; faster and faster down hill and then heavy braking for a

90° left; along the bottom then sharp left and right in quick succession.

It was at this point some years later when I was competing in the Beetle, by then fitted with a very quick 2-litre engine, that I tried a stupid manoeuvre to overtake on the inside. It was too much for the nearside wheel – it collapsed causing the car to somersault.

Over it went with me in it and carried on rolling again throwing me out in the process to land with a thud on the tarmac. I can still see in slow motion the black mass of the car coming down on me. Run! Run! The adrenalin kicks in and I drag myself up and race to the side of the track a split second before the car crashes down again. How did I do that when I can no longer move? I did, thank God, and watch from the verge as the following cars race either side of the Beetle now immobile in the middle of the track. Then red flags are being waved – the race was stopped and the ambulance on its way. Jan arrived totally breathless having been dragged by Rob at a run from her marshal post on the finish line. She'd known I was lying fourth and trying hard as she stood waiting, several laps to run before she could pick up the chequered flag and signal the end of the race. Red flags were not that common but she couldn't see the accident and didn't realise it was me until Rob, who'd watched in horror arrived at a run. "It's dad! It's dad! Hold my hand and run!" I'm OK! Or at least I think I am. Nowadays I would be put in a neck brace, have my back immobilised and be sent for a scan – just in case – but now my helmet, badly damaged from landing on my head, is confiscated by the RAC scrutineers and I am given a very cursory going over by the aged venerable doctor on duty before being pronounced fit to go. I tried to go down to dinner in the pub that night but couldn't make it and the next morning I was so bruised I could hardly move. Despite spending a couple of weeks in a chair the accident shortened my chassis, trapping the nerves in my neck. Evenl now I'm wearing a glove as I write because of pins and needles in the fingers of my right hand.

But that was a one-off. When driver and car are behaving themselves I take Salome into the very steep climb up the mountain leaving the ground at the top; watch the revs!; into the woods and a slow hairpin where the slower cars inevitably hold you up; down, down into a right-hander and back onto the finish-start straight.

This year she knows something's up. She's flying round the circuit passing car after car; really dancing, not with her seven veils more rock and roll. We're with the leaders on the last lap and then we're through taking the chequered flag. Wow. Yes Salome can be brilliant. The same day she performs once more like this; obviously she doesn't want a new owner and I agree. She's too beautiful to sell! We'll celebrate our wins instead. The Frazer Nash Club has set up a private pub in a tent – the 'Dog and Sprocket' and when we finally finish celebrating we realise that we can't leave, we're both too boozed to drive anywhere. It's a very basic tent but we didn't worry too much about the makeshift camping and the lack of beds. Not, that is, until the next morning when ugh! Jan is not good in the mornings at the best of times but she really loses her cool with me when the only thing I can offer her to clean her teeth is a glass of red wine!

As to Salome, after this we can look forward to another twenty years of mutual fun.

On the days when she's good she's very very good – she taunts and tantalises and throws her veils to the wind and we reap in the records at hill climbs and sprints around the country. But on the days when she's bad she's horrid and you can believe she would take the head of John the Baptist without compunction. If I manage to practice she will let me down on the timed run, let loose a chain, oil up a plug, hit a bank – but perhaps that's my fault and not hers.

It may sound trite but one of the greatest honours of my life was becoming, at the ripe old age of 36, Captain of the Frazer Nash Car Club in December 1972. Three years of intense motoring and more than intense pleasure and satisfaction. I loved it. I belong to the best, in every sense of the word, one make car club in the world.

We were already packing in countless competitions over and above the VSCC events in England (and Scotland, Wales and Ireland!). Jan had started driving competitively which made car preparation twice as time consuming – especially as she had little sympathy for the rev limits or the sound of the engine and, although she did well in competition, frequently came back with a useless engine. An understatement to say that it stretched my patience. Any breakdown stretched that in those days and my fuse was normally quite short. There was so much to be done; working flat out and playing flat out too all the way through our thirties. "It's not a race" is a phrase I use instead of grace whenever we sit down to eat with friends or family. It didn't carry too much weight then! We took MV to the Nurburgring taking in a competitive hill climb at Vaals on the way back. I can't remember how I broke the car only that a picture appeared in the Chain Gang Gazette of "Freddie Giles after mending his grease gun, his bevel box and his temper in that order!"

We took her to Italy to compete in the Mille Miglia when it was still a continuous thousand mile event without a night stopover. That was certainly a race despite the fact that the English entry had been told it wasn't. No-one told the rest of the field and so after a while we all decided to forget average speeds and go for it. Peter Still, one of my oldest and best friends, in his comfortable TT Rep travelled with us, clocking out from Padua shortly in front of us at 21:30 in the evening and driving non-stop until we reached Rome around lunch the next day. A whole new experience as motor cycle police in smart uniforms rode as outriders, steering their bikes with their knees while they conducted us with much arm waving through the city traffic, positively encouraging us to drive faster.

25 years after first competing in a Mille Miglia we compete in the Argentinean Millas Sport in 1997

A twelve hour break and off again on the second 500 miles. As dawn rose on the Futa Pass I spotted the outline of a car in front of us and drove like stink to try and catch it. He was not willing to be caught and so his pace increased with mine. What a drive! The silhouette of the ragged mountains against a pale pink sky; a narrow rutted road lacking in any barrier protection against the valley below; tiny twin tail lights pulling us on. I looked over at my navigator and found Jan weeping silently with fear but never saying a word. The top of the pass finally appeared and the tail lights stopped waiting for us. It was Peter, and his passenger Mike Reddaway who had not been weeping with fear but being sick over the side in sheer terror.

Once I was Captain I had to compete in every event there was going and in my first year I won for the 3rd time the coveted AFN[9] Trophy – the most prestigious award in the club awarded for the best overall performance throughout the year in all forms of competitive motoring i.e. to the person with the most points gained competing in any type of event – racing: rallying: hill climbing: trials: sprints: driving tests: everything but concours d'elegance in which we never competed! I won it again in my third year and a couple of times after that, winning the runner up cup several times too.

---

[9] Archie Frazer Nash Cup originally won by AFN himself – the designer and builder of the Frazer Nash Car and constant and successful competitor in the '20s and '30s

The line up at Clink Farm at the end of the season

Having so many points I was also in line for major trophies in our parent club, the VSCC, and was just pipped to the post, quite literally, for the major overall trophy, the Lycett, in the autumn of '73. We really enjoyed the Lakeland Trials. The first one we'd entered in '69 had been so wet and cold and windy it's a wonder we entered again. It was 330 miles from home in the relatively slow Anzani Nash – a good day's drive – but there was inevitably a party at Dick Smith's on the Friday, a storming day's motoring on the Saturday and a full on party in the pub on Saturday night followed by a serious hang over and another good day's drive home again with the driver becoming frailer and frailer as the journey progressed. Quite often a head cold followed by Monday!

As usual in '73 the final trial hill, known as Drumhouse, was the ascent of a slate quarry in the Honister Pass. The steep shale track was used by lorries and dumpers transporting the rough slate down to the splitting houses and their drivers were paid danger money. You needed a lot of grunt to climb it and stout nerves to come back down it with vintage brakes. I had cleaned most of the hills that day[10] and knew I was in with a good chance for the Lakeland Trophy. I'd also cleaned Drumhouse before and so I was feeling optimistic. I'd been trying for 5 years to win the Lakeland Trophy and this was going to be the year – the points for a trophy win should give me the Lycett too. The car was in the queue waiting its turn and I was wandering amongst my fellow competitors chatting when I felt a sudden and sharp stabbing pain somewhere in my groin. Minutes later I was rolling around on the floor in agony and an ambulance was on its way. One little pip of a kidney stone had cost me both the trial and the Lycett! Peter took the car up the hill – full marks – but everyone realised I wasn't driving so although the car won the trial I didn't. Not that year anyway although I finally managed it several years later and was so full of exuberance at the evening's award ceremony that I could do no more than wear the triumphant pot on my head as a helmet, cracking the silver as I did so! It mended.

You have to remember these were the days before HSE and politically correct anything. In the middle of my term we had the usual raid to the Alps, this time based on Briancon. We ran an unofficial hill-climb up the Col de Granon, timing the section up the semi-closed dirt road and what's more aided and abetted by three armed gendarmes. We broke several cars storming up the narrow mountain passes but everyone turned out to give a hand – the club at its best – and all went on their way mended. We drank a lot of free campari at mayoral receptions and were introduced to Ricard and Pernod for the first time. We laughed a lot and on one occasion we forgot the car in the middle of the ancient city, both

---

[10] Got to the top of the hill without stopping and without going outside of or hitting any of the markers 1 to 20 which indicated the route and the points to be awarded for that hill

Jan and I thinking the other had brought her home. For some reason I hitched a lift with an off-duty policeman who entertained me with Bessy Smith and whiskey in his flat before delivering me to the hotel. As it was so late I decided to climb up the fire escape and in through a window rather than wake everyone up but when I arrived in our room it was empty and locked from the outside. So back down the fire escape and up the main staircase to find Jan asleep in the laundry cupboard on the landing….I had the key. The good friend I found "looking after her" tells me that there was a very innocent explanation but I have yet to hear it. I didn't mind. I don't know and I don't mind and he's still one of my best friends!

Jan and the Anzani on a Lands End Trial

I entered everything and tried to lead from the front just as I'd watched Nigel Arnold-Forster do when I first joined the section. I had four chain drive cars by now, MV, my favourite Meadows-engined TT Rep which was superb in driving tests and rallies: PH, Jan's Anzani which was fantastic for trials and for rallies too: the Beetle for racing and speed events including hill climbs and sprints and finally Salome. I was on a high and seemed to be successful in every branch of the sport. It was credited to my driving ability which in a way it was but it also needed enormous support from family and friends and the Nash members in particular who were always there to help out. Tony Coles was always with me, in the paddock, in the workshop, making sure the car was in good fettle. Ron lent me his car, the Cognac, and I took the vintage lap record at Oulton Park which I kept for several years. I was so glad of all of the other good friends in the club who I haven't mentioned but they know who they are. We travelled up to London to the VSCC AGM in a coach which we had organised and it was joked that the coach was needed for me to carry home all the trophies which I'd won that year. In reality it was for the West Country members to get to the meeting and help vote me onto the parent club committee where I stayed for some 13 years.

I took being on the VSCC committee seriously and rarely missed a monthly meeting. Initially they were at the Steering Wheel Club off Curzon Street and Jan and I would spend the day in London before the meeting taking the milk train home. Later they were moved to Newbury, when the VSCC opened its new offices there but that wasn't quite so much of an attraction. I was able to help with the design of the offices later when we had a chance to build a library and Jan also spent hundreds of hours helping the parent club, transferring the entire member's list to a computerised system.

I said that we'd never competed in a concours d'elegance but had forgotten the Paris-Deauville rally in 1980 where the first prize still acts as our front door stop! We had no problem taking the Nash abroad, it was usually reliable, and we had great fun lapping the Arc de Triomphe as a practice for the Peking to Paris Rally we had entered for 1982. Overtaking the course car on the Boulevard Peripherique which was totally forbidden and consuming coffee and cognac at every stop and loads of champagne with almost everything. Deauville was so elegant and the French teams enacted identical elegant scenes as they showed off their cars in the packed stadium; unfurling their parasols; parading their well-groomed dogs; showing off their genuine 20's costumes. We had nothing of that. We dressed as boy racers; white overalls; caps back to front. Into the ring came the Nash with the flourish of a handbrake turn on the immaculate lawn; out of the car and change a front wheel in ninety five seconds and a woman to boot! The crowds loved it and we won first prize for the act! Of course it suited my love of attracting attention to a tee!

Having been Captain I thought I might like to follow Nigel, who had gone from Captain to President of the VSCC. Thank goodness I didn't as by the time this was mooted in the late 80's the role had been changed from competition leader to that of a political director. There were a lot of undercurrents and I'd always been far too outspoken to ever be accepted into the political inner circle which controlled such events. I think I would have been so frustrated and although I would have tried to do the job to the best of my ability I would have felt personally responsible for dealings beyond my control which would have upset me enormously.

Ron and I continued to share our cars. By the time Salome had doffed her seven veils the whole car was no more than 6cwt and gave 80bhp from a 1000cc JAP engine so 250bhp per ton was a lot of fun. We also shared our two road going Nashes. When Jon was old enough Ron had him driving the GN too and using it well. I won various scratch races in it before failing health made Ron think of the future and he wanted me to buy it from him. I was delighted to and went on to set various records for hill climbs and sprints and regularly gained FTD[11] with the COGNAC even holding the vintage lap record at Oulton Park for some years. To be fair to Salome she held her share of records too.

---

[11] Fastest time of day of all cars entered in the event

After climbing Screw Hill on the Lleyn Peninsula – in the rain!

for England and St George

We had always had juke boxes and pin tables in our Farmer Giles cafes but by the end of the sixties we had fruit machines too. They only paid out tokens - no cash - which could be spent over the counter. Before decimalisation and VAT there was an annual licence to pay to Customs and Excise; £25 for a machine costing sixpence a go; £12.10s for a three-penny machine. We always used the 3d kind although on some you had to put in 6d and got two goes. We were always careful to get our licences in good time and to display them, as required, on the wall next to the machines.

One morning I was in the office at ten o'clock when the phone went. Nothing unusual there. It was my manageress, Sheila, from Melksham and there was panic in her voice. Not another bloody break-in I thought: no it can't be: that call would have been either in the middle of the night or first thing as they opened.

"What's wrong Sheila?"
"I've got a problem with the fruit machines. Customs and Excise are in here and they say they're impounding our fruit machines. They've turned them all to the wall with a notice to say 'Property of Customs and Excise' in 3" high letters" My turn to panic!
"What the hell for? They can't do that. I'll be right over"

I put the phone down but it rang again immediately. My manageress from Yeovil, Mrs Cobner.

"I've got a problem with the fruit machines. Customs and Excise are in here and they say they're impounding our fruit machines"

Next the manageress from Frome and she wasn't the last. What the hell was happening? We were being raided. The machines were turned to the wall; the power switched off and huge notices pinned to them; 'PROPERTY OF H.M.CUSTOMS & EXCISE'.

"This is the Excise Office in Trowbridge. We must ask you and any other Director present to come to our offices immediately" It was 9 minutes past ten and I felt punch drunk. Jan and I jumped in the car and got a move on. What the hell was this about?

Brick walls with a fading grey gloss. No windows. A stenographer sat in the corner, fingers poised over his machine. Two men watched us through the door.
"Anything you say will be taken down and may be used in evidence......"
Gestapo or what...What was going on? Were we being arrested? What had we done? We were, they said, operating gaming machines for which we had no licence.

"But we have. We get them every year." Don't lie to us: you know you are cheating. How can I be cheating? You know full well what this is about. No we don't! Another bloody tennis match!
"You are operating machines which require a twenty-five pound licence. Do you have such a licence?"
"We pay twelve pounds ten."
"That's for a machine which takes a three-penny bit."
"Yes, three-pence a game."
"No – a three-penny piece. Is it or is it not a fact that some of your machines take a six-penny piece?"
"Yes, but -"
"So they require a twenty-five pound licence."
"But it's six-pence for two games. That's three-pence a go."
"Your machines take a six-penny piece, and therefore require the full licence. Your customers are paying six-pence for one game and getting a second game free."

There was clearly no arguing with these people. Even I could see that. They were bullies and they were succeeding in scaring us. They let us go at lunch-time. Okay, they said, we'll agree that you may have made an error, so we won't prosecute you. You will pay a fine instead.
"How much?"

211

"Four hundred pounds. Come back at two o'clock with your cheque-book."

It's now gone one o'clock and we have to drive to Frome, collect the cheque book and be back by two. Bloody hell, what a panic, what sort of civilised country do we live in? No time to speak to our solicitor – its lunchtime. We were both stunned by the size of the fine, £4,000 pounds in today's money and traumatised by the treatment. And then things took a turn for the worse. When we came back, ready to pay, they started again. "Anything you say…." They now no longer believed us; they said we were lying, and they wouldn't accept payment of the fine. They were going to pursue the case further. Perhaps we would like to tell them our side of the story – again – from the beginning. We really couldn't believe this was happening. If they thought we had the wrong licence up for all to see why hadn't they just told us it was incorrect and asked for the difference?   Now could we go home and start our machines up again? No. We would await their pleasure.

Back at the office we called our solicitor. What can we do?
Nothing.
What did he mean?
We'll do nothing.
But they've just robbed us of four hundred pounds!
We do nothing. You simply don't tangle with them. Don't even complain. They're a law unto themselves and have much wider powers than the police. Pay up and forget it.

And there it was left - until two weeks later, when we got a call from our friends at H.M. Customs & Excise telling us we could now plug our machines back in. Phew, so that was the end of that. Well, not quite. Three months later a letter arrived. We would now pay a penalty for attempting to defraud the Revenue. One thousand pounds. (£10,000 today!!)

Not long after this we read, in a trade paper, that the law regarding these licences had been amended. The six-penny machines were now deemed to be offering two games at three-pence a go, and for these the lower licence fee would apply. So, we asked our solicitor, can we get our money back? No. You really don't argue with these people. And we never did again.

In the '70s before Game Boys, mobile phones, the net, our younger customers would come in to play some of the innovative video machines which were coming onto the market. This craze took off like a rocket and swept the country. There were no prizes save perhaps the accolade of having the highest score of the week for shooting down asteroids and having their name in lights. These youngsters had no real education but their coordination was fantastic. They could react at such speed they would have made brilliant fighter pilots but sadly of course they would never have been given the chance. I wonder how many such chaps were passed over in the last war because they didn't have the necessary 'officer background'?

Gaming machines were profitable, partly, of course, because of unfortunate people who got hooked on the flashing lights and near-misses as the images rotated and the coins kept threatening to drop but never quite did – or did so just often enough to encourage the player to have one more try. This certainly started to happen when the machines were allowed to pay out cash prizes rather than tokens. Mainly it was women. They'd sit for hours, smoking and playing and hoping. I'd often give them a cup of tea – not so much to encourage them as to sustain them. It may sound self-righteous, but I started to feel sorry for them, and then I started to feel responsible. I wasn't breaking any law, but it did seem unfair to let people gamble in this way when the odds were stacked against them. By the time my contract with the George was up, in 1984, I was glad to be rid of them all

In 1965 I'd bought a combined café and B&B in Warminster. This was an unusual property in that it had once been a Temperance Hotel, "Licensed to Sell Snuff, and Tobacco, Tea and Coffee." In

1969 Jan and I set about transforming it into a hotel and licensed steak-house. This was the era of the Berni Inn; prawn cocktail; steak and chips; ice-cream; all for under a pound. The first thing was to try and get a licence. What a performance. We were opposed by the local LVA – they decided they had too many pubs in the town for everyone to make a living and certainly didn't want me selling alcohol too. They gave us a limited restaurant licence after appeal and it wasn't until years after we sold the place they managed a full pub licence.

Once more I was grateful for George Philip's imaginative design. We opened up the stables behind what used to be a coach-house and furnished the whole place with flat-pack furniture from Habitat. White round tables and beech-wood chairs, a million miles from the traditional brown Windsor chair and dark pub table of the Berni Inns. This marked a further step forward in that we were moving up-market and having to employ far more highly trained chefs. Temperamental beings, chefs. They were either over-sexed; falling into a fit of depression when let down by their current lover – of either the opposite or the same sex; or too fond of the cooking brandy they used in their trifles. Either way it rendered them unable to work while they were under the influence.
We employed a manager there who I later sacked for having sex with one of the young waitresses. I didn't approve of manager/staff liaisons in principle but when it takes place behind the counter in broad daylight it's time for them to go. It meant that we had to work right up to Christmas Eve; I was cooking and Jan front of house. We went home exhausted – we had twelve branches and were running all of the other businesses during the day – and stuffed children's Christmas stockings until just after midnight. Something needed to change.

One of the best changes was Tony Coles joining our team. Tony came to us following an advert for a maintenance engineer to look after the catering equipment but was soon helping me maintain, repair and rebuild my vintage cars which were in use virtually daily and competing all year round. Janice, his wife, wanted him to

214

settle down to a less dangerous way of life. He had completed a full apprenticeship as a mechanical electrical engineer, had a series of very nice pre and post war sports cars and was then a full time diver. I thought his written application said 'driver' but no, he was deep sea diving with all the perils that entailed and he was now picking up lobster, crayfish and crabs from the sea bed and salvaging from wrecks – not of course the historically valuable ones. It sounds romantic but there was danger, uncertainty and frequent fights between the divers and the lobster/crab potters. Added to this there was really little income in the winter months from this form of diving and he and Janice wanted a family.

Much to our good fortune he went on to be my right hand man in repairing, making, developing ideas, anything I put before him. Very little could stump him, be it mechanical, electrical or engineering, and I'm delighted to say that after 38 years we are still working together one or two days a week. He is now naturally a good friend and I would trust him with my life – indeed on occasion when he's been on the other end of a rope and I've been on a roof that's exactly what I've done. There is no way that we could have achieved what we have in business, in competitive motoring or in life generally without both him and his wife.

But Tony wasn't the only change. Being raised in the country I'd naturally been aware of what the arable farmers locally did, and was impressed with how simple it seemed: they turned the ground over, planted seeds, prayed for the right mixture of sunshine and rain and, by and large, raised decent crops which they then sold. They always complained they were hard done by, of course, but they never seemed to go hungry, and they generally lived in nice houses and drove decent cars. Maybe it was time I tried my hand at it. Most of my uncles and cousins had been farming all their lives and it was in my blood from my grandfather Robert.

We bought a little parcel of land, about thirty-six acres, on the other side of Frome and planted it up, mostly with winter wheat, but also, just to hedge our bets, with a couple of acres of potatoes.

Having bought the various outbuildings next to Clink Farm, I'd converted one of the large cow-sheds into a corn store. We sprayed the corn as it came in with an anti-fungal agent, that way I could afford to store the crop and hope the price would rise sufficiently over the winter to offset the cost of the treatment. As usual we did most of the work ourselves, with a part-time milk herdsman to help with some of the more agricultural needs. Tony or sometimes Jan would drive the tractor and trailer some three or four miles across the town and then back again over-loaded with corn: the heavy trailer pushing the tractor down the steep hills of Frome, almost out of control but never quite losing the load.

We only lasted two years. In 1975, a wet spring was followed by a glorious summer and the yield was superb, the stalks almost buckling under the weight of the grain. The price, naturally, plummeted. The following year, 1976, has entered the nation's folklore for the intense heat and sustained drought it brought. The price of corn rocketed, but of course we all had drastically reduced crops. Do I need to spell the lesson out? We sold our thirty-six acres as quickly as we could, benefiting from a huge boom in land prices to net an eighty per cent profit – albeit at a time when annual inflation was over twenty per cent.

While we'd broken even on cereal-farming, we'd taken an absolute hammering in the potato business, and for that we had no-one to blame but ourselves. The corn crop was safely gathered in while the weather was still dry, and the spray did the trick: there was no mould. The potatoes, on the other hand, came in later in the year when the rains had arrived - within days of Mr Denis Howell being appointed Minister for Drought, as it happened. We got them into store all right, and were confident that they'd dry out in the airy shed. They did not. They still looked fine when we went in to pull them out and bag them up. That's when we discovered that the good potatoes just formed an outer layer to what lay underneath. What lay underneath was a sort of pale, yellow porridge, which stank abominably. The entire crop had rotted right there under our noses.

Another shed in which we'd stored the corn was destined to cause us more anguish in the second year. It was only a low old cow skillings, built on a timber A-frame and with a tiled roof. Because of the low cross-beams it wasn't actually possible to get a tractor in with a bucket attached, which was a bit of an inconvenience. Looking at it one day I decided there'd be a lot more headroom if I removed some of the cross-members temporarily. There was nothing wrong with my reasoning at all: adjusting the structural framework certainly made more room. I didn't appreciate though that the sand leaning against the outside wall was seeping its damp into the corn. In six months this 100 tons grew very wet and began to push against the walls. Of course without the cross-members there was only one inevitable result. Jan and I were out in the field walking the dog when we heard a sort of low rumbling sound. It was rather as if someone was tipping a lorry-load of stone. We didn't think much of it until a small boy came running across the stubble shouting and waving his arms.

"Dad, Dad! The barn's fallen down!" At first we thought he was exaggerating. We knew what boys were. Unfortunately, he wasn't. When we got back home there was the barn, or rather the pan-tiled roof of the barn lying on the deck with the timbers poking out from underneath it, a pall of mortar dust swirling about it, and – here was the strange thing - hardy a single tile smashed. The end of my farming career. It didn't matter; I was temperamentally unsuited to the life. There was nothing you could organise for a specific time. If it was wet you couldn't dig potatoes despite the fact you had a crew of women in the trailer waiting to go. If the crop was late it clashed with pre-arranged motoring events. Good job too for what was coming next took all of our energy and concentration.

At the same time as we were trying out 'farming' we were exploring different ways of changing direction in the business. I'd had a shock when I'd gone for my racing medical and discovered that my blood pressure was too high. Next March I would be 40 and I'd had enough of teaching young girls how to make a decent cup of tea. We thought about turning Clink Farm into a pub. It had once been the 'Halfway House' and by now we had houses built all around us. Alas my face didn't fit with the planners. In the spring of 1975 I'd even made an offer for the George Hotel but my £45,000 had been rejected out of hand by Courage Breweries.

The George was a Frome landmark, a large listed building, which dominated the market-place. It was a 17th century coaching inn and in the '60s had still been a thriving market town hotel, hosting the usual Rotary lunches and hunt balls.

By the time my 40th birthday had come and gone the George consisted of little more than a bar, its twenty or so bedrooms shut up for want of repair and the rest of the premises being in a pretty sorry state. The ballroom, sadly, had been sold off to the bank next door some years previously. The tenants were what I can only describe as a hippy couple, with a pretty low standard of housekeeping and cleanliness. Nevertheless, just walking around the old hotel one could sense that the spirit of the place was there, dormant perhaps, but just waiting to be re-awoken. It had a lovely feel to it. I made another offer, £10,000 less than a year previously and this time they snatched my hand off.

Our first job when we took over was to clear away the debris from the years of neglect. A wrought iron balcony on the first floor ran the length of the building facing the market place. The tenants had netted this off and allowed their cats to use it as a sort of recreation area or exercise yard. For cats read "a dozen moggies"; for exercise area read "toilet". There were heaps of cat-shit in various stages of decay – not only on the balcony, where diners in elegant gowns had once taken the air and looked out over the town, but also inside the living-rooms of their flat. Under the bed it lay inches deep. Little wonder the brewery had been so anxious to get rid of the place.

One of the conditions of the sale was that the furniture would be sold separately from the property. The bedrooms were still furnished and we were keen to hang onto as much as we could: there were several lovely antiques which would add a lot of atmosphere once we were open again. Late in the summer the agent for Courage brewery arrived in my office at Clink. He had in mind a figure of, say, £8,000. That was a lot of money in anybody's books, almost a quarter of what I'd paid for the hotel itself. We had coffee and talked around the subject for a while when I noticed him looking at a photograph pinned on my notice-board. It was Salome on the start line at Prescott.

Tony and a young Martin Stretton holding the silencers in place at Prescott

Now why wouldn't they let me compete in my fireman's helmet? Fletch, Jan and Rob were amused anyway.

"Are you interested in cars?" I asked him.

"Yes," he said, "my step-father had a car just like that."

"Really? Where did he live?"

"Bristol."

"Ah, his name wasn't by any chance Jan Breyer, was it?"

"It was. Do you know him?"

"Course I do. That's his car – or was. Would you like to see it?"

"Would I? I used to sit in it when I was a little boy and pretend to drive it."

I took him outside and across to the garage. There, dwarfed by the Bentley and the Frazer Nash sat Salome, my single-seater racing car. My visitor lowered himself into the car and sat holding the steering wheel for a moment or two, delighted to have so many happy memories return. Eventually we got back to business.

"Now," he said, coming back into the office, "where were we?"

"The furniture."

"Ah yes, the furniture. Well I think two thousand sounds about right don't you?"

I called in an old friend, Arthur Sutton, an antiques dealer. He cast his expert eye over the various beds and chests, settees and free-standing cupboards. One thing that intrigued him was a beautiful old desk-cum-chest-of-drawers. The top drawer didn't open as such, but just folded down. Arthur looked it over and declared it to be an eighteenth-century secretaire – or rather a part of one. "There's a bit missing," he said. "What you should have is a set of shelves above it, with glass doors." We found the shelves in the bathroom, covered in toothpaste and dust but perfectly recoverable. No glass doors? Nowhere on site,– until a few weeks later when we were gutting the bar toilets. They had false ceilings, and as we removed them... there were the missing doors. Arthur was delighted "It's made the piece worth about two thousand now I've restored it – do you want me to sell it for you?" I must admit I was tempted. I could have got back all I'd paid for the furniture, but I didn't. I rather liked it, and its been part of my office ever since.

As well as the secretaire there were some excellent antiques in the bedrooms; a suite made of bird's-eye maple, as well as a dressing-table and wardrobe built of satinwood. Sadly, these were too large for what we intended and had to be sold, but we saved a big easy chair for home along with a splendid nest of three Chinese tables. Various bits and pieces found their way onto a pavement sale outside the front of the hotel, organised and run by Rob and Jon who were now of an age to learn a bit of salesmanship – and be paid for their efforts..

The George reeked of history and one of the stories I uncovered fired my imagination. Back in 1832 the locals had become restive over an approaching parliamentary election. Rival factions supporting Sir Thomas Champney clashed with followers of mill owner William Sheppard, and with violence threatening the 7th Dragoons were called in from Trowbridge to restore order. The local magistrate, in time-honoured fashion, then read the Riot Act from the balcony of the George Hotel, although not before shots had been fired into the mob and several people injured.

Brilliant, what a theme. The big room downstairs would be the Riot Bar. Of course, it was a contentious name, and it raised a few eyebrows locally. I found an artist in Bristol and got her to sketch out some scenes I had in mind: the magistrate in his robes, the soldiers in their hats, red coats and white cross-braces, bayonets fixed at the ready; and of course the mob in the street looking surly and threatening. She then enlarged these to make full-scale figures and transferred them to half-inch plywood so that I could cut out the shapes in the carpentry shop at Clink. Back to the artist for painting before we mounted them onto wooden blocks standing them a few inches proud of the bar wall, lit from behind to create a shadowed, three-dimensional effect. I found a few antique guns, man-traps, eighteenth century tradesmen's tools and so on to give the place an air of authenticity, and the effect was dramatic.

The Riot Bar was only part of the hotel. We had to try and fit in heating, en-suites, fire escapes not to mention dining rooms and kitchens. Putting the place together was sheer hard work but once again real friends helped us out. We had drunken carpenters cutting through joists which John Naish had to rescue in a hurry. More aggrieved carpenters deliberately nailing through water pipes which Philip Selwyn-Smith had to rescue in a hurry. The costs were escalating. We threw out expensive plans to replace the disgusting carpets and Lily, Jan's mum, and Togs, our daily, spent hours on their knees scrubbing them up. We mended furniture we thought was useless. We fought the fire officer and found hidden escape routes which gave us a last minute reprieve. Neither Jan nor I had our overalls off for six months other than to rush round the rest of the branches or the occasional motoring weekend. Once more I was going too fast and wearing myself out; drinking whisky at midnight in the hope of falling into a deep sleep and forgetting the rising bank overdraft; throwing best glasses into the fireplace in sheer depressed temper; trying desperately to keep all of the balls in the air. I had been 40 years old, running a good business and with a once more happy family. Why in heaven's name had I taken on this nonsense?

The George was a great hit from the start – even though we lost our management team a couple of days before we opened in March. We had recruited a husband and wife to take over the running of the hotel. The day they were due to move in Jan and I were on our way to London and called in at the café in Melksham around lunchtime. It was a good job we did, because while we were grabbing a sandwich there a `phone call came in from Philip.
"Freddie?"
"Yes."
"You'd better get yourself back to Frome."
"Why, what's up?"
"Your managers have arrived."
"And?"
"Well, to put it bluntly mate, they're both pissed."

That didn't stop us opening on time and we quickly found a new team from the shortlist, husband and wife, who were keen as mustard and worked well together. It was a huge success and we were crowded out. With the hotel and Riot Bar in full swing, we quickly realised that we needed more bar space. Also if we could split the older customers and the hotel guests from the younger element then it would be the best of both worlds. The young were particularly attracted because virtually every pub in Frome belonged to Courage and I was able to buy beer from any brewery. McEwans. Scottish and Newcastle. Wadworths. They were all brilliant beers.

Outside, where the horse-drawn coaches used to arrive, were the old, brick-built stables, a coach house and the staff quarters all unused for the last 80 years. The entrance was from a side road just wide enough for a stage coach – and all our beer deliveries. Perfect, another bar! I could see it and found a local architect who produced some quick drawings and I set to work with my own staff. We ripped out walls – in fact too many and we only just

managed to save it from collapsing one stormy night. Before we started we needed a date to aim for and also a theme for the décor. The Queens 25th Jubilee was coming up in June – that would be perfect. Now we did have to get a move on. The magistrates had no problems extending our licence, the hotel was an asset to the town and we ran a tight ship. Although we were working flat out once more we realised we weren't going to be ready by June 3rd. Most of the building work was complete but the bar wasn't in – nor the furniture and carpets. The electricians had nearly finished and we decided we would open for the day, sweep the place out and put up a temporary bar. Trestle tables and a street party. It worked brilliantly! We had fancy dress and a raft race which started from the front door of the hotel. Run to the river, paddle up and back down the river for 100yds and run back to the bar with the raft. Of course this meant stopping the traffic, the main A361 through the town, which didn't please everyone. We had a Frazer Nash man staying with us for a few days and roped him in to help: Richard was an American, a prison officer, about forty years old, and with a pronounced southern drawl. We wanted to give him an official arm band to wear to help him control the traffic but all we could find were some used by the VSCC in their competitions. A flimsy card, tied with string and printed on it in large letters 'MARSHAL'. He did a great job. When cars thought they had been held up for too long and started hooting Richard would lean in to the open window, point to his armband, and tell the driver "Hey buddy! Can't ya' see Ar'm a Marshal!" Whatever their reply he proceeded to ignore them. As a prison officer he held a prisoner's complaints session every week. The prisoner would be brought and sat down opposite him; Richard would be playing with a 'dime' coin and if he deemed the complaint trivial he would toss the coin across the desk to the prisoner and tell him "Here. Call somebody who gives a f***" Deflated prisoner, end of complaint!
We also had jousting on bikes, a greasy pole, pillow fights and arm wrestling and generally we had a wonderful party and drank well to our Queen.

Three weeks later we were almost complete. One big room was tall and open and we needed to bring it down with a false ceiling. We stitched together a huge collection of flags; flags I had collected over the years; I just like flags and here was the perfect place for them; a kaleidoscope of colour for a ceiling.

Celebrating VE Day on the terrace at home

Naturally our bar was going to be different – and better – than the others in Frome. We had a pool table, pin ball machines, a juke box, fruit machines and the crowning glory was Tony making a wooden box about 18" x 10" x 4" which he fitted with electronic parts. In the front he drilled dozens of 1" holes with a small union flag over them and a Perspex sheet as the final cover. It hung at the back of the bar connected to a button next to the beer pumps, small bulbs inside constantly flashing through the holes. Each time the bar staff served a whole pint, the button on the bar was pressed and every 25th pint the bells would ring and the lights which formed the number '25' stopped on . The lucky customer got a free pint. You couldn't work out when it was going to stop but it was a big attraction and sold a lot of beer.

The Jubilee Bar was an instant success – our town Mayor Sidney Underwood came and officially opened it and on Friday and Saturday nights Jan and I would supervise both doors to it, not for trouble, but to allow people in when people left; we couldn't get any more in and serve them. It was built especially for young people and they loved it; The sad part was they left us at 10:30 to go on to the town's night club. They were having a good time and we were taking good money so how could we change it? We couldn't get an extension to stay open later unless it was a special occasion – New Year's Eve for example. So let's have some special occasions. It started off innocently enough with live music nights but soon these weekly parties ceased to be 'special' in the eyes of the magistrates and we had to find something else. We found an almanac which listed important events, historical or commemorative, for every day of the year and applied for a party for Thanksgiving Day to start with. We had late night licences for all sorts from Anzac Day, when we served free pints to WWI veterans, to Uri Gagarin's flight into space on April 12th. There was, as in my early coffee bar days, a great deal of media interest and we had both radio and coverage in the national press. The police didn't know how to combat the applications to the magistrates. We definitely were having celebratory parties with live music, we weren't causing them any trouble but, with sometimes two extensions in a week, they just felt that it was getting out of hand and that we were cocking a snook at the establishment. They decided to take a stand and object to our next application. The trouble was the application was for the Queen's Birthday and the magistrate shot them down in flames. If Her Majesty's birthday wasn't a special occasion then what was! At the next motoring event I met a good friend, Marjorie Tarring, a magistrate. "And you, Freddie Giles" she said "have been responsible for a major change in this country's laws." According to Marjorie magistrates across the country had received instructions from the Lord Chancellor urging them to regard late night licence applications in a more lenient light.

As well as all the special evenings for which we sought extended licences, we had competitions like arm-wrestling or bottle walking; we had live music most weeks with local bands; we helped make Frome a bit of a hot spot for the local youngsters. Our special nights were so popular we were able to charge for entry.

If all this sounds as though we were busy, it tells half the tale. We were worked almost off our feet. I only knew one way to work in those days and that was flat out. With my quick temper it made me a difficult person to be around when things weren't going well. The most shocking example of this came at New Year's Eve in 1977. I'd just spent an enormous amount of money turning the empty premises next door to the hotel into a second restaurant, putting in a dance floor for cabarets, and employing some expensive staff. It was a big operation, and was something of a risk. That New Year's Eve we had a great band, complete with singer and cabaret and we'd sold out. Then came the snow. Not just a few flurries, but a full-blown storm that blocked off roads and cut off the villages. Early in the evening the cancellations started coming in – and never stopped. By nine o'clock we were trudging home through a thick carpet of snow in total and miserable silence. I slumped in my chair in the living room and got out the whisky bottle. I wasn't going to celebrate New Year, I was going to drown my sorrows before I crashed out. The next thing I remember was the 'phone ringing at about three in the morning. Who the hell could it be? I staggered down to the hall in the noddy and picked up the receiver. I was cold and I was not in the mood for games.

"Are you the owner of the George Hotel?"
""Well, what if I am, what the hell do you want at this time of night?" I replied.
"I'm calling about tonight's event."
Oh, that. And that's when I lost my rag.

"Listen," I said, "if you're calling about the f***g dinner I don't want to f***g hear about it. And if you don't like it, you can f*** off!"

There was brief silence, then whoever it was at the other end said, rather meekly, "I just called to congratulate you. I thought in the circumstances you put on a wonderful spread and some great entertainment. My wife and I have had the time of our lives."

I thought at the time that was a low point. There was worse to come. A year later and Christmas Day 1978 found me on all fours, surrounded by a pool of foul water, with little bits of unmentionable debris floating around my knees. I'd had the call at about nine in the morning, telling me the men's toilets were blocked. Oh, and we can't find a plumber. I tried to think who else I could call on to rod the drains at this time on Christmas morning, and then I gave it up. Years before I'd said I'd never buy another business on my doorstep - you're too damned handy when things go wrong.

Still, life at the George was still giving us enough fun to make all these hassles worthwhile. And today I have enough happy memories of the place to have no regrets. I had some wonderful staff, some great customers, and I know we gave a lot of people in Frome a great deal of pleasure. One person who comes into that category was my friend Richard, the American. He got to know us well enough to confide one night, over a glass of Scotch, that he had had little experience of women. He was, he told us, a virgin. A virgin, in this day and age? How had he managed that? He wasn't sure. He guessed he was a little short of confidence, which was odd, because he was a decent looking guy. Richard, I told him, we're going to have to get you sorted out, old man.

I knew just where to go: over to the George, and one of my barmaids. She was rather gorgeous and wearing a close-fitting T-shirt with a picture of Concorde on it, and underneath that the inscription: "I'm a Supersonic Bang". I had a quiet word with her.

Could she help my friend out of a dreadful fix? She laughed. Why of course I could, Freddie. I went back to where Richard was sitting, hiding behind a pint of bitter.

"There's your girl," I told him. "She'll make a man of you."
"Jeez," he said, eyeing her up and down. "I figured I'd be starting out with a paper kite, not a frigging F-111."

I think I was a natural pub landlord. Although I was growing older I wasn't growing up and I still enjoyed the daft things that people did when they'd had a drink or two. If my customers were up for a laugh I'd generally be there with them. Take the time our lovely receptionist was getting married. She was a farmer's daughter, her husband-to-be a farmer's son. The groom and his mates met up, a few days before the big event, for a quiet sort of stag night. They weren't hell-raisers, but they liked a bit of fun. They ended up drinking at the George, and I ended up drinking with them. As we closed up and left we saw that, across the road, Lloyds Bank was undergoing repairs and was clad from top to bottom with scaffolding. Perhaps remembering my exploits up the church steeple all those years ago, I pointed to the roof and said, "Last one up's a sissy."

We all got to the top, and we all got down again in one piece. I then went home with Jan, who'd just finished the tills and was waiting for me in the car. Next morning I was awoken by a 'phone call from an irate farmer. "I've got a shed full of cows here, bawling the roof down for the want of being milked."
"Well what am I supposed to do?"
"Send my bloody son back home."
"Why, where is he?"
"That's what I'm asking you."

A few enquiries revealed that the lads, after I'd left, had decided to lift a keep left bollard and took it up the hill. Someone had seen us at Lloyds bank and called the law, and the lads had spent a night in the care of the Somerset Constabulary. Not only was this particular farmer's son AWOL when he should have been milking, but he also had a wedding rehearsal to attend that afternoon. In the end, both he and the best man arrived, not in handcuffs exactly, but escorted by a policeman.

The George was by now a family affair. Jan and I were heavily involved, Rob and Jon worked there on Saturday and Sunday mornings, re-stocking the fridges, stacking empty bottles, bringing up stock from the cellars. Our daughter Jill worked as a part-time chambermaid. Jan's mum, Lily was a godsend from the beginning. She and Sid had moved to Frome in '76 and Lily had begun by scrubbing out the place with the rest of the team. Then she ran the lunch time kitchen in the bar, stayed up late to serve the residents until they wanted to go to bed and was back early the next morning to help with breakfasts. Even our friends were roped in. One Easter we had a visiting rugby team for the weekend. They had finished their match and were in the hotel dining room having lunch when trouble broke out. They started a food fight, which not being whiter than white is the sort of escapade I may have got up to from time to time, but sadly the room was also being used by non participants; ordinary guests who didn't appreciate cream pies in their face. By the time we arrived there was considerable damage and I called the law. "Please don't ask us to come out Mr Giles: there's only two of us on duty for the whole town!" So that wasn't going to work, we'd have to turf them out ourselves and yet again a woman proved more useful than a male bouncer. Jan and Velma, our manageress, waded in knowing it unlikely, in those days, that a man would hit them, and got them as far as the front hall with their luggage. My good friend Ron Footitt sat on the wooden settle, his drill in his hand ready to change locks if they didn't want to leave. "You'd better hurry up. I'm on f**** triple time for Easter Sunday and your bill's going up all the f***** time" They got the message.

Our time at the George had started out with a management crisis and was to end in one. In February 1979 Jan and I had just returned from a skiing trip. We arrived home, sat down for a meal with the family, and were immediately aware that Rob had something to tell us. What was it? Oh, you're too tired to deal with anything now; let's have tea first. But no, we needed to know right there and then. All right, Rob told us, your manager has cleared off - with all his furniture. Where to? Well, that's the whole point. Nobody knows. We were on duty by six o'clock without our tea.

Geoff Holes, who had replaced Velma Scott and her husband, lived in the second-floor flat, above the hotel bedrooms. He had re-married shortly before he came to us. Now we discovered that wife number one had paid him a visit, persuaded him that he would be better off going back to her, and had left town with him in hot pursuit. Holes had been just about to be made a partner in the business. We had set up a separate limited company with all of the legal and accountancy work involved and now he'd upped and disappeared. It was this event – perhaps allied with the Christmas morning plumbing fiasco that tilted the scales as far as I was concerned. I was getting out of the hotel business before I lost my sanity.

 Geoff Holes had buggered off and left us with no paperwork. We had no idea of staff rotas, the orders he'd made with suppliers, the advanced bookings he'd made for various parties. Jan and I were running twelve branches between us, including the hotel and we were stretched to the limit. Holes telephoned eventually –he wanted to come and pick up a few things he'd left at the farm when he first moved into the flat – and to collect his salary and holiday pay!!

Before he arrived Tony and I agreed on our plan of action. I was livid at Holes' nonchalant approach and quite prepared for the row to come. As he walked in the office door I fired him. But I still needed a full account of where everything stood at the George and we also needed to dismantle the new company structure which had been set up but not yet initiated.

"Okay, Geoff, are you going to co-operate?"

"No I'm bloody not."

"Well I think I would if I were in your position?"

"You can't just fire me and expect me to waste my time digging you out of a hole. I've only come here to collect my gear."

"Oh, we've got that ready for you. Just turn around and look out the window, will you."

He swung his seat around. Outside Tony had brought the tractor right up to where Holes had parked. The bucket was poised right over his shiny BMW, and in the bucket, teetering on the edge, was our ex-manager's heavy wooden work-bench.

He laughed "You can't do that, you wouldn't dare"

I think he saw in my face as I got up and called across the yard to Tony that I could and I certainly would!

"Looks like I've got no choice, doesn't it?"

By April the George was sold. Trevor Jones and his wife Pat took over and became good friends. We could have waited longer for a better price but the arrangement suited both of us. We kept the fruit machines, the juke box and the pool tables going for them and took a percentage of the takings. For little effort on their part they had the income without having to buy their own machines or rent from a supplier. They sat tight, altered nothing and put it straight back on the market. In five years it was sold again for a much better price but we were all happy. We'd left something in and they did well out of it too. After that it didn't do so well – the wheel had gone full circle and it became a tied house to Wadworths Brewery.

Sailing close to the wind

We hadn't realised how much the George had taken us out of our social circle until our friends welcomed us back with open arms. Before we met, Jan had been almost as wild as I was and we both loved to party. We had missed it. I was barely 43 and Jan was still in her late thirties. Without an evening business to worry about we were free to get back to fun. And fun often seemed to involve water.

I think Princess Ann had already left before I plunged semi-naked into the fountains in front of Longleat House. I hope so! We had taken much drink in the course of dinner and I needed to cool down. "That's a good idea! Why don't we all go over to D's house in Warminster – he's got an indoor swimming pool". I was plastered and certainly couldn't drive; nor could Jan. I put back on my dinner suit and climbed into the boot of some-one's car.

Some had swimming costumes. We didn't of course but I'd gone off the idea by now, I didn't really want to swim and I didn't really want to strip off again. So I was slightly sobering up and slightly aggravated to be called chicken by the fully dressed blonde in front of me. She was loaded and I mean loaded with jewellery: covered with gold and diamonds. I could do no more than pick her up and step over the side into the deep end. Did she lose her cool! Did her husband! Half of the jewellery had fallen off into the pool and he had only borrowed it from the shop in Bath where he worked. There were a few strong words said: my suit was now rather wet and that had to come off: time to leave. Of course we had no transport and it was becoming very late. The one taxi we could muster already had another call but could take us if we would share. Lord Bath's sister-in-law who had been at the same party had been picked up for drinking and driving and we now had to collect her from Warminster Nick. God, did she vociferously object to sharing the back seat with a naked man in a borrowed towel. She was still muttering about it next morning when we went to collect the car – she had to let us in to the Orangery to find our keys hidden behind the ormolu clock! That'll teach us to hob-knob with pseudo-royalty! Marginally better than our brush with politicians at least.

We were friendly with a flamboyant "gentleman" who became a VSCC president and lived in some style on the outskirts of Bath – his estate even featured, should the evil day arrive, a large nuclear shelter for his complete family. Jan and I were invited to a dinner party of some stature with the MP for Bath in attendance – overalls and medals were to be worn! It was a beautiful summer evening. We enjoyed a superb dinner after which the ladies withdrew, presumably to the room of that name, and presumably to gossip, and the men retired to Roger's study to tell dirty stories. This was a first for me. More drink was taken in the study and naturally enough Mother Nature finally caught up with me. I needed to relieve myself. I was told, in no uncertain manner, that I couldn't leave the room until everyone left together. How stupid. But I had to do something; the situation was becoming serious. I reached for one of Roger's many motoring trophies; pint pewter tankards hung around the room and lined along the chimney-piece. Still I was not allowed to leave and so the ultimate action just had to be taken. I can't remember if I apologised; probably not but no-one seemed the least perturbed anyway.

The party continued through the night and as the dawn was breaking a few of us were in the garden admiring our host's fish pond and the beauty of an English morning. Wouldn't this be a great time for a swim? Well Roger didn't have a pool and so the next best thing would be a paddle in the pond. Why not? I suggested to the girl I was chatting up that she should join me but she wasn't at all keen so I picked her up in my arms and carried her down the lawn.

"You wouldn't dare!!" is always the end of a conversation. For goodness sake it's only a fish pond after all. Over the edge we go and whoops. Its five feet deep and I had really made a boo boo.

She was livid and so was her husband. Time to apologise profusely and retreat. Oh dear, I really had blown it this time. Thank you and goodbye is about all you can say on these occasions.

"You wouldn't dare!!" is always the rumbustious end of a conversation motoring – skiing- or sailing

The Bentley made it to the bottom of Bradford on Avon centre before the old girl coughed and spluttered and told me she had no fuel. Hell. It's 5am, I've been drinking and I'm wet through. There is a two gallon can on the side but it isn't as easy as that. There is no electric pump on early Bentleys, only an Autovac, which is a very simple system to deliver petrol to the engine without electrics but a bit of a sod to prime without a funnel, which I didn't have, and while you're worrying about police patrols; it's a good time for them to prowl about just before they go off at six. Roger and Judy still remain very good friends even if they don't invite me to posh parties any more!

But if I'm not getting into trouble in water then it must be snow. Snow is such a natural playground and Jan and I started skiing in the early '70s. Why we went again after our first holiday in Austria I don't know. We went with John and Ann Naish and found very little snow in Serfaus; we had to walk everywhere in terrible lace up boots. There were no drag lifts and no chairs. Poor Ann's ankles swelled dreadfully but John was a natural and promoted to class 2 on the third day. We were stuck with Joseph, he with little English,

236

who exhorted us to turn in our 'hedges' and rub neat whiskey into our aching limbs. The skiing was not good but the holiday was and we thought we ought to try again. We did and by the mid 70's took all four children to Cervinia in Italy which at 11,000ft is quite high. Rachel could faint as the lift in the hotel took off swiftly from ground level to the 10th floor. Oh dear, the girls were not doing so well. I didn't do so well myself when I chatted up the ski rep. She had given me – I thought – a few encouragements including her room number and so I was somewhat abashed one evening when I knocked on her door to find myself face to face, as it were, with a very large very naked young man who wanted to know what the hell I wanted. I think she may have been winding me up!

Skiing in my 65 year old birthday suit. Courchevel. 20th March 2001 The day I collect my old age pension

It was January and bitterly cold but the boys loved it and persuaded me to ski them over to Zermatt in Switzerland, skiing right under the Matterhorn and down to the very old village from which Brits first climbed the un-climbable mountain; four of them died getting down. But the boys thought it all very James Bond and they were hooked. We took them again the following year but this time with a couple who had no children. The girl was a bit keen on me and trying hard to lead me astray. Jan had already 'discovered' us in the drying room of the Scale Hill Hotel in Loweswater after a very wet Lakeland Trial so she wasn't too surprised when they proposed a joint ski trip. The trouble was, Robert broke his ankle and it was my fault. His boots didn't fit properly and so he undid the fasteners to make them more comfortable and I just didn't notice. As he turned on his skis his ankle was able to go over and snap.... I was so angry with myself and so sorry for poor Rob who was stoic in the extreme and my quick temper boiled over and I was taking no prisoners. She came to Jan and asked "My God, is he always like this?" "Most of the time", Jan replied, "but you'll get used to it." "I don't think I'll bother to try!" was the reply and she never did.

Whenever we had snow at home, games had to be played. In 1980 we had a very heavy snowfall. Frome virtually came to a standstill but we could still get around by tractor and so we went to the pub about 2 miles away with 10 to 12 toboggans tied to the back caterpillar style. Great jollity then one of the youngsters suggested we should go to Frome Show Field only ¼ mile from home. In the dark with all our toboggans on the back we set out. Part of the field has quite a slope and taking the tractor down that was fun until I realised from water skiing that the more you swerved about the faster the tail enders had to go; to be the last three or four was hilarious, sledges turning over, losing a body here and there; shouting, laughter, exuberance; at the bottom collect everyone up, swap around and do it again. We all loved it, a few nasty bruises and scrapes but voted a huge success. The snow soon melted and we had to wait another six years before we had enough for another adventure, again in the dark.

The same group would assault Cley Hill just outside Warminster. Very steep and high – in fact the hill renowned for its UFOs. A goodly crowd gathered, the bush telegraph had been working and we duly arrived each with toboggans. There were many strange and assorted crafts. Some were 40 gallon plastic drums sawn lengthways and joined together in which four people might sit. We gathered at the top and after sharing a few drinks from our flasks we decided to send two off to test the water – or in this case the snow. At the bottom they were to shout back to tell us yes or no. Well we waited for some time and we didn't hear anything so decided it must be OK and off we all went. Now this was silly; we had forgotten the huge anthills that grow and stay covered in grass. No-one made it to the bottom without a crash of some sort. Two were hospital cases with broken bits – blood and cuts we could deal with. We went, tails between legs after such a miserable failure, to the Royal Oak at Corsley. In front of a roaring fire and with the benefit of electric light we discovered the hurts that we hadn't noticed until then. Silly buggers and they were all over 18 and I was just on 50. I hope they never grow up.

Two or three years after this these same young people organised a ski trip to Obertauern in Austria. Twelve 'twenty somethings' and two golden oldies. One of the lads, big Steve, had a love for potatoes in large quantities so we each took 7lbs in our hand luggage. A few minutes before landing they were all collected and given to Steve in two ½ cwt sacks – 50kgs. He was left to carry off his trophy but we all had extra spuds for the week. And what a week. Good skiing but most of all the company. A skiing chalet pub about a kilometre up the mountain became our rendezvous for the après ski drinks before skiing home for supper. The CD music collection was terrific – a few bars and you had to dance. I'm not sure what induced our girls, my lovely wife included, to dance in ski boots, each weighing about a kilo, on the tables but the next thing they were stripping off their tops and giving a wonderful display of bare breasts to heavy metal rock. Fantastic. The pub loved it and we left covered in glory, a lovely moon, the snow not quite covering the bare patches on the lower slopes, sparks flying from the skis as they hit a stone. We were so lucky to be included in this swinging crowd and that two of the girls became our daughters-in-law.

The following night we decided on the same pub for our après ski but we couldn't stay. Word had gone round and a large crowd of Germans (yes those Germans keep cropping up everywhere) were waiting in the bar for our girls to 'perform'. No way were we putting up with their arrogant nonsense and this caused enough friction for us to storm out and barricade them in with beer barrels and crates as we went on our way.

In '93 when Jan wasn't able to come because her mum was ill, I went with them again. The snow was not so good and so we decided to swim instead. The afternoon of the first day saw us all in the swimming pool. We paid, changed and jumped in. Suddenly there was a whistle and cries of "Out. Out". Why? "Ver are your 'ats?". What? "Ver are your 'ats?" only louder this time from a stocky irate deutsche frau who had produced swimming caps. Ah so that's the problem. We all hired a cap – fine. Good swim. The next day followed the same pattern with a swim in the afternoon but one of our party, lovely Dorinda, who was then a high powered sexual diseases nurse said we wouldn't need to hire caps. She always carried a large supply of condoms in her luggage and we could all wear one on our heads instead. OK Great idea. We assembled before going in the pool and found it amazing that a condom will stretch to fit over your head fairly easily. With all our 'ats on we jumped in the pool together. The attendants were flummoxed, what could they do? All our hair was protected. Other swimmers and loungers started to notice what was going on when at a signal from Dorinda we all stood up in the water and stretched them over our faces as far as our upper lip. We took a simultaneous deep breath and breathed out through our nose and voila – a space helmet. Much merriment and then after another couple of breaths and blows – bang and they burst, looking decidedly disgusting. We were allowed to change, luckily, but not to swim again. Funny – gross – childish or what!

I was in London for some business which finished by lunch time so as the Boat Show was on I decided to kill time until my train. I'd only ever had a passing interest in small boats and was always getting into trouble with Mirror Class dinghies- turning it over, getting shipwrecked with Brother Frank's children on board and when I swamped it with Jan and the kids crossing the mouth of the Avon and Stour at Mudeford it was the last straw. Then I saw this little stall advertising sailing in tall ships and I was immediately interested. My father had told tales of training in sailing ships in his time in the Navy and I loved heights. When the STS Winston Churchill was launched in the '50s it could only be a dream to sail in such a ship and yet here was a chance to sail in the Lord Nelson – 300 tons and 43 crew, 4 of whom were full timers. It had three masts and was square rigged and the thought of helping to sail her, to climb up the ratlines, out onto the cross trees and up again and then to get out onto the yard arms 100 ft up was another adventure I had to do. I picked up some leaflets and left my name as 'very

Out on the yard arm 100ft above deck

interested'. She had been built especially to take handicapped young people on each voyage – usually six in wheel chairs and six with other disabilities – operating all around our coasts and in the winter in the Canaries. Jan agreed it was a great thing to do as long as she didn't have to.

The first voyage I chose was out of Weymouth, across to the Channel Islands, up to Fleetwood and then to the Isle of Man, 10 days. The ship worked around the clock in three watches each made up of 11 ordinary seamen, a watch leader and a watch officer working in four hour shifts through the night. During the day everyone worked and I mean worked. She was designed with no electric winches except for the anchor. All sails were set and re-set by hand with gangways wide enough for wheelchairs which had the ability to attach to rings in the bulwarks to hold them fast. There was a lift to bring them from the mess deck to the working deck. The mess deck was where we all lived in one big room with two-tier bunks around the walls, male and female together. There were six very small 'rooms' with two bunks and a curtain across for the wheelchair bound and a buddy to help them and in the middle two big tables where a watch could sit to eat with lockers stuffed with oil skins as seats. It was cramped!

Having reported to Weymouth and signed on as a merchant seaman (as per regulations for such a voyage) I was asked if I had ever buddied before. "No? Well with your experience from scouting and the army and your family, you are now!". Only two things to remember. Be on time for watch keeping and DO NOT volunteer to help your buddy unless asked. OK I could cope with that. The lad I was assigned to was great although his limbs were useless. He had motor neurone disease so physically he had no strength but in his mind he was brilliant and as the ship's wheel was powered he loved it and was extremely confident with keeping course, navigating etc. The ship did have auxiliary power if the wind and weather were completely against us. Almost all of us on board were novices as we set out in the Channel, the wind set from the West and we made little progress. The sea got very lumpy and we had to run for Falmouth and shelter. It was all very strange to us; weather dreadful; people sea sick. One girl jacked it in and signed off. I rang home and said I wasn't sure what I had let myself in for, but it all improved and although we couldn't make the Channel Islands we had rounded Lands End when the ship came alive and happy, the wind on our beam, sails set, no engine and we were in business but running late for the huge reception Fleetwood had laid on. The able-bodied had to pay a reasonable sum to work on the ship. 'Work' – how can you describe such voyages as work; even with watches starting at midnight or 4am; cleaning everything including the heads (loos); no privacy; very cramped conditions below and working aloft in every weather. It was worth a fortune and I loved it. I loved being ordered, in the nicest possible way, for certain duties. I had spent my working life asking/ordering staff to do this or that and now the boot was on the other foot and I did every job I was given to the best of my ability but without any responsibility. Would I like to work and study to become a watch leader and then a watch officer? No thank you, this way I had no responsibilities or orders to shoulder.

I made three voyages in the Lord Nelson, the last one in the Canaries, and each time I buddied, the last time with an Italian lad called Andreas. He was very wheel chair bound and for a 4am watch I had to be called at 3:30 to dress him and get him on deck. On a day off in Gran Canaria a crowd of us went to a beautiful sandy beach. It was a hell of a job to get my mate and his chair through the sand to the water but once afloat he could swim like a fish. When he came out I asked him if he knew the name of the man who swam the English Channel with no arms or legs; he understood well enough and when I told him 'Clever Dick' he roared with laughter. "I know what Dick is in English, Freddie!"

Besides sailing on the Lord Nelson I met through the VSCC David Barker who was a qualified watch leader and was organising a watch to sail with the 'STS Malcolm Miller', the sister ship to the 'Winston Churchill'.

Up in the crow's nest on the STS Malcolm Miller

Both of these ships were of a similar size to the Nelson and had been built specifically for young people. Sadly over the years they were failing to attract enough youth even though their passage was paid for by various charities and so they started to take mixed adult crews and I was up for it. Thirteen of us, a complete watch of VSCC members, set sail for the Western Isles off Scotland for a 7 day trip in what was to be perfect weather. We were virtually becalmed for a day off Arran which allowed us to put on all the sails she could carry, 27 different sails, and then we went out in the ship's boat to photograph this wonderful sight of our day's work. Visits to distilleries: tying up with a pub 50yds away and which never seemed to close allowing our watch to come off at midnight and still go for a couple of hours drinking: wonderful comradeship, similar to the Nelson: harder discipline: sailing in harder blows with no motors: peeling spuds: washing up in the galley: sing songs between times: the only booze on board was tins of beer you could buy from the purser during happy hour in the morning and the odd bottle of spirit some-one might have.

I did several of these voyages. One out of Cardiff to Southern Ireland, a three day voyage in such storms that over half our watch was so sea sick or injured that we were very pleased to be back. My final trip, before both ships were sold as being too costly to run, was to the Azores in the Atlantic. Our usual group of VSCC chaps and wonderful sailing among these little known islands, so many of them with steam hissing from the ground. One of our shore trips took us to a virtually extinct volcano. A tunnel gave access to within ¼ mile of the centre and then steps led down the final 200' to a great cavern with boiling mud leaping and bubbling in a pool. Soon the singers amongst us noticed the great acoustics, first came the scales and next the singing - out of this world. Our final sail from a little port back to the capital was to be epic. We were ordered to be back after lunch for a three o'clock sailing time when we were all given yellow tee shirts to wear. Almost all of us were sent aloft and told that at the sound of the miniature canon we were to loose the sails in unison. We stood on the foot ropes beneath the yard arms ready to release the ties; the wind was just picking up; the canon spoke and the sails dropped and filled out with the wind. The Captain was playing 'Rule Britannia' on the record player as she pulled away from the harbour-side completely under sail power. We stood at our positions mesmerised; it was so romantic and so utterly beautiful my eyes now water at the thought and memory of it. That night we set a course that never wavered for 24 hours; my watch was 12 to 4 and it was cold but incredibly beautiful; the moon was full and we had a good wind making 12 to 13 knots and heeled over perfectly; the wind gave a lovely swell to the sea; the stars and the moon reflected in the waves and gave off flashing, twinkling lights like a city. What bliss. As we finished our watch at 4am some of us stayed to watch a sunrise made in heaven. I shan't go sailing like this again. I no longer have the strength in my arms anymore but to finish on such a high could not possibly be repeated.

The only contact since was from the Nelson who wanted to raise funds for an additional boat by instigating challenges involving water. As we live next to the Kennet and Avon Canal it seemed a good idea to ride my 1880 Penny Farthing the 25 miles from Devizes to Bath along the tow path and without dismounting. My good friends Peter and Fran Still cycled ahead of me with a measuring stick warning me when I needed to duck down low to make it under the bridges. By the time I reached the canal side pub at Bath I was so tired I couldn't dismount and had to be practically lifted off but between them my friends had raised almost £5,000 and another sailing friend offered me an extra £100 if I would prove I'd been in the canal on my Ordinary. I was prevented from doing this at the pub by the shallow water and the amount of glass and debris accumulated over the years but the next day the cameras were set up to see me go over the handlebars headfirst into the dirty muddy water. A strange sensation to deliberately have an accident but true to his word Bernard Kain came up with the extra £100 and we were able to send off £5,000 plus towards the new ship.

But despite being hooked on sailing, motor racing remained my true passion.

The 'COGNAC' was Ron's car. The name came from the combination of

'CO'hen – who built it: GN – the early chain drive car, precursor to the Frazer Nash, on which it was based and: AC – the engine used in the car

It was extremely successful in Ron's hands and I was regularly allowed to drive it – in retrospect that was a very generous gesture. The most exciting times were at Oulton Park, taking part in the Vintage Seaman Trophy – a 12 lap scratch race over 20/25 miles.

The big race of the day and we are rolling round the circuit on the warming up lap, ready to take up the grid position we have earned with our practice lap times. The Cognac is a small, nimble car and big, heavy, very powerful cars surround me – apart from the inevitable Morgan 3-wheeler. I am in pole position, with Harvey Hine alongside me in his immense Bentley; Harvey is a brilliant driver in a very fast car and we reach our grid positions together and wait. Two long blasts on the klaxons warn us and a marshal appears at the front of the grid holding aloft his huge yellow signal board "2 MINUTES". Engines are re-started; visors on helmets are pulled into position; marshals race along the grid clearing would-be helpers who have been push starting cars; cars with no starter motors; cars which have stalled, frantic for one more go. The klaxons again and now the "1 MINUTE" board. Heart pumping harder now. The starter is climbing onto his rostrum. Into gear. Build up the revs. Everyone doing the same. Can't hear myself think. Eyes on the starter standing above us. He raises the union flag – pauses for a second – and drops it swiftly.

Thunder: smoke: oil and rubber burning: wheels spinning: Christ this is crazy! 1st right-hander 150 yards and I'm first in – got the line. Harvey very close in mirror but on outside line. Hold line for next corner: down the hill: left – this car is wonderful on corners: ¼ straight to next 180° : steep banking: Harvey up beside me:

straight: hold him off on the bank: down hill, up hill over brow and down again: flat out 6000 revs, 125/130 mph: slow for right hander; up and under motor bridge; slow for the esses through the woods; down the straight under Paddock Bridge into Deers Leap: nasty right-hander; braking; braking; not too much: drop down 20/25 feet and up the other side in a matter of 50yds; up to Grandstand and start straight. He's on my tail never letting up. What a fight. Settle in. Concentrate. Concentrate. Don't over-rev it, could blow up over 6000 revs. How late can you leave braking? Lap after lap; neck and neck. We lap back markers; waving blue flags tell them we're there; cars lie broken around the course; no shunts this time; always a danger. With no prize money brains should rule; but we both respect each other. The pace shows no sign of slacking but on the 9th lap Harvey gets me down the long straight before Deers Leap; a bit more grunt than me but don't give up. Push him on the corners; try to get inside him; make him lose his line. He's good and I can't find the opening. Are we glued together? The crowd is on its feet! My pit signals the last lap. Does he know it? Ought to but you never know; you can't possible count yourself. The last straight; Deers Leap; leave braking very late; I'm on the inside of him. Yes. Yes. Got him. Ah no; he pulls a bit extra from somewhere and we are over the finish line a bonnet length in it! Fantastic. Completely out of breath and my mouth is so dry. We're all in one piece! We drive the slowing down lap together but with Harvey just in the lead. The crowds shout and clap us round. Cars begin to peel off into the pits except for the winner but Harvey beckons me on to join him. He is presented with the winner's garland around his neck – laurel leaved adorned with rose buds – and he picks off a rose bud and gives it to me as we shake hands and congratulate each other. Now that's an exciting game but I do need a pint!

*Winning the Seaman Trophy in the Cognac 1976
from an original water colour by Lionel Stretton*

Oulton Park has given me great joy, frustration and to a degree sadness.

The frustration was there again in the Seaman Trophy Race – named after the great English pre-war driver Richard Seaman who excelled in Sunbeams and later drove for Auto Union and Mercedes. Once more the speed and the roar; the smoke and smell of a heart thumping big race; the Cognac is doing it again and the pace is hot and holy. Cars are dropping out and I've got to the front after several battles. We're on the last lap and I've pulled out a lead of 100-150yds. The Cognac is going beautifully and then – cough – cough – splutter – bang- bang. We're slowing and slowing – it has to be sparks; it can't be fuel I checked that myself. I pull on to the grass 500yds before the finish line. Bugger. I hop out and lift the bonnet – the plug leads are in place; check carburettor floats. No fuel. No fuel not possible. Open big filler cap and look inside – shake car – nothing – nothing! No leaks – would have smelt it. Shit. You bloody idiot. Take my very expensive helmet off and throw it on the ground in temper. You f****** Pratt Giles. The tow truck takes me into the paddock where Jan and Tony are waiting but I am incandescent with rage and need a wall to bang my head against! Should have left Tony to check the car after practice. I don't know how to contain myself; I can't. "Come on Freddie, we're going for a drink" and I follow, hands in pockets, head down, kicking the ground, into the crowded bar. There's a shout from the bar. It's my very good and young friend Martin Stretton (an ace driver). "Fred! Do you want a pint?" "Yes" I snapped back. "Right mate! Beer or petrol?" You have to laugh, it was brilliant. Yes all I needed was a pint of petrol but it was too late for that. We then had several pints of beer and all was forgotten. It's only a game after all!

During my driving career I've won almost 200 trophies and I did go on to win that elusive trophy but my race with Harvey will always remain with me as one of the most exciting.

A few years before I gave up circuit racing the Cognac I had another duty to perform at Oulton. Ron Footitt had won umpteen trophies with the car and had been five times winner of the Seaman Trophy Race. He died in 1990 and wanted his ashes spread at the Cheshire circuit. Ron wanted me to own the Cognac and when I bought it from him we had quite a conversation about scattering him on the circuit from the back of his car. In 1993 the club was back at Oulton and the Cognac was going well. At what point of the weekend, and where on the circuit and how was I to release the ashes? Testing on Friday? Practice session? NO – let Ron do his last Vintage Seaman. Going by the practice times on Saturday, then it seemed quite possible that the combination of Cognac, self and Ron, in a small leather bound box, could win the race. It was not to be – young Majzub in a type 35B who didn't practice until Sunday morning, had beaten our best practice times of Saturday. Never mind – let's not give up before we start! The Sunday weather didn't start too well and soon we were into rain. The expert opinion of Martin Stretton was called for – how to drive Oulton in the wet. It was fast, it was slippery and Old Hall got more and more slippery as the race went on. Ron and I could not live with Majzub but we kept well ahead of Alex Boswell in the Becquet-Delage and then in the mirrors appeared that great giant-killer, Stu' Harper in the Morgan. At one time I'm sure we were welded together and then he made his move which I couldn't stop and he was past, only

to lose it at Old Hall! I didn't get past him and I'm sure Ron was kicking me! Anyhow we finished a creditable third and on the slowing down lap I let Ron out as we came up Deer's Leap under the Dunlop Bridge and just after Knickerbrook. Sorry Ron we weren't first home, but we all three enjoyed it nonetheless.

As I approached my 60s I began to feel that I was losing my edge and didn't relish the challenge of racing especially after a 12-lap race at Mallory Park against an eight litre Bentley. It was a wonderful scrap, lap after lap; you lose count but my pit signalled the last lap and so, staying with him right on his tail until the hairpin corner 150/200yds from the finish, as he took his line I used more revs than I should have done and darted in front of him forcing him to brake. I beat him to the chequered flag and into

Photo courtesy of Derek Hibbert

second place – the leader had left us both way behind from the start. I thought we'd had a fantastic race so as soon as I was back to my pit I took two small screw top beers from my cool box and went and found my opponent, handed him the bottle, held out my hand and said "wasn't that bloody splendid?" His reply "you f****** do that to me again and I'll have you off." Christ I thought, are men so serious to win that you can't trust your life to them anymore? He was a serious racer and was killed in a race in Australia not very long afterwards. That was it. I didn't have another race that day and decided there and then that I'd finished with it altogether.

I loaded the car on its trailer and set out for home. Fifty miles down the road over the brow of a hill and in the middle of the country a car had stopped, turning right into his drive. I stopped too but a motor bike travelling behind me drove into the corner of my trailer and spilled himself, passenger and bike all over the road. As I was jumping out a car came over the brow going like hell. I shouted to Jan to hang on to her seat as she was getting out too and then BANG. Bloody hell was it a bang. My beautiful single-seater had been ripped from its restraining straps and pushed onto the roof of my estate car; the Peugeot had left 40yds of skid, its front end was utterly devastated and the engine was hanging in the road. Jan and I were OK and rushed to open the doors of the Peugeot, which incidentally opened as though nothing had happened to them, only to find an octogenarian friend from our village, a vintage man who had been spectating at Mallory. He was fine but naturally had to lie down on the grass verge. Ambulances and police were called and I was the only one to be breathalysed! Fortunately all I've had all day is the post race 25cl beer so that wasn't a problem but Alex, my old friend, couldn't be breathalysed because he was waiting for the ambulance and claimed that his chest hurt from the steering wheel. Lucky for him!

That was the final decision taken out of my hands. I haven't circuit raced since. We had to hire a JCB to lift the Cognac off the modern car and onto the RAC rescue. Not a happy ending to my 30 years of a very exciting game, no money prizes, maybe a garland or two, but with a huge trust and enjoyment among competitors. Shame really but no matter; as the car was being rebuilt in my workshop son Jon wanted to buy it which he did and we then shared the car at various hill climb events which was fun.

Jon sold the Cognac while we were driving Round the World in 80 Days in 2000. It's much loved and driven by its present owner Trevor John although not in circuit races. I have no regrets giving up the game as it led to long distance endurance rallying with Jan.

Jon on his 40ᵗʰ birthday and we're still into motor sport but this time karting for fun

It's not a race! Is it?

But back in the early eighties having rid ourselves of the hotel business I was also getting tired of the café business. I was tired and impatient with it. I'd had over 30 years and I wanted to get into something new. Rob, our eldest son, had joined us and was working alongside Tony Coles. We had to find something that would suit all four of us.

I've never had a problem selling a business because the first people I tell are the staff. They don't find out from anyone else. I offer them a bonus if they stay until the business is handed over and do my best to get the new owner to keep them on. So putting the remaining cafes on the market didn't pose too much of a problem.

We'd carried on taking Arthur Poulsom's advice and had bought commercial property with any profits we made, taking little in the way of salary to do it. This created another source of income, and a reliable one, but it also threw up a problem. Rent on property that you didn't occupy was deemed to be unearned, and therefore attracted a punitive level of tax, 15% on top of any other income tax level. It is hard to imagine now that this could take income tax to 95%! The socialist legislation was aimed at squeezing taxes from the idle rich, people who inherited property, lived off the income and spent their time frolicking about their country estates here and abroad. But this hadn't been given to me; I'd worked hard and gone without to achieve it. It was our accountant Chris Merrifield who warned us that we shouldn't be selling all of our trading businesses. We needed to keep the unearned income below 10% of our total takings and we would escape, not just the 15%, but the rest of the penalizing charges associated with a property company. The trading income didn't have to be profitable but it had to exist. All we had to do now was find a business with a large cash-flow, one that we could manage successfully, and one that I could get enthusiastic about.

Hugh Steele-Perkins had worked for Pearsons, the estate agents in the area, for some time and had sourced me several good property deals. An old laundry, Modeluxe, which I turned into eight industrial units: a mill complex which made twenty-four starter units; I named them after my cars. My single-seater racing car supplied 'Salome Works'; the engine of my favourite Frazer Nash 'Meadows Works'; both a private pun because both at the time were 'working' well! Now Hugh came to me with another idea – he knew we were looking for turnover and he had found it. A business for sale in Boscombe, just outside Bournemouth, selling men's shoes, but selling them in a rather unusual manner.

It was quite a big shop, and it was full of rack after rack of right-hand shoes. The customer came in and browsed, tried on as many right shoes as he wanted without any interference from staff, made his mind up, and took the shoe to the counter. The chap at the counter, who was the only employee I could see on the floor, read the code number on the item, called upstairs through a hole in the ceiling. Another member of staff located a left shoe in the same size and threw it down through the hole to land in a catch net! Less than a minute. The simplicity of the scheme impressed me, along with the fact that such a large operation could effectively be run by only a couple of staff. Add to that the fact that ninety-nine customers out of every hundred, having selected the right-hand shoe that suited them, then bought the pair, and you'd saved yourself all the hassle of every conventional shoe-shop: running to and from the stock-room, scattering shoes all over the floor and having to stuff them back in boxes when the customer had made his mind up – or, as often as not, walked out without buying anything. The place at Boscombe was a bit grotty. We could do better than that!

Rob was involved in this operation from the start. He was just twenty but had already had experience as a parts manager for Mercedes Benz Motors, so he knew a lot about organising stock. He'd also worked behind the counter in an ironmonger's – in a shop which was rented from our commercial property company –

so he was well used to dealing with the public. In fact he is superb at that.

Hugh had not only come up with Boscombe, he now found us the premises we needed in Bath. The Old Red House in Walcot Street had once been a prominent bakery; producing amongst other things Alfred Taylor's Bath Oliver Biscuits. The new owner had bought it, gutted it and steam cleaned most of the grease and grime off the walls and floors. He jumped at our offer immediately and took us out to lunch on the day we signed the contract. A splendid meal in an excellent restaurant followed by the gift of a crate of Glenmorangie. At a rough calculation it had cost me the best part of £8,000 a bottle! I was to learn that this generous chap had been astute enough to buy the bakery just six months before for almost £100,000 less than I'd paid for it. All he had done was to clean it up and put it straight back on the market. And no I wasn't upset. Good for him I thought; we'd got exactly what we wanted at what we felt was a fair price, and he'd got what he wanted so we were all happy.

Instead of a hole in the ceiling we designed a chute, which dropped the left shoe down into an enclosed area: the customers couldn't get back in the shop or out of the door with a pair of shoes in their hands – unless they went through the till area. That didn't stop more than a few brazen souls 'doing a runner' out of the shop with a desirable pair of trainers; leaping over the barrier and hot footing it down the road, usually pursued by Rob who was by then in charge. We used a more sophisticated coding system to locate the exact partner to the pair rather than a 'similar' pair and a telephone system to connect the stores. Jan designed a computerised stock control system and we set about buying stock.

We knew nothing about shoes and this became obvious quite quickly to the suppliers, some of whom took us for an enormous ride. We had decided we would sell at a discount but we certainly wouldn't use 'seconds' as they did in Street and other factory outlets. These would be good quality men's shoes, Trickers,

Loakes, with a better selection than usual shoe shops. We were the equivalent of a Free House in the shoe world. Or so we thought until we came up against the restrictive practices in the industry. No we couldn't have Dr. Martens – they were already being sold in Bath. No we couldn't have Nike ...... The other imponderable was that most shoes were Made to Order except that you had to order them a season in advance. We didn't have a season. We bought the premises in May and we wanted to open at the end of June. The shop-fitting team: Tony, Rob, John Ford and I could do it but could we get the stock? We compromised that first year and bought from warehouses; taking 'offers' whenever we could, occasionally over-buying and ending up with 100s of pairs in the same style! It was a huge learning curve.

Against our better judgement we were persuaded to stock ladies' and children's shoes; a wider even bigger curve with many more mistakes. We quickly discovered that men actually like the hassle-free shopping experience; they don't need assistants telling them what looks nice! Women's fashions were much trickier. If it wasn't the exact shade of white they wanted there was no compromise – and no sale. The day we opened I was as nervous as I had been twenty six years earlier in Devizes. Although I now knew coffee-bars, cafes, restaurants and hotels inside out this was a whole new environment. Had we got it right? The first person to walk through the door and buy the very first pair of shoes we sold was a friend, Roger Collings, the larger than life VSCC chap whose pot I had peed in after dinner. He knew how I felt and it was a thoughtful gesture.

The Red House was spacious. We had only bought it to achieve a turnover – not even a profitable one. As long as it didn't make a loss was the theory but that's never been my style. Mastershoe had only taken up a third of the property, the shop on the ground floor and the coded stores on the first floor. We still had half of the ground floor and an enormous basement cum lower ground floor which came out at street level at the bottom of a hill. There was also a complete and separate Georgian wing tagged on to this listed

Edwardian building but I hadn't even begun to contemplate that yet.

This was 1982 and snooker was taking off on the box – thanks largely to the fact that most people now had colour TV; it was never riveting but had been even less so in black and white. Alex Higgins and Steve Davis: They were earning big money, turning the sport from an old man's game played in dingy clubs above Burtons into a young man's sport and younger men were wanting to play. There was no dedicated snooker club in Bath although you could queue for the table at the civil service club or the company sports clubs. We could be in at the start of a trend.

There is, I believe, no point in doing things by half. Either you throw yourself wholeheartedly into your project or you leave it alone. Jan says that'll be on my tombstone, cheerful thought.

After a cursory visit to a few clubs in Wales where snooker was growing fast but where the facilities failed to impress us, we jumped in with both feet. Fifteen snooker tables duly arrived and were installed upstairs and downstairs on plush carpets: easy leather chairs were grouped around highly polished tables in the bar: snugs were created into the arched recesses of the Georgian wing basement, a darts room, a TV room, an office: telephones were installed at every score board for ordering waiter service: the ceilings were draped with flags of every nation gathered on our motoring expeditions abroad: walls were decorated with colourful figures rescued from the Riot Bar at the George Hotel. It was very smart and we were going to be the best, most up-market private club in the area.

As in any club open to the public, fire regulations had to be adhered to. We had one perfectly good fire escape running down the outside of the building, but the authorities in their infinite wisdom deemed it necessary for us to install another one, through the basement to the rear. This meant getting permission to access the street behind a row of Georgian cottages, and ought not to have been much of a problem. They were all empty, awaiting renovation; all we wanted was to put a door into a wall that would allow us access into an alley between us. I approached the agent, the same agent who had just sold the building twice in one year, presuming that it would be a mere formality and a nominal sum to tie up the legal side. Not so. The agent realised that if I didn't get access my snooker club would never open. It didn't take him long to name his ransom, £7,500 in 1982 was a lot of money. I could take it or leave it. He knew I had no option.

I've already said, I really believe that if you treat people unfairly then it will catch up with you when you least expect it. Some time later, perhaps ten or fifteen years after all this when the snooker club was just another memory, I was in the garage looking at a car, a Cooper 500, the same type that a young Stirling Moss had cut his teeth on. Rob had raced it for some time but no-one wanted to use it so I'd arranged for a chap to come and look at it. It was sold in an instant. Perfect for everything he wanted to do with it. Not even a haggle about the price. He was really really pleased and I encouraged his enthusiasm. Yes the engine had been rebuilt; it was eligible for all the events he was interested in…..

"Brilliant. When can I come and collect it?" he asked me still sitting in the cockpit.
"Well actually, you can't."
"Sorry. I mean which day next week can I have it? I'll bring cash if you like"
"You can't. You can't have it at all. I'm not going to sell it to you, not at any price. You screwed me in Bath when I needed a fire-escape, remember? Now I have something you desperately want and you're not having it so bugger off out of my garage"

With the fire escape in place and the licence granted we were almost finished. Tony installed a door entry system and a computer system to control table use which Jan programmed. Instead of the old money in the slot and the failure of the table lights at a crucial point, our tables were timed and billed to the minute – it also made it more difficult for the staff to help themselves. We could see how long a member had been playing and as soon as there was a queue we could telephone and ask the earliest table to finish their current game. No-one waited longer than fifteen minutes and then could eat or drink while they waited. All we needed now were members.

During the two or three open days we threw they simply piled in. So did the community policeman. We weren't in the least concerned about him; we'd run several licensed premises by now and knew the laws. But that's not why he came. He came politely to warn us that the area was controlled by mafia type gangs. Gangs who would come to join as members and then take control. We would find our ordinary members slowly fading away as they took over. Well how the hell could we stop them and how would we know who they were?

We weren't operating a colour bar; we had no wish to and we already had members signed up from both Asian and Afro-Caribbean origins. But Rastafarians: smart, well-dressed Rastafarians with voluminous dreadlocks hidden in capacious caps which they wore at all times and elegant, expensive camel overcoats. They came down the wide staircase from the street two abreast. Four of them, their faces in shadow with the sun behind them but their outline leaving us in no doubt.

"Christ Jan, now what?"
"Leave it to me Freddie. Women make better bouncers remember!"

I skulked in the kitchen listening to the conversation. A polite 'Can I help you' from Jan. They wanted to join. That would be fine, of course. We should just point out though that we were operating a strict dress code. No hats anywhere in the club. Well if they must they could remove their caps but they didn't really wish to. Good. Excellent. But the dress code also includes hairstyles. Only conventional styles. No pony tails or anything like that. There was a silence. Thank you for your trouble Madam, we quite understand your position and will not be wanting to join. The figures again blotted out the sun from the open door onto the street and I breathed a huge sigh of relief.

Running the club wasn't without its worries. We were back in the licensed trade for a start; late night working; worrying after we had gone to bed that the club was still open and the phone could go any time; staff were always difficult in licensed premises – although I remember hiring two gorgeous girls who literally accosted us one evening on the street in Bath. They wore bunny outfits and top hats. Naturally it was the top hats which attracted me although their figures weren't to be sneezed at! Would we like to go and eat at some new bijou restaurant they were advertising? No but I like your style and would you like to come and work in a new club I'm opening. They didn't stay to earn a pension but boy were they good for business.

We had a tip off we were going to be broken into at one point. I've no idea who told our manager, Bill, but the police were sufficiently impressed to stake out a couple of officers overnight. All three of them sat quietly in the pitch black of the basement, listening and waiting, until they heard what sounded like an army of thieves breaking in the fire doors at the rear. As the footsteps got closer to the office door and the safe, the two policeman appeared to Bill to get smaller and smaller and there was a heavy thudding and short rasping breathing which frightened Bill to death until he realised it was his own heart beating like crazy. I don't know who was more surprised. Two hefty coppers and a panting manager or the pasty faced weedy youth who was forced to put his hands through the broken glass to have the handcuffs slapped on him.

I could weather those storms with no problem but the day came in February 1984 when I had to sell. We had been open over a year and Jan and I were frequently at the club in the evening; selling; chasing; playing snooker – acting the part of mine host. The telephone rang on the table we were playing at. "I'm awfully sorry Mr Giles but one of the members has just rung me from another table. It seems that you have your coloured balls the wrong way round". This wasn't for us! The club was sold on my 48th birthday, March 20th 1984.

While the shoe activity was in full swing we were also heavily involved in Frazer Nash activities and competing in some form of motor sport every other week-end. In the autumn of '82, between opening Mastershoe in June and the snooker club in November, Jan and I took off in MV for France to organise a competitive raid for the following summer. We had competed in the very first Rallye Neige et Glace in 1970, the only British entry, and had met some great chaps driving three-wheeled Morgans, skidding across the frozen lake in the driving tests and sliding sideways along the snow packed roads just like a Nash. Les Trapadelles. Whenever we were coming to France again.....be sure to look us up......if ever you want any help. We did. Want their help that is. We were heading for the Grenoble area again, their home ground, but this time to find routes, accommodation and hopefully fun competition for over 35 cars – a Frazer Nash Raid. We had the address but in '82 long distance phone calls were a rarity – hard to believe now we all take our mobiles half way across the world – so we wrote. We said we would come and find them on the nth of September at midi and take them out for lunch.

"How far is it from here to Grenoble?" I asked idly after supper somewhere in France.
"Don't really know. Oh. Dijon to Grenoble about 260 miles. In a Nash, doing an average of 40mph including essential stops, that's just over 6 hours. Ah. We'd better leave at 6am!"

The clock in the square was striking midday as we swept under the vaulted arch leading to the passarelle we were looking for. We had stopped twice for less than ten minutes each time. It was already unbelievably hot and we were wind battered, grimy faced and badly in need of a beer. But we'd made it on time and all we needed now was to find the house and see if we could recognise our Trapadelles.

"Freddie Giles?" an unfamiliar face thrust itself in front of us, hand outstretched in greeting. "Bienvenu".

There was no house. The address was merely a poste restante for the collection of club mail. A letter-box in the middle of Grenoble! Having got our letter, our friends had been waiting for us in half-hour rotas since 10:30 in the morning. That was lucky!

Now with their help we could start the organisation. The diary of the recce reads like the itinerary of a highly pressurised sales rep. We seemed to be on the go from early morning to late in the evening and covered 1704 miles. Eight days later we were back at work, our 'holiday' over but with the hotel rooms found, the competition planned, the mayoral visits organised and only the inordinate paperwork remaining.

The following summer the raid began with a bang. Our job was to be last out of everywhere but also first in to the next stop. A daunting if self-imposed obligation. So the accident happened behind us. A woman had come out of a side street and T-boned a Nash, totally wrecking the car and putting both occupants in hospital. At the first night stop in Arras everyone had to make a huge effort to overcome the gloom. Not a good start but thankfully the injuries were not as severe as they first seemed. The competition had begun in a light hearted and treasure hunt sort of way from the moment we stepped off the cross channel ferry. At Chateau Thierry on our recce trip we had seen another ferry, a one-man band with a small skiff, and so there were points to be gained for 'crossing the river without using a bridge'. No-one found the ferry-man – he was probably at lunch – but one of us, Tony Jones, was so ultra competitive that he swam this wide fast-flowing river. Not content with that he even swam back again! Full marks!

I think extracts from an article written by one of my close friends Dick Smith, who was captain of the club in '83 is a brilliant record.

The character of the road changed near Grenoble and became a hairpin, after hairy hairpin climb. As we progressed so the character of the driver changed also as I became more and more irresponsible and the Nurburg[12] was driven flat out hairpin to hairpin. My rev limit of 3500 was discarded, and almost immediately my new one of 4000 was also ignored, and then the one of 4500 and so on! But my word when we got to Villard I felt a new and younger man; Martin Stretton, overcome with excitement for he'd been following me, shook my hand, and Rosemary went off to wash her feet with Swarfega for the first time.

The Trapadelles had been as good as their word and had arranged all manner of tests – not all motoring orientated; I seem to recall one which involved peeling a hard-boiled egg with one hand, except that the occasional egg had not been cooked! And another, reversing over walnuts to crack them open, not as easy as it looks. They laid on a typical French lunch starting with a huge buffet and buckets of wine. The Nash men gorged themselves on the buffet – and the wine of course – and we were all mortified to discover that it was only the first course – the first of many in fact which we ate with some difficulty for the sake of entente cordiale. We made a lot of poor speeches in schoolboy French and the French thanked us for coming in flawless English so as a gesture of solidarity we pulled off our polo shirts with Nash logos and offered them to our French counterparts who responded in kind. Jan got a heavy Guernsey sweater which had never been near a washing machine and reeked of BO. She spent the rest of the day with her arms glued to her sides but was far too polite to take it off again! These were the days when there was no breathalyser in France and a vin d'honneur was de rigueur so the journey back to base was equally exciting.

The Trapadelles had also helped us to organise an unofficial speed hill climb which is once again recalled by Dick Smith.

---

[12] A very quick Frazer Nash indeed which was raced pre-war and is still campaigned in European events by Dick. It looks and behaves like a racing car!

[13]*The roads round Villard de Lans were made for Nashing. There were hairpins galore, tunnels, roads winding down gorges next to dashing torrents, incredible climbs and the most breathtaking scenery. During our stay we had a splendid five or six mile speed hill climb on a "closed" public road with several hairpins. I say "closed" public road guardedly because on one of my runs I came very sideways round one of the hairpins to find another Nash man leaping up and down in the road making signs so I gave some signs back and proceeded flat out around the next blind curve – and came nose to nose with Francois Scrud inching his way down in a Renault, face as white as a sheet, for had he not met Martin Stretton about a minute earlier no doubt going as sideways as me? I missed him, just, and reconciled myself to keep a strict look out, which was just as well because the next obstacle was an ice-cream van pottering up the hill at about 5mph round another blind corner.*

It seems so irresponsible in today's politically correct environment but it was fantastic fun and there were no accidents. When you are driving your personal 10/10ths, maybe slower maybe faster than the next car along, you are also concentrating 100% and the adrenalin is ensuring you are fully alert and your reactions are at their speediest. You can't spend your life being careful and thank goodness there are even now friends like Dick who still want to drive their cars flat out. Dick competed in our Alpine Day with another good friend Chris Chilcott – also a little mad and deluded into thinking he's a reincarnation of Nuvolari.

Martin Stretton and Mike Gibbs thundered past without any exhaust system, shouting jovial ruderies, and tore into the distance. More adrenalin from me and we screamed off in hot pursuit. I noticed Chris's hands were shaking and asked if he was concerned. He replied definitely not, but he added he was almost overcome with excitement and couldn't believe how splendid it all was. I saw Martin screaming away, sliding corner after corner in a

---

[13] A quote from Dick Smith again

shower of dust and stones and it was too much and so I closed and started a fantastic battle. It was during this time that Mike Gibbs apparently had a word with his Maker but I fear his Maker wasn't listening or took no notice because the dice continued unabated. After a while Chris leaned across to me and brought me back to my senses by shouting "If you don't drop back, either Martin will have a very bad accident or you will break the Nurburg" and so I slowed once again and kept watch at a distance of about half a mile.

Some people have more sense than others, though as Chris said, no one could have had a more exciting ride than ours. We rode with the Gods that day and I shall never forget it....neither will Chris. Next day he was covered with bruises and burns where he had been tossed all over the cockpit

Still a very good friend – Chris Chilcott at my 70th birthday party

The whole event was a great success – everyone really enjoyed it and the motoring was as exciting as we had ever known it. But it was hard work – leaving late and arriving early, making sure that the hotels were all up to scratch and the civic receptions attended on time. I felt personally responsible for things which were outside of my control which I know is crazy but just can't help. In everything I do the devil's in the detail – and it has to be right. One of the then senior members of the club came to me one night to complain that a previous occupant of his room must have been smoking as he could smell it and what was I going to do about it? It was just about the last straw and I had suddenly had enough of it all and wanted to go home. Mike Gibbs found me wandering round the town and calmed me down and after a few beers we converted the peak on my hat to one which could be turned up when required. Written on the underneath was F*** off in bold letters and I was told to use it the next time some idiot confronted the 'organiser' with a bloody stupid question or complaint.

We had organised a fortnight's events for some 80 people and by the time we got home we were exhausted but straight back into the daily grind of shoe shops, snooker clubs and two remaining cafes.

Competitive motoring was of course not taking a back seat and almost every weekend through summer and autumn there was a race meeting, hill climb or sprint. Then came November and the trialling season, having to repair the Anzani Nash after the ravages of the rough muddy hills on every outing; driving the seven hours to the Lake District in the beating rain. I was on my knees, almost ready for one of my periodical 'collapses' when I was once again rescued by a good friend.

We met Michael in the Lake District in 1969 and he promptly persuaded us to let his company insure our vintage cars. They still do that now, together with the rest of our insurance, but the point of this story is the way he and I became instant great friends. Somehow we just sparked off against each other and we have been in scrapes, japes and general mischief all over Europe and South Africa together.

Jan and I got married on February 14th, Valentines Day. How romantic I hear you say but of course it's so that you don't forget your anniversary. We had a small wedding with close family and friends; there was snow on the ground and we drove in the open Bentley with the four children to the Registry office; I was so lucky and so were the children; she had become mum in every way possible. Late in the afternoon we set off in the Bentley again for our honeymoon in London, but not before Frank had rolled in the snow in nothing but his underpants and not before Roger Richmond and two or three good Frazer Nash friends had held me down and chained to my ankle a length of 'Nash chain and a large metal ball – a lobster pot marker buoy. I didn't know but Jan had the padlock key and let me out down the road.

As happens in well organised circles the VSCC AGM was being held during our honeymoon in Heals Department Store on the Tottenham Court Road. Who should be there on the sixth floor but Michael who by strange co-incidence had got married on the same day and the same time as ourselves. The business meeting was over and the party was in full swing when I went down to the car and retrieved the ball and chain. He had no idea what hit him when half a dozen stalwarts laid him out and pinned him to the floor, ball and chain firmly padlocked in place. Great fun. We both now had new balls and chains. This one was uncomfortable to wear, same as some human ball and chains I suppose, and he wanted out. He tried desperately and unsuccessfully with a small hacksaw as we teased him with the key. We were next to an open window and I simply threw the key out. Or so he thought. He had no idea it was sixpence that had hit the window and disappeared down into the night. He did lose his temper to the amusement of the gathering crowd until we set off to "look for" the key.

Two warriors in wode capture a virgin slave with a pig net
Scottie, Jan and I at a Round Table do around 1970 – shortly before I was
thrown out of the club for stripping with a stripper at an all male evening.
The retiring chairman took her to bed but that was OK whereas my public
performance was 'unacceptable'

Scottie, as he became known, developed a motor racing club, the 96 Club, for wealthy insurance clients interested in fast sports or racing cars. They could get together at various circuits around the country and have a day's unofficial racing – quite legal and great fun. He also organised a three day trip to the 24 hour race at Le Mans where they might watch, join in peripheral events and generally have a good time. He would hire a chateau for 25/30 paying guests to wine and dine them in style – a fantastic three day party. I went along to chef and generally help the party – an unpaid worker first and guest second. Scottie was always good at 'getting in' to places and he had chatted up some-one for enough tickets to the Moet et Chandon marquee; free champagne unlimited. An 8' wall surrounded a magnificent garden in the centre of which stood a palatial marquee, a huge stone obelisk decorated with a mass of hydrangeas the centre piece. Just let's attach this medical-style marker band to your wrist then you can come and go as often as you want. Fabulous. We'd been ensconced for some time, ten to twelve of us drinking and chattering quietly enough when a very huge, very drunken, very noisy young German staggered unsteadily past us and stopped, swaying, at the edge of the flowers. I still don't like the Germans.

"Have you ever seen a drunken German rolling about in a flower bed?" and with that I ran full tilt at him, shoulder full into his chest and over he went into the hydrangeas. He never knew what hit him and rolled about like a stranded fish, whilst I nipped back into our little group. We all thought it was hilarious especially as four burly gate-keepers ripped his wristband off, picked him bodily out of the flowers and threw him out of the enclosure. Jan still doesn't find it funny and nor may you but it was at the time!!

So in December '83 Michael rescued me once again. The organisation of the Frazer Nash Raid to France in the summer had taken it out of me. I was working too hard and no doubt heading this time for a nervous breakdown. He could see that I was at a very low ebb and told me there and then that I was going to South Africa with him in two days time. He had some motoring business to do and was to stay with friends and for the first time I was to travel first class! Drambuie on your cornflakes! Naturally we got up to mischief. We were asked to leave an animal safari camp because we skinny dipped with a female guest in full view of other guests. They all found it funny that evening but some people can be very narrow in the morning! I generally left business behind for two weeks except that Michael talked and talked at me to sell all of the businesses which were bothering me. What was the point of being a rich man with broken health and this time it wasn't just physical energy I was out of but mental as well. Even though I had good staff and fantastic support from Jan it must be admitted that I don't delegate well enough and must always lead from the front. When we got home I took his advice. Sell. Sell. The snooker club was sold the following March and the two final cafes in July 1984 leaving us with just Mastershoe to run.

Scottie has taught me a lot and I shall always be thankful he made me see the light – money isn't the be all and end all of everything. Life is a one-way ticket and family and friends are the most important part of it. Sadly motoring friends aren't as available as the local Lions or the Golf Club. They are scattered all over the country and all over the world and you never quite know when you are going to see many of them again. Perhaps whenever and wherever the next motoring competition takes you.

And so it was in 1985 when we took MV 1764 to a Frazer Nash Raid to Boulogne, a repeat of the first event I'd been to with the club some 20 years earlier, and once again the combination of this super car, a little motor-sport and two good friends made for a brilliant holiday. Two days after the end of the Nash Jolly and we'd finished meandering around Northern France, crawling up canal tunnels after chain drive tugs and in awe of the awesomeness of the many military cemeteries which inescapably reduce me to tears. Both the Nash and we needed some sun to escape the incessant rain. Forget the leisurely trip, we would go for the South. In the '80s the D roads were still well chaussees deformees but by nightfall we were just north of Avignon and ready for a laid back couple of days before Dick and Rosemary Smith arrived. But what's in the local papers? Mont Ventoux Hill Climb this weekend and only 15 miles from us. What's more it's still raining even in the South of France and it might be something to do. The Spartan beast of the Nash is welcomed all the way. Non it is not too late to join in the fun. Sign on the dotted line; see the man with the white hat who will run his pencil round your spokes to make sure the wheels will not fall off. Non you do not need a licence or a tin-lid, oui you run with your passenger, have a glass of wine.

But within hours of arriving at somewhere like Ventoux you are being greeted by friends you last met years ago. Birds of a feather; like to like; whichever cliché you choose it works which means you almost always finish an event in the company of a seriously compatible competitor who is as pleased to see you as you are him when next you meet. Erik Koux, the Dane in a Bugatti is one such after a chance meeting in a bar half way back down Ventoux.

After the 14kms of hairy hairpins and a dice with a chain-drive Damont we needed a glass of wine. With Erik and Randi we celebrated our practice times, changed into best bib and tucker for the gala dinner and celebrated further. My idol of early days, Nigel Arnold-Forster appeared, he was also competing in a Bugatti, and we settled down for a long evening. Not being competitive it isn't surprising that as the wine loosened tongues we had challenged two Bugattis to a race up Ventoux. We were staying at a small hotel in Vaison called the Chapel of the White Penitents which had once been a nunnery and continued to retain some of its puritanical qualities. It was after 2am before we rolled home only to find we were locked out - but men always keep ladders in more or less the same place and it wouldn't take too long to climb in through our first floor window. "What is this? (Qu'est-ce que c'est que ca?)" demanded a boorish voice grabbing at the ladder as I was almost at the top. The inn-keeper! Jan appeared at his elbow and called in her best French "But Monsieur, it is a ladder". For some reason this seemed to antagonise him further and it was another half an hour before we persuaded him not to throw us out before the Smiths arrived the next day.

Another challenge for which MV is lovingly stripped and oiled and spoken to in fond entreaty before we join the throng. The sun is warm on your back, the crowd bustles and jolts, there is the background music of motorbikes and raucous 500s. It sounds like a Johnny Morris impersonation of a French crowd intent on pleasure. All we need is Tubby. The chains are displayed for the nth time – fantastique – incroyable – diable! Nigel has given me a 4 minute handicap as he has 8 cylinders to my 4 and says 17 minutes is a good time for anybody. Erik in the type 37 has given me par! I am a little concerned by the time I come to the third hairpin. There is nothing wrong with the car but there is a mass of spectators lining the route. They group in the road until the car approaches and then dive for cover as she sweeps by, sideways into every bend, accelerating out. I can't see where the road goes because of them but finally twig there is an elevated marshal waving a yellow flag in the direction of the next bend but it is still several bends before I trust in this. The top gets steeper and the drops more dramatic but the car scrubs her speed on the sideways drift through the sharp corners and thank goodness the crowds have thinned out up here. 17m 35s! Fantastic. Fancy the old girl holding 4 ½ thousand all the way. We're miles from home and all three of us are breathless!

The Bugattis are coming. No! Nigel has run out of petrol 100 yards from the flag and we all leap onto the course to push him over the line. It costs him 18m! Erik appears next and we crowd round the results to see his time. More than 17'35". A Nash has beaten two Bugattis up Ventoux! But it's not an antagonistic race! Before long we are full of sporting spirit and French wine and another party begins. Another race. Another friend.

Back to the wild wood

Although we'd been very happy at Clink for 25 years things were beginning to change and we had a particular neighbour, who I could never find, who virtually drove us from our home. When I bought Clink I had the chance to buy seven acres of field with it but I didn't want to borrow that much more money then. As we were more than half a mile from the outskirts of Frome I didn't see that in years to come it would become very valuable building land. It has never worried me that some-one else did see the potential and of course hundreds of houses were built turning our large farmhouse and buildings into an island, completely surrounded. Our quiet lane, where Ben the terrier would sleep in the middle of the road, had become a busy thoroughfare and from living in the country we were now in the middle of a housing estate. It made no difference to us as a family but of course we Giles have always been a noisy lot with fairly wild parties, both grown ups' and children's.

In fact one day Margaret, Togs, our help in the house, had an irate phone call telling her "to shut those children up. They're playing around that swimming pool again and we aren't going to put up with it!" Fair enough you might say but Togs could tell this anonymous neighbour that the children must be very loud indeed because in fact they were all in Lyme Regis for the day and she was the only one at home. Collapse of stout party but it didn't finish there. Whenever we had a party or whenever I started one of the racing cars some-one rang 999 and the police had to turn out. One particular summer's evening we had a fancy dress barbeque, mainly young people and our kids, it was Fletch's 21st. I was dressed as a woman, in a long red dress, high heels and a glorious silver wig and we were all in the lounge when a large burly copper put his head in through an open window, the result of yet another 999 call. He was escorted off the premises by a very angry me, still in my red dress and heels and with my wig swinging in the breeze but with the addition of some ripe and unladylike language.

*Cross dressing for a panto party
New Year's Eve early '90s*

The final straw was Rachel's wedding. The reception was at home, it had been a lovely day and the police had been told that at eight o'clock ten rockets would be fired. They would be noisy but then the happy pair would be leaving on their honeymoon and that's how it was. But the cop car, sirens blazing, was with us in no time flat.

"We have to answer a 999 call"

"But you knew about the rockets!"

"Yes"

"So did you take a name?"

"No, but even if we did we couldn't tell you"

The following day, Sunday, I was door knocking every house around us. No, not us, not us, then who, don't know! I'd had enough, it was time to sell and move on. Selling in 1986/7, property boom time, would be no problem but our menu for somewhere else was a bit ambitious, a very tall order!

> Had to be in Wiltshire
> Had to have some land
> An old property that we could convert to our style of living with the ability to have noisy parties
> Must be next to water, a river, lake or canal, but not too remote

We read estate agents brochures and drove hither and thither but there was nothing. Do we give up? We were coming very close to doing so when we found Seend Park Farm. Robert came to see it with me – we stood on the bridge over the mill stream and looked up at a horribly neglected farm house; in the distance were Roundway Hills where I'd played as a boy; behind the house ramshackle out-buildings and the Kennet and Avon canal with a bridge leading to part of the farmland that came with the house. That's it he said – you have to have it!

The auction was in June '87 but we would be on holiday in Spain so Bernard Kain who was a friend as well as our solicitor offered to bid for us. We told him how much we could afford and at the appointed hour sat in the sunshine next to a stream in Andalucia wondering if we'd bought it or not. Bernard is astute. He waited for the first few bids and said nothing then when the bidding appeared to be sticking he came in with a jump bid trebling the increments and effectively shutting out the other bidders. He had bought it and for less than we anticipated. All we had to do now was sell Clink.

We'd decorated for Rachel's wedding so the house was looking good and our local agent suggested a price and for that he would charge me 2.5%. It wasn't enough. Look I said, get me another £20,000 and I'll pay you 4% of the total. We can exchange as soon as you like but we need to stay here for nine or ten months. Half an hour later he called back. Could he come up then and there with a buyer? They were with us for less than an hour; agreed the full asking price and my extended completion, and that was it. We could start planning for Seend.

Interestingly enough the flight back from Spain had been delayed by eight hours and we'd sat in Malaga airport with a notepad and sketched out the layout of the house as we wanted it. Exactly as we have it today. The timber framed house had been built around 1620 and the walls bricked about 150 years later. The foundations simply sat on a series of big stones resting on the clay sub-soil and moving with the water table. It was going to be an exciting project and first of all I asked an architect friend to come and look it over with me. It was of course by now empty and looking the worse for wear as any house does when the furniture is taken out but architects can usually see through this to the potential of a place. We both had a bit of a shock.

"Let's go down the pub, Freddie and get a drink"
It was only half past eleven and hardly time for the whiskies Richard put onto the table. I couldn't understand what he was thinking about.

"I'm sorry to have to tell you this Freddie, but the house is falling down in a big way." Silence from me.

"One of the main rafters is rotted right through and could drop at any moment and the house would collapse in a heap around it"

I've always found it easy to deal with big problems rather than niggling ones and suggested that if that was the case we'd better get out of the pub and get on with it.

In the dining room was an exposed beam resting against the outside wall except that the end was so eaten away that the wall was offering no support at all. By the afternoon we had acrow props holding it in place and before long the blacksmith had forged a huge shoe to set into the wall and support the rest of the beam. It wasn't to be the only beam in trouble as we found later!

George Philip came over from France and lived with us at Clink for three weeks to get the feel of how we organised our lives and to help us with more detailed planning of the layout. That made it easier to talk to builders and get prices, settling on one of the best builders in the area, Butchers of Warminster. Once they had started we changed nothing so there was no reason for them to vary their quotation but it was quite a job. Joe and Betty Tolley had lived there for forty years and were proud, in fact positively boasted that they'd never spent a shilling on the place even stuffing sheets of ply or hardboard over the holes in the roof. We gutted it from top to bottom, wrapped it in a cocoon of plastic sheeting against the winter rains and began again from the damp course upwards.

At the same time I was turning some of the outbuildings into my vintage workshop and so was on site every day which proved to be invaluable as I was always available for an instant decision and the job wasn't held up for the want of one. We had no catering left, no snooker club to run and Robert was getting on with the shoe shops with the help of Jan in the office. I could semi-retire and took the opportunity. It was exciting and rewarding, creating exactly the home we wanted and finding surprises along the way – like the huge inglenook fireplace totally bricked in by a contemporary tiled fireplace or the original timber framing of the roof. Butchers concentrated on the building and I managed the transformation of the outside. Tarmac was to be a much later addition after we had moved in and for a whole year we seemed to be permanently walking in black mud.

The hysterical historical planners didn't help much. In between us buying and completing, some kind soul had arranged for the building to be listed. That meant we couldn't knock anything down – not even the grotty breeze block dairy tacked on the side – without countless meetings with their inspectorate. Chris Hyde my architect at Butchers saved me from disaster on more than one occasion when my short fuse got the better of me and I threatened to tell the planning officer my views on his intractability. Chris was much more laid back and still finished up getting his views across while I would slope off and attack something physical as an outlet for my frustration. We began the rebuild on January 4th 1988 and moved in on September 28th. After three weeks it felt as though we'd lived here for ever. By Christmas we were able to resume the parties we'd had to give up because of our anonymous neighbours at Clink.

The first Boxing Day set the scene for several years with a raft race on the canal followed by a bicycle extravaganza to the local pub.

Here the winner of the various tests along the way was obliged to ride across the garden tables and headlong into the canal. After an hour or so it was home by tractor with a trailer full of wet bikes and scantily clad youngsters to hot showers and a super lunch. There were usually about 50 of us, our children and their various friends, the whole day filled with laughter and pranks. Boys lost their trousers up trees, girls were sunk in floating baths but all innocent, noisy fun. A wonderful time for us between our children grown up and them producing children of their own.

Overleaf: Nephew Edward at the Barge, Seend Cleeve on Boxing Day

After the success of restoring Seend using Butchers I felt we could enjoy another project with them. I found a beautiful set of redundant Victorian farm buildings near Tidworth. Money country! They were perfect for five detached conversions and we soon got planning permission. We had the plans worked out and a price from Butchers and had agreed to go ahead. Electric and water were on site, as were builders' offices and stores, the mess room and even toilets. The start date was scheduled for three to four weeks but I had seen storm clouds gathering in the property market. Could we do the job and market before the crash in house prices which I felt was looming ever closer by the spring of '89? No. I could have a million pounds hung around my neck with expensive money, falling prices and rare buyers. I decided to pull the plug. Butchers were naturally upset but they accepted my opinion and I felt morally bound to pay them their projected profit and to put the site on the market. It cost me dear and I lost over £170,000 on the deal. The only thing I salvaged besides my sanity was a very old wooden case lock with a huge key from the stable block which now locks my beautiful millennium barn!

It was the correct move. Property did crash and there was negative equity for hundreds of thousands. The developer who bought from me went bust – as did Butchers later – and the following buyer finished the job. They look rather splendid now but my first loss was best loss.

One of the reasons for buying our house at Seend was the land surrounding – or almost surrounding it which we now owned too. It was a great pleasure to walk the dog on our own acres. The dogs – Bonny our Jack Russell who was in essence a huntress and Katy a Jack Russell Border Cross were in their element. Bonny had already gained a reputation in Frome hunting urban rabbits, unfortunately belonging to neighbours and still in their cages, and taking the new puppy Katy off to hunt too. In the process of this venture they had successfully unseated a motor cyclist who was happily too concerned with the fact that Katy had broken her hip to press charges! At Frome we had managed to restrain both dogs in the back garden but that was now impossible and they sallied forth on a series of adventures which was ultimately to lead to the downfall of one of them. They would run away and hunt badgers or foxes for days and days. On one occasion Bonny limped home with her front teeth impaled on her bottom lip, Katy would arrive with her tail in tatters but they never seemed to learn. The longest they were missing was three weeks and they were finally found further along the tow path making for home but too exhausted to carry on; both wasted to almost nothing with their fur totally dishevelled. One day Bonny disappeared down a known badger set and we never saw her again. Katy came home a day or so later, once again the worse for wear, but although she would hunt whenever we were walking, she'd lost her leader and never ventured out for a long term adventure on her own. She lived to a ripe old age of 18 so it didn't do her too much harm.

But aside from a hunting ground for dogs we needed to utilise the land in order to look after it. The canal people were truculent and refused us permission to establish water onto the 14 acre field on the other side of the canal so long term grazing for cattle was out.

We reseeded most of the grass and let it to a local sheep farmer and that worked well for a while but the lack of water was a problem. One of the things I had always wanted was my own wood. As a boy I'd loved the woods at Cling Hill, we'd spent hours making dens, playing with bows and arrows, looking for birds' nests, climbing trees and as a Scout in Spye Park Woods we'd had the most fun. We decided to plant a wood and to make it a community wood so that local people could walk, picnic, play and enjoy the peace and tranquillity relatively close to 'civilisation'. I was back in Wiltshire which had always been good to me and now I felt I had both the time and money to give something back.

I was lucky to find a tree man on my wave length. I wasn't looking for a cash crop and I didn't want 'foreign' trees. They had to be indigenous broad leaved varieties; an exciting wood which changed organically and was full of surprises; a proper wood. We managed to get a woodland grant which helped towards the cost of planting as our scheme had 5000 British trees; oak; silver birch; ash; hornbeam; crab apple; hazel; chestnut and many more. For a while it looked like a war cemetery with row upon row of pale posts and pink plastic guards each containing a tiny sapling reaching for the light above. But like many other things in life planting and maintaining a wood is neither straightforward nor as easy as it looks. We expected to lose about 5% in the first year but we lost well over seven hundred trees. The field mice got into the tree guards and made it their winter quarters, eating their way through the young shoots. The weather was too hot and too dry and the soil couldn't hold on to the moisture. We sprayed for weeds and overdid the culling of the grass around the young trees leaving them even more vulnerable to lack of rainfall. But we replanted and replanted and the following three or four years we kept on filling in the gaps until finally they were all established. We walked the length and breadth of every row a dozen times at least; re-staking here, loosening off a support there, putting in a post, taking off a tree guard, mowing the 3 metre path between the rows. That was in 1993 and now we have a beautiful living wood, some of the trees are over 6 metres already and the locals both walk in it and plant trees themselves in memory of friends or family. What's more it's called Giles Wood and I'm very proud to have created something so wonderful which can be enjoyed by future generations.

There are several footpaths across the fields and a bridleway runs past the house. We've mown many paths throughout the wood to encourage as many people as possible to enjoy the complete peace and tranquillity it offers. Everyone who finds us for the first time comments that it's a little bit of paradise and we're more than happy to share our good fortune. Scouts and cubs camp here in profusion. Local people plant trees in the wood in memory of their loved ones or to mark an auspicious occasion in their lives. Our own family come often in the summer to swim in the river or the lake in front of the house.

We've built them a playground with redundant slides and swings thrown off the village green by 'elf and safety, if you use a plastic sheet and wet the slide you can land in the catch net over the stream!

Our family Christmas Party happens in summer time – if wet in the barn!

It's quite a lot of work to keep it up but it really is beautiful and I want to go from here in a box – and then only as far as the wood to be buried!

I'm proud too to have created our Millennium Barn! I was so outraged at the Government's feeble attempt to celebrate a new millennium with the 'Dome' I thought we should have something nearer home. Most of my working life I have been restoring old buildings and I'd never built anything new but this time I wanted to create something which would complement the wood – on the other side of the canal. So I built a replica of a 16th century Wiltshire barn, aided and abetted by a wonderfully supportive team which included John Ford, our builder and carpenter, Len Brewer who normally helped with the garden and on the farmland, which by now had grown to 60 acres, John Naish, as usual a stalwart, and Lesley Earp, our secretary, who 'found' all the bits we needed – including tall boys and small boys after we had convinced her that it wasn't a wind up.

As usual 'hands on', from the stone base wall held together with lime mortar upwards. It was going to be as authentic as the planners and modern regulations would allow and after explaining to a slightly dubious planner that I was not planning a new house in disguise and this was to be a purely agricultural building. Some men go to work in a Rolls Royce and others go in a Mini but they both arrive at the same place. I could have a magnificent oak framed barn or a grotty old tin shed (existing!) but the result would be the same. The planner accepted the analogy and we could start. The frame was oak and came with Masonic like Roman Numerals as markings which fitted together like a jig saw puzzle.

Lesley helping with the daub

The roof battens were riven oak and the stone tiles were held on by wooden pegs. Once we had the roof on we could start the process of infilling the walls. We interwove riven oak battens between the oak frames to create the wattle and then we had great fun plastering them from both sides with the traditional daub. Everyone loved this messy job, plunging both hands into the tub and slapping the clay mix onto the waiting wattle, the person on the other side doing the same so that the mix was truly pressed in. A coat of lime wash and our barn could have been there for hundreds of years. We christened it in September 2000 with its first party when we celebrated winning the Round the World Rally.

The topping out ceremony when I climbed to the top of the structure and fixed a branch of young oak in place as a symbol that the building is made of living wood and also as a token of good luck.
Photo Trevor Porter Wiltshire Times

Why finish last indeed?

Although I no longer circuit raced by the mid '90s I still had Salome my faithful little single seater and was using her for sprints and hill climbs but I wasn't getting enough motor sport. Reading reports of historic motor rallying all over the country and Europe set me in action. These events were re-driving the courses of events of the '50s and '60s using cars manufactured pre 1965. They were very competitive rallies rather than social tours. The Monte Carlo. Liege Rome Liege. Rallye des Alpes.

'Out of guilt for being a naughty boy', four or five years earlier in my mid-fifties, I had bought Jan a beautiful red 1960 MGA. She used it as her summer car. It was good-looking, very sexy to look at, one of the best looking cars BMC made. A lady of a car, not particularly powerful but beautifully mannered, good brakes, comfortable, enough speed and excellent handling. As I said, a lady! Yes that car would suit very well for the type of event Jan and I could do together. So what did we need to go historic rallying?

> A reliable car for a start – the MGA for example
> A very good competent navigator – Jan fitted the bill perfectly
> Have a sense of adventure – yes we had that
> Find no problem with sometimes being on the road for 12 hours or longer or even 28 hours as in the Monte Carlo. OK.

Our first event together, talk about a blooding. If we were still talking to each other after that, and we were, then this was the game for us. This was the Monte Carlo Rally which started at Brooklands, the historic 20th century circuit. We went on a one day course to familiarise ourselves with the historic rather than vintage rules for navigation rallies but the only one I can remember is that "the navigator is in charge. THE BOSS!" Timing is to the minute with the exception of special sections and regularity sections where timing is to the second. This rally allowed you to make up lateness as long as you didn't exceed the maximum average speed (50kph in Europe) by more than 25%. That doesn't mean you get your lateness penalties wiped out by making up time on the next section, it means that you can avoid the situation where you are running permanently 30 minutes late – the result of which is that you might as well never have been through a control – and persistently pile up penalties all day. It lets you build up a buffer against maximum lateness. It also means the rally doesn't get too spread out time wise which is for the benefit of the organisers.

You know where the main time controls are and the special sections but not the finish controls for the regularity sections where you are timed to the second for keeping to an average speed. Maps are issued a few days before the start so you have chance to plot the course for the whole event. Organisers deliberately take you into rural situations where a mistake in finding the correct route leads to losing time and a frantic drive to catch it back up again. In the mountains this is very difficult especially as they use as many unmade tracks or roads as possible. Needless to say GPS or mobile phones are not allowed. A very exact odometer as used in the post war rallies can be made accurate to almost 100% and as all rallies work in kilometres we calibrated the MGA accordingly. We were very new kids on the block to this game and to throw ourselves into such a prestigious event which included driving for a day and a night until the following lunch time in January was pushing our luck.

A timed climb of the Stelvio on the Rallye des Alpes

We thought we had prepared the car. Chains for snow, shovel, torches, extra lights, reversing lights, tow rope, various spares, hood, Perspex side windows, one of which we lost before the start, large competition numbers stuck to the doors. France was in darkness as we left the channel tunnel and we couldn't keep to the times expected of us but it was serious fun finding the night stop in the dense winter fog. The following day we improved until we hit our first regularity section where timing was + or – a second which that first time was all totally beyond us.

We have improved since then and have become quite good at it. In '04 on the Rallye des Alpes we lost just 6 seconds in the whole day and won the coveted yellow shirts as rally leaders. We were presented with these at the first night stop in Burgenstock overlooking Lake Luzern, one of the many magnificent hotels the organisation find, at the champagne reception before dinner. It was a shock to us when our names were announced and we were called to the rostrum. Jan could do no more than take off her silk blouse, leaving herself in just her bras and looking rather Boadicea like, before putting on the canary shirt. The competitors loved it and applauded loudly. We had to wear the yellow shirts the following day only to be baulked by two German competitors in a Healey who weren't out to compete themselves and wouldn't let us through on a tight mountain section. This cost us 55 seconds and put us into 8th place. Jan lost her rag and was all for starting World War III but funnily enough I didn't bother. The organisers could only reprimand them but couldn't give us our time back. Anyhow it's only a game and we were lucky to be playing the game and in the big scheme of life it really didn't matter. Annoying all the same.

But those first Monte Carlos were awful, especially the all night drive. Having driven all day with a three hour stop for food and drink but nowhere to sleep or get warm we drove into the night on snow and ice. The next morning Jan had to pour cold water into my hand for me to splash into my face to try and keep awake. We could have given up at the breakfast stop but hot rolls and a wash saw us rejuvenated and heading for the lunch time finish on the quayside at Monte Carlo. We had been seeded by this time and we were way down the field, the little car was running hot and I had to keep refilling her with water. Then we were baulked for miles by a huge truck on a very snowy road and once it turned off I pushed the car too hard to make up time. The temperature climbed and suddenly we had water and steam everywhere – oh bugger. A core plug had blown out of the side of the engine – about the size of an old penny. We didn't have one but we were on a mountain road in a forest of young Christmas trees and I thought I could make one from a chunk of wood. With my small hacksaw I jumped off the verge and into the trees and ugh! I'm up to my shoulders in snow; those trees were bigger than I thought and the snow very deep. No matter; this was an emergency and although I didn't like doing it I cut part of a tree down climbing with it back up the bank like Mallory on Everest. With my large knife, never be without one, I whittled and tapered a piece of wood about 4" long and drove it into the hole in the engine with my big wheel mallet, a good temporary bodge. I used all of our spare water which was just enough to get us to one of those village water troughs fed by a mountain spring, filled up again and pressed on as we were so close to our goal, the sea front and final control on the quayside in Monte Carlo.

The road winds down from the mountains in a giant corkscrew with myriads of dead end roads and one-way streets criss-crossing the arterial – dead easy to get lost if you've never been there before. Finally Jan had to resort to a young man on a moped who was persuaded to lead us through the maze and down to the final check-in. Brilliant, we made it, we were almost last but on time to be qualified as a finisher in this famous winter event, the Monte Carlo Rally! Over the finishing ramp and time to celebrate with a few drinks. The winners had long gone to their respective hotels but we tail end charlies still celebrated before following our usual routine and bedding down the horse for the night.

Into our DJs and off to the prize giving dinner at the Hotel de Paris. What a night with free booze flowing freely! Well it had been included in the entry fee – champagne all the way and very rude to leave it. The Casino on the other side of the square now beckoned and seven new found friends made a concerted assault, our wallets well nigh empty but counting on the cash we were about to win. Check we all had our passports, you can't get in without them, but naturally one of the chaps didn't have his on him. We worked a clever scam swapping passports and peoples and got seven of us in for the price of six. Winning already! Not with pontoon, 21s, blackjack at 100 francs a card and the roulette wheel 500 francs a roll! We didn't exactly get into heavy gambling but wandered around observing the frenetic activity for some fifteen minutes until the heavies arrived. How they found us, how they knew we were seven and not six, we didn't know but we found ourselves back in the square very quickly. Thrown out of the Casino in Monte Carlo, now that is fame and without so much as a bruised wallet. The only alternative was another drink or two. The lack of sleep, too much booze, it didn't take all night for us to want to find our beds but before we got there Jan managed to fall backwards over a low wall. Drunken hussy! Still she had six men to hoist her back onto her feet and unhurt – there aren't many female navigators on winter trials. What an event. We were hooked.

The Trial to the Nile in 2002

Across the Balkans, Turkey, Syria, Jordan, Egypt
3 days in the Western Sahara and sandstorms instead of snow storms

The Monte is a wonderful adventure and we did it three more times in the MGA before we decided we didn't want to cope with thirty hour drives any more. I love driving on snow and ice and the MG handles like a Nash, sticking to the road like glue. Well almost. On one occasion we were lying 13th overall when the organisers gave us a 12 hour penalty by mistake. Jan didn't spot it until too late and so the following morning instead of setting off with 12 cars in front of us we had more like 112. A real back marker and travelling with cars which either aren't very competitive or have mechanical problems, both of which can hold you up on the narrow mountain passes. I approached the 10 or so cars immediately in front of us before we set off and explained the problem. If I gave them a toot on a hairy section would they mind letting me through. They were all super and agreed to this and sure enough as we came up behind them they pulled over and let us past. We must have overtaken about eight of them on a very fast downhill section when Jan warned me of an approaching right hander. Hairpin right! A short pause and then a louder warning. Hairpin right!! I had heard but I was going too fast and there was nothing I could do on the frozen snow so I slid gracefully on until my front wheels came to rest on the edge of the precipice. I was now blocking the road until the convoy, which we had so brazenly overtaken, duly arrived behind me to lend a hand to pull us back out of the snow drift which had broken our slide and send us on our way again. Truly embarrassing.

The last Monte was in 2000 when we used the Hillman Hunter. It was 'ready' for Around the World in 80 Days, a rally starting on May 1st. That was a great lesson. You think after a huge effort over two years that you have a car prepared for any kind of event. Not so, the new brake pads on the Hunter wore out on Day 3, right down to the metal. We had no spare pads but managed to shape down over-sized pads from a Sherpa van with the help of a hacksaw and a friendly garage. We were back on the road but with no idea what had caused the problem and only after a complete strip down of the front brakes at home could we diagnose and sort it out. A valuable shake down for a huge adventure drive. A competitive drive around the world. The first ever.

It doesn't sound much. Tower Bridge in London: through Europe to Turkey and Georgia: across the ex-Russian Stans to the deserts of Northern China: an airlift from Peking to Alaska: the Yukon and down the Rockies to Vancouver: across America to Niagara and down to New York: another airlift to Morocco: a flurry around the sand dunes of the desert and back up through Spain and France to London and Tower Bridge. A challenge for the millennium that had to be done. 22,000 miles – 80 days – only 270 miles a day average – easy! Or so we thought. We hadn't taken into account the full on competition it would engender; competition timed every minute of every day for 80 days. We couldn't envisage the stress and the strain we would have to endure and the totally devastating fatigue which would overwhelm me. I was to drive the whole way round with Jan in charge of navigation and paperwork and we couldn't know that for some days I would be driving 13 hours non-stop for days on end.

We had agonised long and hard about which car to use? It could be any model made before 1968. The MGA was too small, the Bentley too heavy and ponderous and the Frazer Nash positively hopeless. The insurance to retrieve a car from anywhere in the world was £10,000. Ridiculous – you need a throw away car; if you blow it or smash it you leave it behind. It must be simple, cheap, have spares available, be fairly quick and comfortable. Volvos and Mustangs were not allowed, they had apparently blotted their copy books on previous classic events and – until he needed the cash from the extra entries later on – the organiser wasn't having them.

We found a Hillman Hunter which had competed in the '97 Peking to Paris, the same model which won the London to Sydney in 1968. It had to be the car to use. What we didn't know was that the car had suffered a nasty bump in some far distant country which had left the chassis an inch shorter on one side. Driving her home the car spun out of control the first time I braked in anger, it didn't augur well. It was partially rally prepared with roll over bars and, amongst other things, foot plates on the back for the navigator to stand on and bounce me out of the sand I would no doubt become entrenched in somewhere in a desert. Tony and I systematically took the car apart and systematically rebuilt or replaced every major component. We read Andy Cowan's book about winning the London to Sydney, "Why Finish Last?", and copied a lot of modifications that had been used on that event. We were after reliability. We wanted to finish the event and thought that in itself would be a fantastic achievement. After the short sharp shock of the Monte we still had much to do and worked frantically every day throughout February and March, my patience and my temper growing shorter as the deadline loomed closer. By the 20th April the car was loaded and ready to go.

The blue bell woods outside of Marlborough were an essential detour. We have to see them every year in May, it's so beautiful, England at its best! A champagne reception and we left the Bear Hotel in Devizes to the sound of the same hunting horn which had sent me on my way to London back in my bed-pushing days. The last Saturday in April and a day of calm. A view of the city from the London Eye, supper by the Thames where we meet up with other early arrivals. Noise levels rise. Anticipation is taking us over. Sunday is a blur of signing on, of scrutineering the cars, of questions about insurance, driving licences for China, the principles of rally timing. We are hungry but can't eat and certainly we can't sleep; checking the car again at 5:30 on a fresh May morning and at least five hours before we are due to start. Then before we know it we are off on our allocated minute to thousands of cheering, flag waving crowds including our lovely daughter Jill and her husband Andy. It was all very emotional. The oldest car on the rally never made it past Greenwich and was never seen again but what I thought was to be a gentle start was anything but.

The first seven days were so competitive we couldn't believe it; night sections; terrible tracks; cars breaking down; engines smashed on rocks; what were the organisers thinking of? We are behind a big Healey as it overtakes a huge vintage Rolls Royce; his wheels slip into a gully on the nearside and he accelerates to get himself free but loses control and shoots off the road and over the edge of the mountain. Bloody hell! We stop in the middle of the road and I rush over the very steep side slithering my way down. The car had smashed its way through trees the size of lamp posts and rocks like armchairs, strewing its personal contents and bits of car for 40 to 50 yards. The crew were hanging in their full safety harness and I had them out and sat down before more help arrived. On the face of it they were OK but their race was run and ambulances and fire-fighters were on their way. They were left in good care and we pushed on, just making the time control at the bottom of the valley. Full harness was immediately put on and we all realised this was serious fun.

After 7 days still relaxed enough to thank the belly dancer in Istanbul

In this game if you have problems you are left behind as long as rally staff know where you are. Later in the rally, cars and crews went missing after smashes, waving the rally on its way and rejoining it as long as three weeks afterwards. The rally had been divided into three legs with three simultaneous rallies. A 7 day rally to Istanbul for the full 100 cars which set out with 20 cars dropping out at that point. A half way rally London to Peking where the next 38 cars would drop out and 42 for the full circumnavigation, London to London. By Istanbul we had lost two of the 42 and we found ourselves leading the whole event including the London to Peking competitors. Where drivers had been pacing themselves, saving their cars for the next 73 or even 33 days, I was throwing the Hillman into every special section as hard as she would go, driving 10/10ths wherever it was necessary. We hadn't been seeded and in order to reach the stage controls on time we were forced to overtake slower cars in some hairy places. Roads which had disappeared in a slurry of gravel and silt, the car sliding from side to side on the rough surface and falling sideways into a muddy wash-away. Climbing 1 in 3 ascents and holding onto the steering down the hazardous descents. I tell Jan I am in control but it's only just. All of my trials experience with the VSCC comes into its own as the car weaves and swerves to avoid the sump breaking rocks on the course. After 12 hours a day for 7 days the car is not broken and we are in the lead.

We really didn't set out with any intention or thought of winning this very competitive rally but we hoped that we had prepared the car well enough to be able to finish it. We took very little in the way of spares; a main leaf rear spring, a radiator strapped to the underside of the roof, fuel pumps, oil filters, electrical spares and brake pads of course! Enough to carry out two full services on the way. I had a good tool kit, this was essential, and axle stands and a scissor jack. I could always borrow a hydraulic jack for lifting the whole car in times of need. We were travelling as light as possible, the more weight the harder the car had to work. Clothes were limited to three sets - one to wear, one to wash and one to dry. We washed our undies every night and if they hadn't dried by the next morning they were strung on the clothes line in the back of the car; the same with shirts and trousers. Early on we established a long-term routine. Half an hour before the final control, Jan would make a note of the things I needed to look at when we arrived. I looked at the suspension almost every day to make sure nothing was working loose but there may have been a squeak or a rattle which warranted further investigation. While I was doing this Jan would clock in, find where we were sleeping and sort out the maps for the next day, then she would bring me a beer. One. And I wasn't allowed it before I had finished all of my jobs. A shower, if there was hot water, where we would wash our clothes, food and an early night. Sorry, no sex for 80 days. You're on a rally!

So our preparation and our regular routine were paying off. No-one could say we weren't competitive but it wasn't meant to be like this. To be in the lead after 7 days meant we were going to work as hard as possible to stay there. And we did work hard. Over Turkey's rough roads, moving out of the way of huge lorries who took no prisoners, and into Georgia, a poverty stricken but beautiful country, and a fantastic reception. The Russians had moved out, taking all factory equipment with them plus all the tractors and farm machinery. So many people looking after one cow or two pigs on the side of the road. Wonderful farm land with

just small plots being tilled by hand or maybe a horse or oxen. So many men stood about with no hope of work but yet we had this terrific welcome, a buffet and entertainment hosted by the president. We were treated to colourful national dancing, acrobats, school children in national costume singing Georgian ballads.

On the balcony overlooking us were a group of fifteen or sixteen huge men, we all thought they were the President's bodyguards. Not at all; they were the finale of this colourful evening and they suddenly began to sing, with no instrumental backing. They really were splendid, talk about the best of Welsh miners in full throat, we all cried for encore and they gave it to us. It was a tremendous evening, giving us wealthy Westerners the very best they had, poor devils. We retired to bed in the 'new' Sputnik hotel, an old concierge guarding each floor in this poor worn out sleep over, carpets in holes, dubious plumbing, welcome to the ex-communist countries!

The Georgian roads leave much to be desired. We were heading through the foothills of the Pataa to Samtredia, 150kms of rough roads strewn with pot-holes. Pot-holes like pits and I needed to concentrate hard to avoid the crumbling tarmac or the cracking concrete. A Mercedes-driving German amongst us who had regular business in Georgia tried to persuade me to use a main road which wasn't part of the official route but would have been better for both car and passengers. He knew for certain there would be no secret passage controls on the narrow rural roads of the competition route. No way was I doing so and I made no bones about telling two other Mercedes drivers who took the easy option, both English, that they had cheated and that if either of them beat me in this event then in my heart they hadn't! The reply from one of them was immediate. "Are you calling us a***holes?" he asked. "Well, yes" I replied, "I suppose I am".

As it turned out one of them was second overall but not without the inadvertent help of a control marshal in the deserts of Morocco who saved him the 30 minute penalty he could have incurred by approaching a control from the wrong direction. Indeed I watched him go into the control and thought that he had received a penalty so commiserated with him for his loss of second place. He was six feet tall and much younger than me and his reply was to take me by the throat! By then the competition had become more than serious and I was saved by our SAS trained paramedic who leapt in and separated us. By that stage all of the difficult driving had been done and he could only have beaten us if our good and faithful Hillman had suffered a major mechanical problem through Spain or France. But before then we were to have further adventures.

The driving through the Stans was very hard, Azerbaijan, Turkmenistan, Uzbekistan, Kazakhstan and Kyrgyzstan. Jan was scared crossing the Caspian Sea, she hates boats. It was a very rusty bucket of a boat and we had no cabin. We'd bought supper in Baku which we ate on deck in the evening drizzle and I left Jan lying across three unbending uncomfortable seats with another girl stretched out beneath the seats and found a quiet corner above deck. One engine failed an hour out of port and the toilets, such as they were, lasted about an hour longer. It was grim. After a 24 hour crossing, the authorities in Turkmenistan wouldn't let us off the boat until six in the evening and we had 500 miles in front of us before that night's check in. Sleeping camels on the road in the dark, crazy driving from the locals and tiredness all took its toll. I found that I had to stop about every hour and run up and down the road for 100 yards to revive myself. In Ashgabad the youths had taken down the directional arrows set up by our marshals, there were no other instructions to find the time controls and it was turmoil. When we finally arrived in the early hours tempers were frayed but food, drink and dancing girls were still waiting for us and the tiredness was soon forgotten.

Along the old Silk Road towards Samarkand and pressing towards China. It wasn't getting lost which was the problem now but the heat and the sand and the wind which caused blinding sand storms. How they coped in open cars I don't know as we wore face masks inside the Hillman. Across the Karakum Desert with the road, the railway, the telegraph poles and a canal all running together between the edge of the sand and the steep sided mountain range. No traffic, only horsemen with nothing but their eyes on show as they wrapped their faces against the biting wind and sand. For the first time the car let us down and as we spluttered to a halt I pulled off the road – into deep sand! We were stuck. The next car through was the film crew and while Jan stood on the back of the Hillman to bounce us out of the drift, the crew towed us back onto the road and filmed Jan's backside at the same time. The intense heat had caused a vapour lock and we were forced to cut the rubber pipe from the pump to the carburettor to let the air pressure out but I later re-routed it lower down in the engine bay.

Cell block B! No, we are not incarcerated at HM Turkmenbashi's pleasure, our home tonight is a redundant sanatorium. There is no sanitation: there is no running water – luckily I filled the water carrier from a stream earlier in the day: there is obviously no washing powder as although the sheets are 'clean' they carry the stains of many sleepers: there is nowhere to go to the loo. Jan is now adept at having a wee between the two open doors of the Hillman no matter where we are but the confined grounds at Chardzhou finally defeat her! Once again we are amazed by the generosity of those who have nothing. We have a band: we have a bar selling coca cola and beer: we have a barbeque and we sleep like innocents.

At Samarkand I carried out my first 5000 mile service. A father and son, local Uzbekistanis helped me find a tyre depot to change my tyres and then invited me home for breakfast! An enormous bed filled the simple veranda outside of their bungalow. The bed, where the whole family have slept for the night, was still warm with woollen blankets, tousled and tossed. The women rushed out to gather up the bedclothes and spread an ornate kilim and grandfather appeared and beckoned me to join him sitting on the newly made bed. Father noticed a pile of night soil made by a small child and gathered it up with a shovel from the foot of the bed. We couldn't communicate. We could gesticulate and they offered me bread and nuts which I accepted with nods and smiles. How wonderful. I hadn't seen the grand markets of Samarkand where Jan had been but this experience was only happening because we were rallying – and were not tourists with demarcation lines of safety.

My service turned out to be a bit of a disaster. The following day the car was fluffing and spitting and I was convinced we had fuel problems.

We made it to the start of a special stage in the foothills of the Naratau Mountains and watched by the local schoolchildren I emptied the fuel tank onto the grass and tipped in my spare jerry cans. We'll be OK now I thought, I was sure it was fuel. We had 70kms of undulating mountain road in front of us and 55 minutes to the next control. Every time the car approached 3000 revs there was a total loss of power. After two or three abortive stops to check if the plug leads were in place or the fuel pump was working we decided that we had to try and make it to the control with the remaining power. We were going to lose some time but I could crawl up the hills and fly down the other side as fast as the gradient would take us. But I hadn't bargained for the wadis at the bottom of the hills and I hit one at full speed, the front wheels dropping into the deep ditch across the road with an almighty bang. I carried on and we made the control with a minute to spare but I limped the remaining 250kms to Tashkent with a powerless engine and now a dodgy steering. We had put the tracking out quite badly. There was going to be no supper for us tonight until the car was mended.

The tracking was relatively simple. Once again the generosity of the locals came to our aid. A young man who was looking at the cars, in his Sunday best, was a mechanic and his garage had the equipment to sort us out. Despite being both Sunday and late he was delighted to open up his immaculate workshop and set to work on the Hillman. A fantastic job but we still had no power or supper! I tried all suggestions from fellow competitors, taking the car on a short test run each time and returning even more disconsolate each time. Jan decided we needed to get back to basics. What had I changed at the 5000 mile service? Nothing. Well only the distributor cap which looked as though it had a crack in it but that was for a brand new part. Well change it back she insisted. The power is faultless!

We were still in the lead but next morning we very tired and concentration was poor. Heavy road-works meant the route out of town was a diversion but by the time we were due to leave the traffic police had gone off duty and information was scanty. Jan felt as though we were leaving in the wrong direction, the compass was still pointing west, and without waiting for my navigator to give me any instructions I threw the car round in a U-turn and set off to the east. It was a one-way road and round the next corner came a huge Mercedes taxi. Crash. The 'roo bar was bent and the nearside wing was twisted onto the tyre. What could I say to him it was my fault. I took out my wallet and offered him $60 but with that, out of the bushes at the side of the road, appeared two policemen. The taxi driver shook hands with them so I did the same. They looked at my $60 and shook their heads, looking at the wallet in my hand. I took out a $100 bill and they nodded in unison. The police took the money, not the driver, and they waved us on our way. Phew. A further embarrassing moment until I had jemmied the wing off the tyre and we were free to go.

We were to go through a pass 12,000ft high into North West China and had encamped some 120 miles before the border. The camp should have had us all sleeping in yurts – the local thick felt round tents made from yak hair – but for whatever reason we were billeted in ex-Russian concrete barracks. It was a terrible rat infested place with no sanitation and made the sanatorium look like a palace. Beds with filthy mattresses were crammed eight to a room and the food had been laid out on trestle tables for hours before our arrival, exposed to flies and heat. It would be preferable to sleep in the car so a few of us took off to the village some miles down the road. We discovered of all things an English B&B – it was already full with the German and Swiss contingents but they let us have a space on the floor of the TV room! It was beautifully clean and very acceptable.

Next morning we had a stage section of exactly 120 miles all on gravel, mud and rocks. We were at 7000ft so had 5000ft to climb. We knew it was going to be tough as running number 89 and still not seeded we had to overtake most of the slower field in front of us if we were going to stay on time. Why Philip Young, our organiser, put the potentially quickest cars at the back and never graded them by results I don't know but he did and so when we were given the average speed of 60mph for 120 miles on unmade roads we knew a real race was on.

Looking back it was so dangerous but now at Day 24 and still leading it meant we were going to drive our hearts out. The 'road' was a raised causeway covered with stone marbles and with deep treacherous ditches on either side. If you went off you weren't going to get back on again without help. Most vehicles let us through when the track was wide enough and they saw our headlights in their mirror but the TV crew in the Land Rover, no matter how we tried, just wouldn't move over. They were driving flat out, as we were, on one stretch, both of us at 90mph, when they suddenly veered into a wider track and just as suddenly we were showered with stones that fired at us like bullets. Three smashed the screen in my line of sight, not breaking the screen but leaving three big stars. Hells bells! Keep up speed and crouch down to look through the steering wheel. Shout at Jan to release her safety harness and find, from the back of the car, coats, or anything, to go under my bottom – I couldn't do the next 60/70 miles like this. We didn't stop or slow, I just sort of stood while she stuffed our luggage under me: that's better, now get on with it.

The car was going beautifully, flat out was just over 90mph but we were climbing hard, the Northern side of the Himalayas in the distance, fantastic, but we didn't have time to admire the view. We had a job to do. We didn't speak other than for me to ask Jan for my water bottle, my mouth was incredibly dry, or for her to tell me we were still on time, in fact about 4 or 5 minutes ahead. With over 110 miles done the engine started to lose power; bugger, now what? But suddenly I had a Mercedes and a Porsche in my sights and we were gaining on them; strange; then it dawned – our altimeter showed over 12000 feet and we were running out of air – or at least the engine was, unable to properly burn the fuel it was receiving; running rich if you want to be technical. We were all struggling but my simple SU carburettors were coping better than the more complicated systems of Mr Mercedes or Mr Porsche and our common or garden Hillman was proving her worth. The KISS system came into play – keep it simple stupid! Out of the eighty cars still running five of us made it on time; brilliant; what a race; now we were all knackered and short of oxygen – I had to change a wheel I'd manage to dent on a rock and that took a long time at this altitude, not the three minutes Jan and I normally took to change the spare.

China at last. If you are a tourist and have time to stop and stare you will never see this China. Dirty China. Polluted China. How can you breathe in Llanzhou? A lorry driver is whipped for daring to cross the road in front of us. A poor country with tarmac only in the towns and the narrow country roads full of government-owned blue-painted lorries hauling coal.

Repairing a puncture at a ' tyre station' in the Gobi Desert 200kms from anywhere

We couldn't possibly get lost as a policeman stood at every junction, road or track, pristine white gloves even in the middle of the desert. No roads, just hundreds of miles of track, rutted, with sharp puncture inflicting stones. Dry river beds. Sand. Narrow steep gorges and astounding dust storms which attack your eyes and throat. For fifteen days we took all that China could throw at us.

We picked up the Great Wall when it was a low mud barrier, sometimes only remnants left in situ, and we followed it off and on for 2000 miles until we came to Badalong – the sight we are all familiar with, its stone castellation walls and towers running up and down mountains in spectacular fashion. Over thirty-eight days of competitive motoring and we were still leading this rally, ahead too of all the competitors who were leaving us in Peking for home. We had lost just 18 minutes in 11,000 miles.

Now we could set about loading our 40 cars into the belly of a Russian Antonov cargo plane which would fly them to Alaska for the next leg of this epic drive. All had been weighed and when the rally crew were safely aboard it was decided that this huge monster of the skies was too heavy for take-off! The air temperature was too high and they were forced to wait until late at night when it had cooled down before they had enough lift to get airborne. I must say we were pleased not to be on that flight and equally pleased to see it land safely at Anchorage the next day. June 10th and then June 10th the next day – we had just crossed the International Date Line. One more day and Jan could have had two birthdays. One birthday present was a brilliantly packed new windscreen which meant I could discard the three pillows I had sat on for the 15 days across China.

My Avon tyres up to then had been superb but Anchorage seemed a good place to change them – the half way point. What a disaster; three days of hell on terrible tyres which felt as if they were going to let go on every serious corner. Then, in the middle of nowhere, we came upon a garage which had six new Goodyears stacked in the corner. I was a little loath at first having shelled out for tyres in Anchorage but was quickly persuaded by Jan that we had no chance of staying on the road if I didn't change them again. We were just hanging on to our slim seven minute lead but we had a hell of a lot of motoring still to do. We had a new Clerk of the Course, who had been set the task of organising the whole route through North America. From Anchorage, north to the Yukon then down through the Rockies almost to Vancouver, across the Big Country of Montana and Wyoming to Niagara and down to New York – and he'd been told to make it tough. Indeed he followed orders and at times the weather must have had the same orders because it threw snow, hail, dust, huge storms and the Police at us! Our new Clerk of the Course had told no-one in authority that a road race for 8/9000 miles was taking place in the States and the Police were just waiting for speeders. By now we had, thank goodness, been seeded and were the first car away every morning, quickly followed by second and third place. By the time we three had gone through the locals had called the law and sixth and seventh man were frequently stopped and booked.

For eight days I drove non-stop for 500 miles a day; thirteen hour stretches with nothing more than a short break. The clever stroke was to keep us off as much tarmac as possible: we virtually had a strike at the end of one day in Canada after 350 miles on dirt roads: not just any dirt roads but logging roads. Because we were always first away we didn't realise the dust we were creating and which hadn't settled before the next car was due through a minute later. It must have been horrendous for the later cars. Not long after setting off we were flagged down by the driver of a logging lorry who wanted to know what the hell we were doing driving on these roads. He must have been 100' long and loaded with unimaginable tons of felled trees. Well, we're in a rally, we told him, 40 of us. Were we in radio contact with base? Well no. He stopped all of the logging trucks on the road with one radio call, explaining that base contact was not just a legal obligation but a survival necessity. It was the only way that the drivers knew the position of the other

314

trucks; they certainly couldn't see anything in the dust they created and would have run over any one of us without even realising it. That was the only time I was really annoyed with the organisers – we hadn't come on this rally to kill ourselves nor did it seem had the others. The route was changed for the following day.

A pre-war 4 ½ litre Lagonda had its suspension collapse in China. Only 50 of these cars were ever made and yet there were two of them in Anchorage. The Alaskan owner was pleased to help them and spent two days rebuilding their car with parts from one of his own cars. Ten days down the road they blew their engine and called Anchorage again. "Yes, I'll take an engine from one of my cars and have it sent to you on a lorry; you take yours out and send it back!" They were missing ten days but turned up in great form determined to finish the event and that was the attitude taken by one and all. Competitors all helping each other as much as possible.

The camera crew were skilful at finding very fast tricky sections where they knew there would be some action but as a driver you looked hard for them, slowing as soon as you saw them to avoid the pitfall. They cottoned on to this and began to camouflage themselves superbly, twice catching out Claude Picasso in his big Mercedes. On one occasion he lost the back end and hit a tree just behind the rear wheel; this got fairly well sorted that evening but within two days the cameras were rolling again when he rolled the car in a big way. It was driveable but it was a wreck; good job it was a hard top. That evening a screen was found – 12" too high but taped into place: hydraulic presses, crowbars, hammers were put to good use to get it roadworthy for the next morning by a whole team of competitors. The results were tremendous; the car was rough but ready to take off on its appropriate minute in the morning.

Photo Courtesy of Philip Young Endurance Rally Association
Photographer Mike Johnson
The camera crew were skilful at finding very fast tricky sections but this time
they had used the ford to water the course for the first car through.
"Keep it on the island" said Jan as I executed a less than graceful pirouette.

By Bonanza Creek near Dawson City a lovely Frenchman and his wife, Yves and Arlette Morault, had got up to second place and they were really trying. His sportsmanship truly shone through in a special timed section deep in the forest. We had set off first and within a few minutes were confronted by a huge bear in the middle of the track. I stopped to take a photo – Jan was not happy about my decision as the timing was very tight but I took the photo anyhow and as I was doing so Yves roared past us. A mile down the road and Yves was stopped, waving us through, he understood what we were doing and had given us our place back – how generous can you get!? Many days later, in another fast wet section, he lost the car over the side incurring a penalty of one hour and was out of the running. Being the sportsman he is, he found me out to give me some good advice. "Freddie, you have only twelve special sections before the finish in London and therefore you can afford to lose two minutes per section and still win by fifteen minutes. It will mean you can ease back and not drive flat out each time" I had a job to obey but prompted by the navigator to slow down I did lose seven minutes. We won by a 29 minute margin over 22,000 miles so it was quite close.

The Hillman was running splendidly, not putting a foot wrong, until Duluth on Day 61. We had a day off here and I needed to change the rear brakes and fit my new linings. We were housed in a dark and dismal multi-storey car park which was not easy to work in. The car was sat on its axle-stands minding its own business while I was fettling away on the vice attached to the back of the mechanics' Land Rover. One of the back up crew told me that he had just felt my half-shaft bearings on the back axle and one of them was shot. "Needs renewing" he told me. "Never! – it's been perfect". But he spoke to another member of the back up crew who confirmed the 'fact'. I quickly put the car back together and one of the crew and I set off to a local garage. Having confirmed that they had the tools and equipment to sort out the problem I left the professionals to it and went on repairing my collapsed seat. They removed the half-shaft and without thinking or asking me if I had a spare or even examining the bearing it was put under a 50 ton press which burst everything apart.

It's mid-afternoon on a Friday and everything is due to close down not just for the weekend but Tuesday is July 4th – Independence Day – and nothing moves or opens until Wednesday 5th! There are frantic phone calls but no bearings and I go back to the hotel totally distraught. The car wasn't broken this morning and now it isn't going anywhere: all this after the huge effort we had made in this mundane Hillman against the Porsches and Mercedes. I cried, I blubbered when my navigator wife and best friend appeared from town. What the hell has happened? I explain and she leaves me and heads for the workshop and the car. I don't know how she achieved it but hell and high water weren't going to stop her finding a new bearing. No, she wouldn't allow them to close; they were going to find and fit a new bearing.

Thanks to our sweep, Andy Inskip, one was found, not the correct one but with the same outside and inside diameter. It wasn't as wide but they could get over that and it wasn't a sealed bearing so back axle oil escaped through to one of the rear wheels which meant no brakes on that side but at least the car was mobile. All this time I had taken to my bed in sheer anger, frustration and grief and then three hours later Jan stormed in the door and announced that the car was back in the car park and ready for the morning. What a woman, my wife of then thirty odd years, how I love her. Next morning, more determined than ever, we set out on our minute, but not before Jan had rung home and related the problems. Tony Coles, my friend and engineer, who had helped prepare the car, was very upset as the bearings were new and they would have sung to us for days before they screeched and then let go – there was nothing wrong with them. Another good friend Philip Selwyn-Smith and he then sorted out a pair of half-shafts with new bearings fitted and had them air-lifted to us in New York. We decided not to fit them until our day off in Morocco – the car had to catch the Antonov and fly to Africa whatever happened.

It was hot. 54 degrees centigrade at midday! It was the organiser's last chance to change the leader board and Jan was tossing and turning all night before the final special stages across the Sahara, the route of the Paris Dakar. Instead of the final test promised they had added two additional passage controls with the potential to lose ninety minutes in penalties and put us out of the running. They had also reduced the target time by several minutes. We knew we could afford to lose minutes here by driving slowly but we couldn't afford to lose our way on a complicated series of desert tracks. We would end up stuck in soft sand or we would miss a passage control and it would be all over.

"Where the bloody hell are you going? I didn't tell you to fork right. Keep left now!" Jan was shouting in my ear. We had been overtaken by the Mercedes, the second car which had started a minute behind us and the third car, the Mustang of the Irish boys was catching us both. "I'm following the Merc – he's headed for that track on the right". "Well don't. Keep left!" She didn't lift her head, just ticked off the next instruction on her road book and tugged at the Halda to clear the intermediate reading. "45 degrees left. 480 metres and 90 degrees right........150 metres....here." We had circled a huge sand dune on our right and hidden on the other side was a passage control which we were now approaching from the right direction!! Sat at the control and facing the wrong way was the Mercedes, who then backed up and followed our route around the dunes. The Irish had followed us. "I knew Jan wouldn't go wrong" he said, "so I just caught you up and followed you round." It was a long and complicated stage and boy were we relieved to pass that final control. So relieved I drove off the track and was immediately stuck in the sand.

By the time we arrived in Tangiers I could hardly stand. I had driven every mile of the way, kept the car serviced myself and had used up all of my spare adrenalin with the tension of being in the lead. We walked down to a beach café for supper but I couldn't stay and I couldn't walk back, Jan all but carried me and put me to bed. Matt, our travelling doctor administered some knock-out drops and I slept. We had a 04:30 start to catch the ferry to Spain the next day.

The only row Jan and I had was the last afternoon in France. We pulled into the final control of the day mid-afternoon. A lovely hotel and the French contingent were laying on a huge celebration; bottles of champagne were being lined up along the bar. What a party we were going to have. "Sorry but no" said Jan, "the organisers have passed a new rule and we can book out for tomorrow morning's time at any time before our due minute. They want the rally to finish on time on the 80th day. We are booking out now and leaving for Calais tonight". Jan had worked out that if the Hillman let us down on the last lap, the 140 miles to Calais to catch the 08:30 boat, we could easily blow it and our huge effort over 79 days would have been in vain. I reckoned that the Hillman wasn't going to do that and I wanted to go to the party. "No, you are not.

319

You are going to drive to Calais tonight". I kicked and hollered, I wanted to go to the party but after some time she had her way and we set off, leaving behind a great celebration. It took an hour before I got over it and realised she was perfectly right. Strangely enough both 2nd and 3rd place cars were in Calais that night and of course the Hillman didn't miss a beat.

Tower Bridge London with flags flying from the car, 'Rule Britannia' blazing loudly from the CD and the whole of our family there to meet us together with a huge number of friends from all over the country and the bonus of a first cuddle with Sarah, our eighth grandchild. Lesley, Jan's PA, produced champagne for everyone and we celebrated in the grounds of the Royal Mint with the cars all around us. Incredible. No-one believes us when we say we set out to drive around the world, not at all thinking that we might, with our simple Hillman Hunter, be the winners. Having found ourselves leading after only a few days our competitive spirit kicked in and we were going to fight and by golly we did. I doubt if another such rally will be organised again.

Rallies have taken us all around the world. All over Europe, Argentina, New Zealand, South Africa, the Middle East – countries with borders which are now closed to us. The Bentley was due to compete in the centenary of the Peking to Paris Rally in May 2007. The original rally in 1907 was a challenge for a bottle of champagne – Mad Motorists indeed – with 5 cars setting out to drive across China and the Steppes of Russia and only 4 making the finish.. This would be the third time we had entered the event and Jan and I were hyped up about the whole adventure. Mongolia – ten days camping in the desert. Siberia. Moscow and a grand finish in Paris. We had entered for the event in 1982 but it never came off. We tried again in 1997 but we lost my co-driver Fletch. This time Jan and I could do it together. We wouldn't be competitive. I was still competing at 71 so we were going for the adventure and to finish! For the third time, it was not to be. My own chassis, rather than the car's, demanded more attention and a back operation on January 13th (again!) banned lifting a wheel or a tool bag until the end of July. Bugger it.

A euphoric post rally tango in Buenos Aires – the only British entrants in the Argentinean Mille Miglia '97

Photo courtesy of Trevor Porter and Wiltshire Times and News
We lost only 52 minutes in 22,000 miles of timed competitive motoring to win the Around the World Rally outright.

A lame excuse

I've agonised over this chapter for ages. It seemed that there was a problem with the book's progress until one day last autumn in the Italian Alps. The editor, Jan of course, was dragging her feet to finish it off. We had enjoyed a long laid back lunch in the sun with several glasses of red nectar when I was suddenly jolted back into real life.

"You have to tackle a chapter about your lady friends"

It took I'm sure only a couple of seconds but it seemed like hours. Am I hearing this? How does she know? I spluttered in my wine. "What lady friends are you talking about?"

She fired back with very accurate arrows quoting names I'd forgotten about so I put my hands up and surrendered. "Yes," I admitted, "there were a few. But honestly, they had led me astray. I didn't mean to be naughty"

"What a lame excuse!" She wasn't angry. She just said "Well, you've got to write about it other than that the book will not be complete nor even finished! So, you'd better get thinking; now let's have another glass of wine."

She was laughing at me all the while and I sat there with a complete jumble of thoughts whirring around in my head.

Home again and I talked to our eldest son, Rob, whom I turn to whenever I need some honest advice. "Father, we all knew about it, yes Jill and Rachel as well. In fact can't you remember about 20 years ago Jon and I invited you to a meeting to tell you to cool it and you did? Of course mother knew, as did all your friends. As Rob said, "you can't keep a bottle of champagne and two glasses in

323

a 'hidden' compartment of the Porsche and not know what you're like!" He's perfectly right and I can't find real excuses.

I've always got on very well with the opposite sex and over the years we've employed hundreds of females, before gender discrimination, as manageress of restaurants, pubs, cafes, coffee bars; women who had brought up a family well and now in their forties wanted still to achieve something else in life. One thing I didn't do was to have affairs with staff although I really enjoyed working with them and their sense of humour. You could never get the same response from men in the catering trade but maybe I'm too red- bloodied and don't understand the sexual orientation of so many of them.

It's no excuse but being brought up as a milkman was such a temptation and then I never played the field enough before my first marriage. Two years in the army on the barren wastes of Germany and eighteen months later I threw myself into working 14 hour days with the first coffee bar – 7 days a week except for Sunday mornings.

Later, with competition driving, there was so much excitement, wildness, and women were attracted to me because of it. It's nearly unbelievable now but I didn't have to know a girl very long before I had to test them by feeling their breasts to see if they had a 'British Standard Handful'- always in public. I never had my face slapped or was threatened by husbands or boyfriends but the girls love to be made a fuss of and it was just a great joke. A bottom felt was the same although I do remember having a pint poured over my head at a wine and cheese party in Frome in the brief time I was in Round Table. In the '70s long skirts were de rigueur for evening dos but a local solicitor's wife appeared in a pair of hot pants with the cheeks of a very tidy bottom peeping out. Naturally there was talk among the men and a bet was taken as to who could be the first to feel said bottom. I had to laugh – she did ask for it and her husband was only a pint sized wonder himself.

I've never been a man's man.

I was thrown out of Round Table, well asked to leave which amounts to the same thing. There was a party, an all male do, at the local motel for the outgoing chairman and the committee had organised a voluptuous stripper. The chairman and I just joined in to strip with her and everyone loved the fun. Of course we'd had too much to drink but all I did was put my clothes back on and go home to Jan with a bottle of champagne that seemed surplus to requirements – she made me take it back the next morning. The retiring chairman had a room for the night and spent it with the stripper. The new chairman came to see me the next day to tell me that stripping for fun wasn't the sort of behaviour he was going to tolerate. The night before he'd been clapping and cheering with the rest. How hypocritical. I resigned on the spot.

So some women found I was attractive – I really don't know why. Maybe they felt that I liked women and women's company and I was usually playful and happy and often doing something exciting. What attracts? At a party recently a young man came into the room to collect his parents (role reversal or what) and all the women without exception stopped talking and gazed at him. Jan said he was utterly dishy but to me he looked like a normal chap so how do men tell?

I'm not going to name names or relate other than amusing experiences especially when I have a wife who has accepted my behaviour with never a word while 'clever old me' thought I was pulling the wool over her eyes. She has threatened to add an appendix with 'the list' and to make it available in a brown paper envelope if I'm not careful! She did get her own back on one occasion - the annual Nash Christmas Party in Hereford. She knew that I had a fantasy about having two women at the same time and organised the friend who had introduced us, Jane, to meet us in our room before supper. When I arrived they were on the bed clad only in scant undies. Wow, I thought, this is my lucky day as I stripped off and jumped onto the bed. Then they began. To tickle me unmercifully. I am ashamed to admit that I ran for the bathroom and barricaded myself in until they promised to leave me alone. Of course they never had any intention of doing anything else and my fantasy was shot to pieces.

When we talked about my escapades Jan said that most of them were friends whom she liked and knew they were no threat to our life together but there were one or two she positively disliked, thought them tarty and predatory and would have nothing to do with them socially. I never worked it out stupid sod that I am! She also said that we have a fantastic life together whether business or pleasure; the children had been through one break-up and she couldn't see the sense of another when she knew that I was like a dog and always came home to be fed and watered.

If I thought I was having secrets, Jan and the four kids had plenty. Bumps and scrapes in motor cars, personal upheavals all kept from me. I walked past a red Sierra, which Jonathan had scratched, for three weeks, thanks to some 'careful parking'. Father knew nothing and it's only now I am finding out all sorts of things which went on and quite rightly so.

Am I lucky or what? Jan still loves me and without her I could never have achieved what we have done in business or our wild adventures together.

Incredible.

And so?

So Must I Grow Up?

We grow up without realising it – our progression through life ensures that we do. But being grown up doesn't have to mean boredom, conventionality, never again being spontaneous.

My life still involves cars and will probably always involve competition and a craving for adventure. But there is more time for our nine grandchildren, our own family, newly found golf for its social rather than competitive element and of all things bridge – competitive bridge to keep my mind active when my body begins to creak.

There is, I believe, no point in doing things by half. Either you throw yourself wholeheartedly into your project or you leave it alone.